D1351209

POTTERY

the essential manual

Harrow College
Harrow Weald, Learning Centre
Brookshill, Harrow Weald
HA3 6RR
020 8909 6248

POTTERY
the essential manual

Doug Wensley

The Crowood Press

First published in 2002 by
The Crowood Press Ltd
Ramsbury, Marlborough
Wiltshire SN8 2HR

British Library Cataloguing-in-Publication Data
A catalogue record for this book is available from
the British Library.

ISBN 1 86126 520 4

Frontispiece *'Dancing Bottles', soda-fired stoneware,
by Ruthanne Tudball. Photo: Ruthanne Tudball*

Right *'Monolithic Landscape Form', by the author.*

Typefaces used: text and headings, ITC Giovanni;
chapter headings, ITC Tiepolo.

Designed and typeset by
Focus Publishing
11a St. Botolph's Road
Sevenoaks
Kent TN13 3AJ

Printed and bound in Singapore by
Craft Print International Ltd

Acknowledgements

Jude, my wife, has given unstinting help, support and technical advice, both ceramic and I.T., when proof-reading drafts of
all the chapters. Her contribution to Chapter 9, Decoration,
her practical help with demonstrations, and her photographs
of some of the practical elements of the making processes,
have all been invaluable.

Thanks go to Rosie Wensley for word-processing Chapter
14, Personal Approaches, and for photographing some of the
making processes.

I would also like to thank Sally Michalska for expertly
word-processing the main body of the text – her patience and
tenacity were much appreciated.

My sincere thanks go to all the artist-craftspeople featured
in Chapter 14, Personal Approaches. They have generously
shared their thoughts, have given transparencies, and have
spent a great deal of time providing written information (an
activity few potters relish), all of which has added valuable
breadth and insight into the ceramic creative process.

I am especially indebted to Mike Powers, Ruthanne
Tudball and John Wheeldon who welcomed me into their
workshops, to talk with them about their procedures,
philosophies and working lives, and to take photographs for
this publication. My thanks in this respect also go to the staff
and students on the B.A. Decorative Arts course, School of Art
& Design, Nottingham Trent University; in particular to the
programme leader, Tony Ingram; to the ceramics lecturer,
Jude Wensley; and to students Phaedra Cozier, Sarah Hillman
and Karen Lyons.

Special thanks go to Pamela Wood, Keeper of Decorative
Art, Nottingham Castle Museum & Art Gallery, in making it
possible for me to photograph just some of the ceramics in
her care, including the Ballantyne Collection.

Also to Comte Robert Bégouën, Association Louis
Bégouën, Laboratoire de Préhistoire de Pujol, for providing
the illustration of *Bisons d'Argile de la caverne du Tuc
d'Audoubert*. To Emmanuel Cooper, for his photograph taken
by Michael Harvey. To Michael Evans and the trustees of the
Weston Park Foundation for their permission to reproduce
photographs taken from the ceramics collection at Weston
Park, Staffordshire. To David & Charles Ltd, publishers, for
permission to reprint an extract from *The English Country
Pottery* by Peter Brears.

Also to Allan Ault and Valentine Clays, for their generous
help and support, and for the clay samples and technical
advice, and for the series of photographs they provided.

I would also like to thank Laurie Joyce, Fuji Processing
Laboratory, for generously supplying film and processing.

Most of the photographs used throughout the book
were taken by the author. Others are acknowledged within
the text.

Contents

Introduction

One of the most exciting features of present-day ceramics is the incredible richness and breadth of creative activity. Technical expertise along with imaginative creative thinking is evident in most exhibitions of contemporary studio pottery, as is the urge to extend the boundaries of ceramic activity.

The possibilities for the clay worker/maker have never been greater, and it pretty much follows that a participant's enjoyment of the craft has therefore never been greater either. Traditional practices and procedures have been embraced, extended and/or revised to adapt them to more recent technical advances. Hard-and-fast rules or taboos that might hinder creative activity have generally been put aside. The only significant constraints arise from what is, or is not, available to the would-be maker.

In addition to the rich depository of knowledge acquired by past cultures, and also the creative output over several thousands of years, today's potters have at their disposal stimuli and insights unknown to previous generations. Information technology has given rise to a great sharing of specialist knowledge, together with a clearer awareness and understanding of what is happening in the ceramics field elsewhere in the world. Potters are no longer restricted to their immediate vicinities for either practical or conceptual needs. Materials and ideas are readily, if not always freely, accessible, as is craft training.

Development and change have always taken place, in pottery as in other areas of human endeavour, but things really began to speed up with the onset of the Industrial Revolution in the late eighteenth century. During and since that time in the West, arts and crafts movements have been exposed to radical change, this being particularly true of ceramics. Thus, whereas in earlier times the needs

of those who could afford pottery were provided for by local craftspeople, the introduction of mass-production in depersonalized factories took over such outlets. Factory production had the tendency to increase the desire, and hence the market, for these wares, and threatened still further the existence of the low-volume producers of hand-made pottery. Their products were cheaper, both in cost and design quality, and the new manufacturers were quick to develop their new markets.

The cost to society was arguably twofold: some, if not all, of the intrinsic value of hand-made pottery was lost in the mass-production processes; and skills unique to the craft were buried and almost lost under a mountain of often very inferior goods.

During the next 150 years counter-revolutionary figures such as William Morris, the Martin brothers and Doulton of Lambeth, among others, began to re-examine the contribution of the individual makers to ceramic processes. Bernard Leach, often credited with the birth of the studio pottery movement in the twentieth century, spent years studying the craft in Japan and Korea, then returned to the UK and in 1920 set up a workshop in St Ives, Cornwall. The unique experience afforded to Leach in the East was in part due to changing cultural attitudes there, and in part to easier travel access worldwide. Oriental pottery had inspired technical refinements and some superficial copying of surface pattern in Europe since the seventeenth century, but Leach could be seen to have introduced a genuine understanding of the oriental expression of creative, inspirational potting in the West.

With the publication of *A Potter's Book* in 1940, Bernard Leach became recognized as the prime motivator of a pro-studio philosophy. Arguably his life and work are instrumental in revitalizing the craft and in bringing about its renaissance, as he led by example. Like William Morris before him, he championed a move away from sterile, factory-

Opposite *Lidded milk jug, tenmoko glaze, by Ray Finch.*
Nottingham Castle Museum & Art Gallery

made pottery, often over-designed and over-decorated, with inappropriate and insensitive appendages and patterns. Individual potters regained control of the various stages of making, enabling them to produce sympathetic, intrinsically pleasing wares reflecting humble materials and technologies. In post-war years the craft enjoyed an expansion of participant involvement at both professional and amateur levels.

The renaissance was largely craft-led and tradition-led at the outset, with emphasis on the pleasure to be derived from making and using simple, well designed and well made objects. However, due to the desire to emulate Leach, coupled with constraints of contemporary technology, studio pottery appeared to become a little bogged down. The desire to produce work with the characteristics of wood-fired, reduced stoneware tended to promote

a range of wares that were predominantly brown or speckled oatmeal; stoneware was the buzz-word, cone 8 the benchmark, and reduction the quality kite-mark. Potters even felt obliged, at times, to resort to desperate measures, such as introducing smoke into clean electric kilns, in order to keep up with the trend.

That is not to say the work was the worse for that, but some people working in the 'swinging sixties' found the constraints imposed by available technology unacceptable. And so started another revolution, this one slower and quieter.

In conjunction with chemists working in the ceramics industry, some potters began experimenting with glaze formulae, underglaze colours and body stains, with the ultimate aim of extending the colour range at high temperatures. These developments in glaze chemistry, and changes in firing

Sculptural form, by John Maltby, c. 1970. Nottingham Castle Museum & Art Gallery

processes, have significantly increased the range of possibilities available to the studio potter.

In a similar way, practical production possibilities have been extended or improved over the past fifty years or so. The increased participation in pottery has given rise to the establishment of specialist firms catering for these interests. There is little need, nowadays, to set up a workshop alongside a convenient bed of local clay since suppliers offer a wide range of reliable bodies, either ready for use, or they will blend specific bodies to suit individual requirements. Neither is a would-be potter restricted by kiln design or the ability of someone to build one: what cannot be purchased over the counter can be designed, built and installed by experts who understand the processes involved, including health and safety, and planning considerations.

Increased contact between studio potters and industry has also altered perceptions of what a studio potter can, or should not do. For many people, studio pottery has become synonymous with 'good' and mass-production with 'poor'. However, it does not follow that all hand-made items have an intrinsically greater quality status than factory-made pieces simply because of the production method. It is worth remembering that materials and techniques have always provided a link, and recently this mutuality has enjoyed a greater focus. Students on ceramics courses at all levels have been encouraged to develop skills that might previously have been considered as primarily 'industrial' and therefore inappropriate to studio ceramics. The acquisition of such skills has significantly extended the visual vocabulary of the studio potter, and has resulted in the enrichment of the ceramic experience, as witnessed in the breadth of activity remarked upon earlier.

Studio potters have also benefited considerably from experience in the industry of health and safety considerations. Until relatively recently, for example, all potters were at risk of lead poisoning. As a result of precautions taken, however, reported cases of lead poisoning in the UK fell from 432 in 1897 to nil in 1944. The development of non-toxic fritted lead, facilitating the formulation of safe 'low-sol' glazes, has eliminated the need to use raw lead ingredients. Other poisons such as antimony, barium, cadmium, copper, chromium, selenium and

Vase by Hans Coper, c. 1963. Nottingham Castle Museum & Art Gallery

Square platter, earthenware, by John Pollex, 2001.
Photo: John Pollex

Above *Three bowls, stoneware, multiple firings,*
by Emmanuel Cooper, 2000. Photo: Michael Harvey

zinc are still in use, but our knowledge of them is now greater, and we can therefore take the necessary precautions when using them.

Coincidentally the growth in awareness of the potential dangers of some pottery materials has been counter-balanced by a similar increase in the range of safe alternatives available. It is now possible, for example, to obtain reds without resorting to the use of lead, that do not rely on a reduction atmosphere in the kiln, and which do tolerate high temperatures. Reds achieved by reducing copper oxides are at best fickle and unreliable, and copper's reputation in health and safety terms is, in any case, somewhat tarnished. So it is reassuring to know that specialist potters' suppliers can offer safe and reliable red stains and glazes, most of which are of excellent quality.

One hazard that cannot be ignored as long as we use clay is the illness known as 'silicosis': when particles of silica are inhaled into the lungs in the form of fine dust they are surrounded by new lung tissue. The silica remains embedded, however, blocking lung capillaries and causing the lung to clog. Nevertheless, awareness in the industry has brought into force regulations in most countries to protect workers from this condition. We can protect ourselves significantly by simply avoiding dust.

Health and safety, as an issue for today's studio potter, should be informed by industry's experience and practice, and tempered with common sense. Whenever possible, use wet or damp material; wash clean all tools, working surfaces and machinery after use; do not wear dirty, dust-encrusted overalls; and always wear a face mask when dry-mixing glaze materials. Clay, and splashes of slip or glaze dropped onto the floor, get trodden on and quickly become dust. So avoid dropping materials on the floor in the first place, and clean up thoroughly before treading anything in.

If all this suggests a morass of danger and restriction to creative activity, be reassured. There has been a significant increase in the numbers of participants at all levels who enjoy being involved in an almost timeless craft as it develops into an exciting twenty-first century form of expression largely free from any impediment or hidden danger.

Note from the Author

It should be said at the outset that the author has not invented or developed all the ideas outlined in the chapters that follow. Some of them have been collected and used by him over the years, often in conjunction with students; others have been tried and tested by other craftspeople, who have generously offered to share their innovative ideas. Much other material is the bedrock of ceramic activity as it has evolved over several thousand years. It was with that in mind that some historical and other background information has been included in order to provide a link between tradition and what might be considered *avant-garde*.

1 Clay and Ceramics

The plastic nature of this unique material has been utilized by human beings for many hundreds of years. Evidence discovered deep underground in caves at Tuc d'Audoubert, in the Ariege region of France, indicates that some 20,000 years ago during the Palaeolithic period someone modelled with the medium to produce ritualistic sculptures. The pair of bison in high relief (see photo) were apparently cut from clay found on the floor, and the figures lifted and stuck to the wall of the cave. They were then modelled and given true rounded contours, and tools were used to create texture suggesting manes and beards. From at least that time, clay has been used extensively in wide-ranging manifestations of human creativity and self-expression.

For most people today, clay is probably synonymous with the art of pottery. It is perhaps worth remarking that, whereas the material itself has been used for a very long time, possibly in excess of 50,000 years, its use for specifically pot-making purposes is rather less ancient. Indeed, there is no evidence of its being used for this until some time between 8,000 and 6,000 B.C., by which time clay pots were being made in areas as remote as Asia Minor, Syria and Anatolia, and South America.

What is 'Ceramics'?

From that location and period there developed a craft based on the 'ceramic' process – which begs the questions 'what is "ceramics"?' and 'who invented or discovered it?'. The Greeks were well aware of the concept, *keramos* referring to the man- ufacture of objects from clay metamorphosed by fire into a new material: the potter's trinity of earth, fire and water – for 'earth' read 'clay', which contains free water. As the material dries out, this free water is released to the atmosphere, the clay remaining chemically intact; by reintroducing water it can be reconstituted into a workable, plastic state.

The crucial change from one material to another is brought about by the action of fire. This metamorphosis involves driving off the water that is chemically bound up in the molecular structure of the clay, the result being a new material that is hard and porous; this is usually referred to as 'biscuit' or 'bisque' ware. The *ceramic* nature of an object simply implies that it is made of clay; that it is (relatively) thin, so as to be able to withstand thermal shock; and that it is *fired*, the action of heat transforming it into a new material. Unlike the first, drying stage, this metamorphic change is strictly one way.

Background and History: an Idiosyncratic View

No real evidence exists of early awareness of the ceramic potential of clay. Sculpted clay models made during the Palaeolithic period in Europe have been preserved by subsequent coverings of flowstone – calcium carbonate deposits, as stalagmites – but any form of primitive unfired or 'raw' pot forms would have been obliterated long since, even supposing they had been produced in the first place. Nevertheless, at some point clay would have been brought into contact with fire. Some anonymous being must have noticed that clay could be formed into crude containers, and allowed these to dry out in the wind and sun. They might then have been used to store foodstuffs, such as nuts, berries, or even liquids. And it is tempting to think that, in collecting melted fat, or even attempting to cook, a clay artefact may have been accidentally dropped into a fireplace: discovery of the material's transformation, and realization of its potential, would have had a profound effect upon any early society.

Whether accidentally or consciously occasioned, at different times and places, such discoveries would have led to the gradual appreciation of *ceramics* as a concept. Whenever and wherever the ceramic process emerged, a technological revolution came about, with or without immediate awareness of the event. Its processes and skills would

have slowly emerged, been developed, spread out to other peoples, and been refined to suit the needs of the societies it came to serve. And there is plenty of evidence of later ceramic activity throughout the world, which has often been developed independently.

What is clear is that the ceramic process has been understood and utilized much longer than pots have been thrown on some sort of wheel; it has older, stronger traditions based on forms of hand-building with clay. Both useful domestic ware and decorative, ritualistic or sculptural pieces have been produced widely by many societies; and before the advent of the potter's wheel, these makers were frequently women.

Such hand-built pottery normally reflected the vigour and growth associated with nature, and the closeness of the maker to it. Forms were natural and grew almost casually to fulfil desired functions. Decoration was direct and reflected the intimate experience of the maker, often influenced by traditional women's occupations such as basket weaving

Bisons d'Argile, Tuc d'Audoubert. Photo: R. Begouen

and textiles manufacture. Motifs were frequently associated with plant and flower forms, as well as human and animal detail, and again referred to the maker's closeness to his or her environment and way of life.

Recognition of the two technologies – making in clay, and transforming it via the fire – provides any primitive society, past or present, with profound issues: ideological, philosophical or pragmatic. Trial or purification by fire, as applied to pottery, is a fact of life. For example, peasant potters who 'bonfire' vessels using dry grasses or dung as fuel suffer considerable losses in the process, and to off-set breakages due to the uneven distribution of heat, more pots have to be produced than are actually needed. These losses are inevitable, and in such circumstances the potter must be philosophical, while at the same time he attempts to overcome the basic problem by designing a more effective means of firing. (*See* Chapter 3, project – pebble, cast and bonfired.)

Earliest kilns were probably mere bonfires or very moderately modified versions of them. Fires were sometimes built into shallow pits, and some wares produced as deliberately expendable and placed so as to protect others placed deeper within the fire. By about 3,000 B.C. the first true ceramics kilns were evolving in Egypt and Mesopotamia; this coincided with the emergence of a form of potter's wheel in Egypt at about the same time. It is tempting to speculate whether or not the one came before the other, but in any event the ancient craft of pottery was again subjected to a revolution, both cultural and industrial.

Development of the wheel was attributed to the Egyptians some time about the third millennium B.C. and was to have far-reaching effects on the craft. Hitherto pottery had been produced at a leisurely rate, consisting more or less of one-off pieces, usually made by women. The wheel, representing 'technology' and probably developed by men, became the tool of men. Pots could now be mass-produced, and were usually decorated in a more mechanical manner, it now being possible to apply decoration onto a revolving, truly circular vessel. Banding could be easily and accurately applied, and geometric forms and motifs superseded the gentler, lovingly executed artwork of the more sensitively conceived hand-made pieces.

It is pretty safe to say that, since its development in the Middle East, the wheel dominated the production of ceramics, generating an influential stereotype that has been difficult to change or avoid – at least until now.

A Current View

Contemporary studio pottery, hand-made by artist-craftspeople using traditional, time-honoured methods, encounters all the pitfalls, problems and delights inherent in the primitive approach to the craft. At the same time it embraces some of the advantages of modern technology that are considered appropriate to the specific needs of a workshop or classroom, such as 'designer' clays and 'computerized temperature controllers' (of which more later). After all, there is no merit in putting work at risk in the interests of a misguided 'back to nature' acceptance of the crude or inept, nor is there any sense in wasting valuable resources such as materials, fuel or time.

But to return to the basic reason for writing this book. The combination of an almost timeless craft tradition, and of practical skills that appear difficult, if not sometimes closer to mysticism and alchemy, is often somewhat daunting. Talk of glaze formulae and recipes can be intimidating to the novice, and probably one of the first and most potent images a beginner has to come to terms with is that of the potter working at the wheel: it can be as off-putting as it is compelling to see such skilful dexterity, suggesting almost magical control over an inanimate material. We hope to offer reassurance and guidance, in down-to-earth terms, so the novice can meet these challenges with confidence.

It takes millions of years for feldspathic rock to be eroded and rotted down into the raw material we know as clay; against this timescale the development of the potter's wheel is extremely recent, and post-dates other known usages of clay and the earliest attempts to create a 'ceramic' material. This means that the wheel is not actually synonymous with pottery.

Many peasant and artist potters, both contemporary and from ancient civilizations, have produced artefacts without recourse to the wheel. They have exploited the properties of the medium in many and varied ways, producing fragile porcelain pots and models, or huge projects such as the recently discovered life-size Chinese warriors. Anyone with a love of, and a feeling for clay, and an understanding of the basic processes involved in fashioning it, can produce exciting, fulfilling ceramic artefacts. You may feel that what you really want to do is produce wares on the wheel: but if you don't want to face that particular challenge, you must not feel that you are somehow disadvantaged or inadequate as a potential potter.

Historically, wheel-work as a mass-production process was superseded by new technology: now, virtually all industrially made pottery is produced by other means, and potters have increasingly felt themselves freed from the dominance of the wheel, and in a better position to challenge rules and conventions. The field is therefore wide open for experiment and innovation: nowadays you can make whatever you choose. You can utilize traditional studio pottery methods, altering them to suit yourself; you can borrow and modify industrial processes and materials; and you can introduce such innovations as are appropriate: in short, almost anything is permissible and possible.

The creative potential of clay can be experienced and enjoyed in a shed, a back yard or an evening class, as can the fascinating processes of making, decorating and firing. Maybe your first experiences were at school or college or at home, or perhaps you are still looking for a way to get started: whatever the case, I hope this book will assist and encourage you to pursue your interest to the full, and give you the confidence to attempt a wider range of ceramic activity. For example, a principal aim is to dispel some of the mystique surrounding firing kilns, so that those involved less frequently in firings will be better able to manage both the kiln and its contents successfully.

Above *Food vessel, Bronze Age. Nottingham Castle Museum & Art Gallery*
Right and inset *Large Nigerian jar, probably 19th Century. Nottingham CM&AG*

2 What is Clay?

It is difficult for children or adults not to respond to clay in an imaginative and creative way because it simply begs to be used. It invites manipulation, and defies the logic of clean hands, clothes and kitchen work surfaces. It prompts most of us at some time to play with it, exploring its possibilities, and to somehow transform the humble material into something more enduring. We poke it, squeeze it, pat it and manipulate it with our hands and fingers. We smooth it, pinching and coaxing until we are satisfied with the result, even attaching appendages to our newly created artefact. Then we find that its substance develops too many cracks to be acceptable – we realize that we have handled it for too long with our warm, dry hands, and so we return it to the riverbed or plastic bag and start again. After all, it's only mud…

Clay, found in the local churchyard.

The creative process intently under way. Photo: Doug Wensley

Or is it? In fact the simplicity of the material is deceptive, because mud does not have the same potential, as many young children have discovered. Nor is a mixture of sand and water an adequate substitute either, however fine the sand. So what is clay, and what is it that makes it so special? The answer to the first part of the question is easy: it is rotten rock.

Over millions of years igneous or metamorphic rock slowly decomposes, producing the unique material we know as clay. Its scientific name is 'hydrated silicate of alumina', it has a theoretical clay crystal structure with the formula $Al_2O_3 2SiO_2 2H_2O$, and it should certainly not be confused with mud. It is extremely common, and as a raw material it is easy to find and usually relatively cheap. Its major attribute is its plasticity in its damp, heavy, natural state, and it is this that gives clay its versatility. In this context the term 'plastic'

refers to clay's property of being malleable, or capable of being manipulated by numerous means into shapes that can be maintained while the material is still in its plastic state. It is this characteristic that is regarded as the key to most ceramic endeavour, allowing the material to be pinched, rolled, thrown, cast or spun into virtually any form; it can be extruded, stamped, pierced or scored in its moistened state. After drying out it can be broken down, re-moistened and re-used.

Understanding how this plasticity occurs can therefore be useful in maintaining this property. Perhaps the first thing to say is that not all naturally occurring clay bodies have the same degree of plasticity. As mentioned already, clay is actually slowly decomposed rock, such as granite, which upon decomposition first yields silicates, salts and feldspar. This feldspar can further break down into the end product kaolin(ite), at the same time releasing mica, quartz and further salts and silicates. As a consequence of the nature and degree of the breakdown, coupled with accidental factors such as contaminants picked up during the prolonged geological timescale involved, there is no 'one' clay, but a wide range of differing bodies (of which more later).

The Properties of Clay

In use, clay is described as being in 'wet state' or 'dry state'. 'Wet state' refers to the condition of the clay when it has been prepared for use, and when its properties are first likely to affect the work of a potter. 'Dry state' is when it has dried out and loses the 'free water' contained within the body.

'Wet State'

When first quarried, clay can often appear almost rock-like: lumpy and hard, and like this its real qualities are easy to miss. Ball clay in its fresh-dug state looks particularly unpromising as a potter's medium – yet in spite of this we still refer to it as a 'plastic' clay. In its purest form, mined from the site where it originally decomposed from the parent rock, clay is usually referred to as 'primary clay'. The most important of these residual clays is china clay, noted for its whiteness and purity; but because of its relatively large particle size, it lacks plasticity. Another important primary clay is bentonite, which conversely is extremely fine and plastic.

Due to the ravages of weather and erosion, clays can be carried – as a suspension in river water, for example – and deposited well away from the site of the parent rock. Such clays can collect a wide variety of impurities en route, these altering their appearance – iron oxide, for example, can add the characteristic terracotta colour to clays such as red marls. As a consequence of these processes –weathering, abrading, frosting and leaching – particle size is broken down to produce finer, more plastic clays.

Such bodies that have been carried away from their points of origin and dumped elsewhere are known as secondary clays. In a fine-grained body such as ball clay, the particles – think of them as minute single crystals – are so small that an electron microscope is needed to see them; in such a clay there are often in excess of 3.5 million crystals in one cubic centimetre. In addition, each grain is plate-shaped, rather like a discus; when all, or most, of these particles or plates are arranged to lie in a similar plane, and lubricated with water – so that each minute particle is wetted on all its surface area – the body is likely to have achieved maximum plasticity.

Like primary clay, clays containing significant quantities of sand will also tend to be less plastic, or 'short', a condition that may be modified by blending in a more plastic clay. Naturally occurring ball clay, being extremely plastic, is frequently used for this purpose, particularly as it is virtually impossible to use on its own, being too sticky and unable to support itself. Its name refers to the practice of digging such clays from open quarries in handy-sized lumps – 'balls' – of about 25lb (11kg). Ball clay is also frequently included in glaze recipes to provide adhesion before firing, and to help keep the glaze in suspension. Fireclays are also naturally

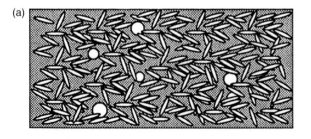 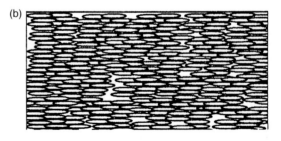

(a) Disc-shaped particles scattered haphazardly throughout the body reduce plasticity, causing the clay to appear 'short'.
(b) When particles are aligned in the same plane the clay becomes more plastic. Discs, lubricated with water, slide easily one against the other.

short, but these can be crushed and blunged to produce extremely plastic clays that reflect their origins as shales or flaky, compacted sedimentary clay (*see* the photos on page 21).

'Dry State'

When clay dries out it loses the 'free' water contained within the body; obviously it loses plasticity as this drying occurs and, perhaps not surprisingly, it shrinks a little. In this condition it cannot be worked except by scraping, scratching or sponging, as finishing-off procedures – although it can be returned to its plastic state, in other words, recycled for further use (*see* Chapter 4, Clay Preparation, page 38). Its shrinkage also affects working procedures, a state of affairs that will be considered later, as it has serious implications for any sort of assemblage.

A source of 'found' clay: a trench dug in the bank has revealed terracotta clay, some of which has fallen into the stream below.

Where is Clay Found?

Clay is usually found buried beneath more recent deposits of rock, sand and earth, perhaps transported by glacier and/or river, washed down and deposited in caves, riverbeds or back gardens. Many local potteries were established in close proximity to sites where clay was found near or at the surface, not just because the clay was gratuitously obtained, but also because it would have been impossible to have transported such a heavy raw material over any significant distance. The characteristics of local potteries were thus determined to an extent by the characteristics of the locally available clay bodies. The Honiton Pottery, for example, was a family business established on a red clay dug from its own back garden. In the long run, however, this source proved to have too many unreliable properties (colour, shrinkage, resistance to damage in firing, and so on), and eventually more consistent supplies had to be sought elsewhere.

The following short excerpt from *The English Country Pottery*, written by Peter Brears, paints an intriguing picture of the chaos and distress that arose in the sixteenth century as a result of the potter's quest for 'proper clay':

Having obtained a site, the potter then proceeded to dig his clay, the depth and size of his 'pot-hole', or 'potter's pit', being determined by the situation of the clay and the amounts he required. These pits were a continuing source of trouble for the local community, for the potters appear to have rarely refilled them. These open pits, often flooded with water, were dangerous, and numerous complaints were raised against them. In manorial and burgess courts throughout England there were hundreds of complaints and pains made against the potters, usually because the pits endangered the lives of both the local people and their livestock. In areas where the clay deposits lay just under the surface it was not uncommon for the potters to dig large holes in the roadways, were the clay was rendered down to an excellent consistency by the combined action of the weather and the passing traffic. At Burslem in 1549 Richard Daniel came before the courts for digging in 'the King's Way', and a little earlier, in 1533, the Wakefield Burgess Court ordered that 'the Cuppers from henceforth shall get no clay within eight yeards of the hye waye side'.

Some self-reliant potters still seek local clays, and are prepared to work hard to obtain low-cost material, literally from the earth beneath them. Others tend to blend own-brand bodies using ingredients purchased from a supplier; these will possess characteristics as required and determined by the individual craftsperson. More often, however, blended bodies are mass-produced and purchased for a specific purpose.

What Clay to Use?

In the past, potters had little choice, and would have used the clays that were available in the immediate vicinity, either directly from the ground or blended with other local bodies to improve the working or visual characteristics. And where no suitable clay could be found, there would have been little or no ceramic activity. Clay could be bought in at great cost from outside sources, but even the expense of this would not have been the major issue: the mere fact of transporting large, extremely heavy loads would have been impractical, if not impossible – an ironic situation, as some of the difficulty was probably because of the ill-advised digging of other potters. Only limited trade would have been possible, in white bodies likely to be most suitable for slips (*see* Decoration, page 118), and such material would have been used sparingly because of scarcity and cost.

Contemporary craft participants can almost be forgiven for thinking that clay is a product manufactured in some vast factory complex, rather like washing powder; after all, it comes in the same sort of handy packages, plastic-wrapped, with its name and catalogue number clearly printed on the packaging. And the consumer has an almost dazzling choice of 'designer' clays, far removed from the

Red marl – terracotta production.

Raw fireclay – stoneware production.

Above *Fireclay 'picked up' by shovel loader.*

Right *Fireclay being 'fed' into the blunger.*

Above *Another view of fireclay being fed into a blunger.*

Left *After blungeing, slip is passed through a vibratory sieve, leaving a collection of residue.*

Right *Cakes of clay being removed from the filter press after pressing: a cycle of three to seven hours at 180 p.s.i., depending on the clay.*

Cakes being fed into a de-airing pugmill, pugged clay cut and stacked on pallet.

Clay being bagged after pugging.

Finished stock ready for despatch.

Photos above and opposite: Alan Ault, Valentine Clays, Stoke-on-Trent.

original quarry sites, in every sense, and which offer a choice of specialist options to suit almost every circumstance.

This invaluable resource is entirely justified here, since potters need to be able to select clay bodies appropriate for their intended use. Preferences will depend, among other things, on the making and firing processes, the nature of the glazes proposed, and the colour and texture of the body. These days we are no longer confined to local materials because modern transport is quick, convenient and not excessively expensive. Suppliers can make available to us clay bodies either from stock, or blended to meet individual requirements; and most are pleased to give practical advice or even samples to experiment on at home. This gives you more time to be actually making things, and also side-steps the risk of back injury, and the unpredictability of digging clay from an unreliable source.

The advantages of such a system are varied and obvious. In short, we can usually obtain a readily available, reliable body to suit our particular requirements, with the assured prospect of being able to reorder on a long-term basis. We can also expect delivery to our door, at a price…

Buying Clay

If you need to purchase clay, you might consider the following options:

- Contact a local, established potter;
- Collect your clay direct from a local supplier to save delivery costs;
- Join with other interested potters to purchase collectively in bulk;
- The same goes for buying other raw materials too, more of which later.

Convenience does cost, however, and not just in financial terms. The satisfaction of obtaining and blending our own bodies is gone, and we have lost touch with one of the more fundamental aspects of the craft – contact with the earth. In order to re-establish contact with this element it is therefore worth digging to discover local clay, just as a break from using standard bodies, as a return to basics, and as a means of realizing the qualities and potential of what is, after all, the craft's basic raw material.

To engage with this idea, and to put it into the whole ceramic context, refer to the project on page 25: Introduction to the Ceramic Process.

What Clay: Factors, Choices, Decisions

So, how do you decide which clay to use? Well, it rather depends on how are you involved with ceramics. For instance, if you are a student and must make use of the resources provided by the establishment you attend, there may well be no choice. You may perhaps find two bodies on offer: a red earthenware clay, probably best suited to the production of press-moulded dishes and smaller thrown things; plus a grey stoneware throwing body, the latter being the preferred choice of experienced students who extol its virtues in reduction firing, whatever that may be. Peer group influence may well overshadow practical considerations here, so try to experience both before making judgements.

If, on the other hand, you are setting up your own workshop, with or without experience, and you have yet to acquire clay, the choice is yours. Start by browsing suppliers' catalogues, and try to identify a clay that seems appropriate to your requirements. If you intend working within earthenware temperature ranges, then a good red clay may well be best; if you intend to build large sculptural pieces, then a heavily grogged grey clay, such as raku or crank, will almost certainly be more suitable. In subsequent chapters there will be specific advice and comment on different bodies, and on the making, decoration and firing of pieces, all of which may help you come to various decisions. But the most important point is that you get your hands on some clay (any sort will do to start with) and play your way in, sorting out your preferences as your experience increases.

What Happens Next?

In 'playing your way in' you make a few pots or other artefacts. The intention is to change these into ceramic pieces by subjecting them to intense heat. In order to bring this about the artefacts must be made out of clay; they must be completely dry; and they should be relatively thin and of uniform thickness.

The fundamental concept of a potter's trinity of Earth, Water and Fire is as inescapable as are the consequences of it to the craft we have chosen to follow, and to ignore any one is to put all our efforts at risk. Subjecting dry clay artefacts to heat means putting them into fire, and there is a real risk at this point of damage or loss due to thermal shock. Temperatures must be raised very gradually, to reduce shock, but also – and this is almost more important – so that any moisture remaining in the clay is not forced out too violently.

All these points will be raised again in the contexts of making and firing, but it is worth repeating that (a) thorough drying out, and (b) very slow initial heating up, are both essential to successful firing.

Smoked pots.

3 Introducing the Ceramic Process

In this introduction we hope to cover, in a basic yet challenging way, most of the processes involved in the production of a ceramic piece. No special tools or equipment are necessary, only a willingness to become involved with the craft at the humblest 'hands-on' level; you will also need plaster of Paris, superfine dental or casting plaster, obtainable locally in modest amounts from some chemists, arts & crafts shops, and in rather larger quantities from builders' merchants.

Slip-Casting a Mini Pebble Pot

First, the messy bit:

1. Dig some clay, as found in a garden, a workmen's trench or a river bank. Incidentally, the clay illustrated in the photographs comes from a trench dug close to the foundations of a local church during a successful attempt to save the building from serious subsidence. About 1lb ($\frac{1}{2}$kg) will be sufficient, depending on impurities. If it is obvious that the material contains a great deal of pebbles, more may be required.
2. Soak the clay in a bucket, adding double the volume of water. Overnight should suffice. If necessary, especially if time is short, break up any lumps by stirring with a blunt instrument.
3. Ideally try to form the mixture into a creamy consistency, though it *will* still have lumps in it.
4. Now force the mixture through an old pair of tights (or anything else that might do) to sift out

'Found' clay soaking down.

any foreign bodies and to render the whole into a smooth consistency. If the mix seems too runny, allow it to settle, then decant off the excess clear water.

Now comes the creative part. Select a largish pebble (2–3in/5–7.5cm maximum) from the trench (or other potential source if necessary); the selection process is the creative bit in the sense that only *you* would have chosen that particular stone. Also required is a cardboard box, large enough to contain the pebble and allowing about 1in (2.5cm) space on every side, as illustrated.

Pouring the slaked-down clay into an old pair of tights.

Squeeze gently to force clay through the foot.

1. Take $\frac{1}{4}$ cup of the sifted clay and, using the brush, mix in water to make a slip of single cream consistency; then apply a coat to one half of the pebble.

   Note: Slip that is painted onto the pebble acts as a releasing agent, preventing plaster adhering to it. Other cost-effective DIY agents include old engine oil or washing-up liquid, either used separately, or mixed with clay into water-resistant slip.

2. Mix up sufficient plaster to fill the cardboard box to one third of its capacity. Then follow the instructions in the captions that accompany the illustrations.

3. Pour the plaster into the box, checking possible leaks, and if there are any, quickly apply clay to the outside of the container to avert loss.

Plaster of Paris sprinkled into the water, and allowed to settle without stirring.

Making a Two-Piece Mould

Have at hand the following:
• One or two plastic bowls, capable of holding a pint or two of liquid (ice-cream or margarine tubs are ideal)
• A plastic kitchen jug
• A paintbrush (any sort, such as 1in/2.5cm household paintbrush)
• A cup or yoghurt pot in which to mix up some slip
• The pebble, cardboard box, and a water supply

Continue adding plaster until a crust (islands of dry powder) begins to build up on the surface. This indicates approaching saturation point.

Now use a hand to stir and squeeze out any lumps, ensuring an even, creamy mix.

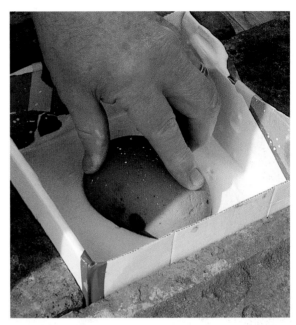

Lower the pebble into the plaster, up to its widest girth, so that it is half submerged (see note 5).

6. The plaster will get quite warm as it sets; once it is firm, make two or three indentations (keys) into the plaster surface (*see* illustration below), then coat pebble and plaster with slip.

Plaster is poured into the box.

4. Gently tap the sides of the box, or bump the supporting table to agitate the mix, so that minute bubbles of air are sent to the surface.
5. Allow the plaster to begin to set; this could be anything from 5–10 minutes, depending on the mix. When it is firm enough, carefully insert the pebble, painted side down, up to its widest point. (Ensure the plaster does not cover the upper side of the pebble, or it will be locked in when the plaster sets.) Make sure there is about $\frac{1}{4}$in (1cm) depth of plaster between the pebble and the bottom of the box.

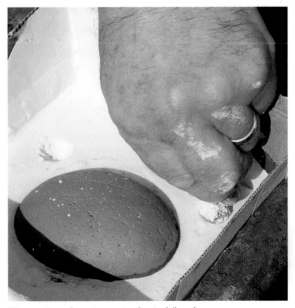

Use a coin to bore in semi-spherical 'keys'.

When the plaster has set, paint its surface, and the pebble, with slip.

7. Mix more plaster and pour it over the pebble to cover it by at least $\frac{1}{4}$in (1cm), forming a level surface.
8. Allow the plaster to dry thoroughly.
9. When the block has cooled off and is hard (try poking a finger-nail into the surface), the cardboard box can be stripped away, and the sharp plaster corners chamfered off.
10. The task now is to separate the two layers of plaster, so as to remove the pebble. Try gently knocking the upper layer sideways; if nothing happens immediately, don't worry: place the block on its side and trickle some water onto the joint between the two layers, allowing it to soak down the slip-lined seam. Try knocking

A second mould being cast, using a tomato.

The cardboard container removed.

'Pouring' channels, also referred to as 'risers' or 'spares', are carved into the moulds using a knife, file and/or surform tool.

The two-part mould separated. Use a surform blade or 'riffler' to clean up the edges.

again; on small moulds this will almost always succeed. If it doesn't, use a very blunt chisel to prise them apart, using water, and gentle but persistent wiggling and tapping.

11. Once separated and the pebble removed, each half of the mould can be seen to have a hollow in the shape of the pebble.

At this stage there are two options. The two plaster blocks could be used as 'pressed' dish moulds – though this would not make use of the creamy mix of clay as 'won' and filtered, above; this option will be referred to later in Chapter 7, Hand-building. The other is slip-casting.

Take care to match up both halves of the channels.

Slip-Casting

This project involves filling the pebble-shaped space with slip, allowing it to coat the hole, forming a hollow shell of clay that then becomes a ceramic vessel. In order to achieve this, it is necessary to make a pouring hole in the mould, through which the slip may be poured in. The illustrations show how this is accomplished. In fact, as will be seen, *two* holes are necessary, one to fill and the other to vent air; though on this small scale it will be rather difficult to pour in slip anyway, and the holes may need to be widened.

1. Carve matching channels into both parts of the mould. On this scale two holes are necessary: one for filling, the other to allow air to escape.

Either try to blend these into the shape so that both holes can become spouts on the finished form; or allow scope for modification after casting, disguising or reinventing the holes to suit the vessel.

2. Reassemble the mould, using the locating keys to ensure correct alignment of the two pieces. Firmly attach them together, using rubber bands (car or bicycle inner tubes can be cut into excellent strong versions).

3. Check that the slip (creamy mix of clay) is of a pourable consistency. Stir, and dip a finger into the mix, and withdraw it: if the nail has a very thin coat and the quick is filled, the consistency is probably about right.

Completed moulds, one set with pouring holes for slip-casting, the other for press-moulding.

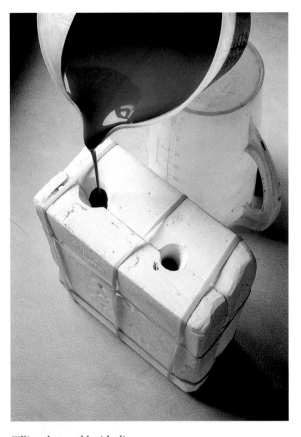

Filling the mould with slip.

The mould is left to drain, resting on two supporting laths over a bucket.

4. Carefully pour in the slip, allowing air to exit via the other hole. You will find that as you pour, the slip tends to stiffen and dry, blocking the entrance: poke it free with a thin stick or grass stem. Completely fill the mould until both holes are full of slip.
5. Tap very gently to ensure all the liquid has run in, and top up as necessary.
6. Do not leave too long. Pour off the excess slip, leaving a coating on the plaster walls inside; by carefully scraping away excess slip across the top of the holes, it should be possible to get an idea as to the thickness of the build-up inside.
7. This is the critical part. Leave the deposited slip cast to dry out before attempting to separate the mould. If the mould was very dry before pouring, the slip will not take too long to stiffen; if the mould was very damp it will take longer.

Cleaning off excess slip to prevent unnecessary 'locking' as the clay stiffens and shrinks.

The resulting cast could be left in the mould until it is completely dry. The chances are, however, that curiosity will lead to the vessel being exposed and examined before this, probably whilst it is still leather-hard. As a rough guide, try leaving the cast overnight to firm up, and then *gently* shake or tap the mould, listening for sounds of loosened contents. This being the case, it would be possible to fettle, attach to, or remodel parts of the finished piece before the clay became too dry to work. Tap the pot down onto a flat surface to flatten a base.

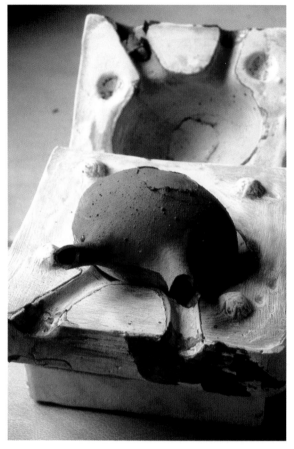

Above *The slip-cast pot revealed after separation.*

Left *Fettling off the 'feather'. Use a potter's knife, a metal kidney tool or an old penknife.*

Slip-Casting Tips

- It is easier to carve out pouring holes while the plaster is still 'fresh', i.e. hard, but not yet dry and brittle, or as soon after separating as is possible.

- After cleaning up (even washing) the mould, allow it to dry out thoroughly before casting; putting the two separate parts on a radiator overnight will usually be sufficient. (The process depends on plaster absorbing water from the clay immediately in contact with it in order to build up a clay wall/shell.)

- Each casting causes the plaster to become less absorbent (being wetter), so second and subsequent castings will take progressively longer to build up similar wall deposits. Watch for indications (thin walls, collapsing etc.) that drying out is necessary.

- Be prepared to adjust the consistency of the slip – add more water to assist filling.

Whichever way the job is completed, there should now be an interestingly curious pot as evidence of your efforts. Now cast up several further editions of the same.

Picture sequence of pressed version. *Flat slabs of clay can be gently, but firmly, pressed into the moulds.*

Score, and apply slip to the surfaces to be joined together.

Use a damp sponge to coax the clay down into all the irregularities to reproduce all the interesting detail.

Use a wooden tool (modelling, or an old ruler) to remove excess clay, dragging against the plaster mould to prevent the clay releasing from the mould.

The completed 'tomato' released.

Firing

The final stage may be described as 'ordeal by fire' – literally. The finished pots, having been dried out completely, are still only made of clay, and are fragile, brittle and still recyclable at this stage: so they are now put into a bonfire.

Any sudden thermal shock could prove fatal, so it is essential that the wares are protected from this, as far as is possible. All-round heat will be less stressful than heat concentrated on one side only, so if possible avoid sitting the pots on the ground – at least to start with. Use your ingenuity to support the pots on something that will not burn away quickly, so that a fire may be built up gradually around them. At the start, use fuel with a low thermal output, such as dry grass, shredded paper, thin twigs and the like. Dry wood shavings, as sold in pet shops, can be scattered on and around the pots to slow up the firing.

Above *Leather-hard surfaces can be burnished using a very smooth pebble, spoon or similar implement.*

Below *Pots awaiting the trial by fire. Most are burnished, one is not.*

Protect from initial heat: use wood chippings or sawdust inside a tin – or not – to slow combustion. Density reduces oxygen supply.

A slow, gentle start to the fire.

Gradually increase fuel to build up heat.

Hot charcoal provides enough heat to achieve metamorphosis.

Allow the fire to die down completely. Uneven or sudden cooling can cause 'dunting' – or cracking, flaking or collapse.

A selection of bonfired and pit-fired pots, cleaned up and wax-polished, revealing a rich terracotta body with arbitrary carbon-black 'decoration'.

Increase the fire's intensity gradually, trying to heat the ware gently and evenly throughout. Individual pieces or small batches can be placed inside old tins if a bit more protection is preferred. Aim to get a reasonable base of glowing charcoal under the wares, and once there is a good fire burning, stoke it as necessary to ensure thorough, and if possible red, heating of the pots. Let the fire do its work, then allow it to burn right out, and the ash to cool down; then withdraw the wares.

With a little luck they should have remained whole, changed colour (depending on the original body), and become relatively hard and porous. If they were made in a terracotta-coloured clay they may now appear to have assumed an almost chestnut colour, probably with black, smoked patches as a result of the fire. Finished wares can be cleaned up and washed (if the firing has been successful), and treated with an ordinary wax polish to enhance the colour.

In Retrospect

The end products may be under- or over-fired, or a mixture of the two, and may not be as attractive as might be anticipated. They will, however, have served as an holistic ceramic experience, the process of creation from mud to stone; the metamorphosis involving the ceramic 'trinity', and introduced practical making skills.

Health and Safety

With care and common sense this project can be carried out in a private garden or yard without significant risk to anyone. It would, however, be wise to wear protective glasses when stoking. Particularly during the early stages there is a chance that the ware might shatter due to unexpected moisture remaining present in the body. This is very unlikely here because the walls will be remarkably thin, but it is better to be safe than sorry.

Note: Firing, and avoiding the problems therein, is discussed in detail in Chapter 13. However, in the interests of both maker and pot in this particular context, remember to allow wares to dry out thoroughly before subjecting them to the fire.

4 Using, Reclaiming and Preparing Clay

Most casual encounters with clay, the raw material, might give the impression that it is always in excellent working condition. Seen in the hands of an experienced craftsperson it will appear to have life, vigour, and a desire to adapt itself to the will of the maker in a most co-operative manner. It will be wonderfully plastic, malleable and homogenous; though the latter will not be immediately obvious, even to anyone aware of its significance.

Conversely, the clay may be either too sticky and unsupportive, or excessively hard and unyielding. In group classes, for example, the condition of the clay may well suit some, but be less than ideal for others: if it seems right for throwing, it may well be too soft for hand-building processes, and could prove extremely difficult to roll out into flat slabs. The individual maker is therefore responsible for suitable preparation of his or her own clay.

Nowadays, clay purchased from a supplier will normally come in plastic bags containing 25kg (55lb), having been de-aired and prepared in average plastic condition. These bags are best stored in a cool place until required, and will keep very well if wrapped again in further bags, or contained in a bin, for instance a dustbin, preferably airtight.

Storing Clay

- Clay, stored in bins for imminent use, should be covered with wet cloth and/or plastic sheet to avoid drying out.

- Clay stores well in basements/cellars.

- Potters of old had been known to have buried clay, often for two or more generations, to conserve and enhance plasticity. 'Resting' clay can help, although a time-span of months may be all you can give it.

It is quite possible that when a new bag of clay is opened, it will be found to be too stiff. Suppliers do not wish to be accused of selling water, and so have to tread a wary path between introducing too much or too little moisture content to their products. Clay in plastic bags can, and will, dry out in time, and storing it in dry conditions – such as in the same room as a kiln – will hasten the process. So do remember that although polythene looks waterproof, the contents can in fact dry out even if bags are unopened, or undamaged. A damp, cool environment is best for long-term storage.

Reclaiming Clay

Most of us have a bag or two of hardened clay that we intend to reclaim 'some time'. Unfortunately there are usually more interesting things to do, and so the bags just sit around waiting. As usual, prevention is better than cure; nevertheless, to effect a cure, the following procedure will have to be carried out:

- Break up the dry lump, probably by battering it with a heavy hammer. The drier the clay, the easier this will be.
- Put the small (as small as possible) pieces into a bin.
- Cover with water.
- Allow the dry clay to slake down and settle.
- Decant or siphon off excess (by now clear) water.
- Slop out clay onto an absorbent surface, usually plaster of Paris.
- Allow to stiffen up ready for preparation (*see* below).

Soaking the clay down.

Cracking up a hard lump of clay.

Slopping out onto an absorbent surface.

Where the bag of clay has not dried out completely but has retained water, but is just too hard to work, and cannot be broken up by violence as above, try the following: leave the hardened bag outside to the ravages of winter weather: frost will achieve what strong arms and soak-bins cannot. This is because water trapped inside the clay freezes. This seems to have a twofold effect: water is physically separated from the clay, causing a break-up within the mass; as it begins to melt, the now small, broken clay lumps are wetted, making them more inclined to accept additional water. They sometimes become very soggy, and can be recycled much more easily.

Ideally, discarded clay should be kept damp after use so that it can be mixed up (wedged or kneaded) and restored ready for use again. Clay that is too stiff for immediate re-use should be allowed to dry out completely, broken up into small pieces and soaked down in water to be recycled later.

It is obviously important to separate 'reclaim', as we often call the recycled material, to ensure that different bodies are not mixed together unintentionally. Two or more clay bodies may be found in use in one establishment, so make sure you are aware of this if you have just arrived.

Clay is not improved by the accidental addition of foreign bodies, either. These can cause unsightly lumps or 'blow-outs' later; the author has 'found' potters needles when 'slopping out', unfortunately by becoming impaled by a finger. Possibly an 'occupational hazard', but decidedly unnecessary (*see* Tools, page 59). Reclaim bins should be adequately covered to prevent all such incursions.

Preparing Clay

Whether or not you have your own studio, or rely on the technical support in an educational establishment, a knowledge and understanding of the preparation processes is essential. You will want your clay in ideal condition for its intended purpose. Furthermore we all have preferences, based on different expectations and experiences; though it is usually not difficult to ensure that these prefer-

ences are met, despite the fact that it entails some extra work.

The easiest method of reclaiming clay is, as we have seen above, to collect *used* clay in its plastic state, and to knead it up ready for re-use. As clay is used, it will tend to dry out to a lesser or greater extent. If it remains reasonably damp, it can be mixed together with softer clay so that the overall mix is of an appropriate consistency. This is often a useful way of dealing with wet, sloppy slurry and collapsed pots resulting from throwing on the wheel, and still-damp 'turnings' produced during the finishing or turning stages.

Drying Out Wet Clay

Preparation is crucial, and there are basically three traditional methods: allowing the clay to dry out naturally; using an absorbent surface; and via the hands-on processes of kneading and wedging.

Drying out naturally: The clay simply dries out in the atmosphere. Allowing clay to stiffen up naturally sounds the easiest option. Unfortunately, it can take time, and usually results in rather uneven drying. To at least partially overcome this, the clay can be squeezed into long, sausage-shaped rolls and arranged, arch-like, on a board, allowing air to circulate over a greater surface area.

By using an absorbent surface: Such a surface will absorb moisture from the clay; it might be plaster of Paris, in the form of kneading slabs and moulds. Spreading out 'slops' on a plaster slab or into a plaster mould results in the water being absorbed by the plaster, and again, is a useful means of stiffening clay.

Via the hands-on processes of kneading and wedging: These two processes augment and resolve the shortcomings of the above options.

Kneading is similar to the method of kneading bread, except the idea is to achieve a totally even consistency throughout, ensuring that all air bubbles are eliminated. (*see* page 40). Usually this process is attempted using approximately football-sized lumps, or smaller. If kneading is difficult, then probably the body needs to be softened, as per 'Wedging', below. Remember, if you can't knead it, you probably won't be able to throw it, either.

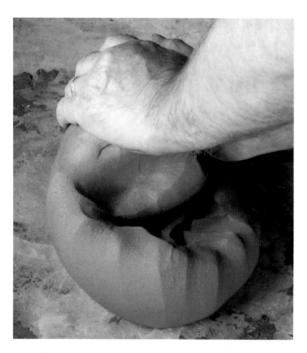

Kneading: using a single twisting, spiral movement. The lump has to be lifted, using the fingers, pulling back towards oneself before applying pressure with the heel of (usually) the right hand.

Alternatively, pressure can be applied via both hands.

Progression of the spiral pressure.

This produces a double spiral. The aim in either case is to stretch and de-air the clay, rendering it homogeneous – that is, with an absolutely even consistency: no hard lumps, air pockets or foreign bodies. The latter are forced to the surface during twisting and stretching, and can be removed by hand.

Wedging is done by cutting a large lump of clay in half, lifting and turning the freed piece, and slamming it down into the piece left on the bench, thereby spreading, stretching and mixing the clay (*see* photos). The intention is to bring the two lumps together without a loud slapping sound, because this actually signals entrapment of even more air, rather than less. This vigorous method of homogenizing clay is perhaps best seen as the first step, getting a large quantity into semi-acceptable state; followed by the second step, of kneading up smaller lumps into prime working condition.

A Mechanical Alternative: the Pugmill

Pugmills are rather like giant mincing machines, namely ram-fed worm-screws forcing clay through narrowing extrusion exits, churning it up and compressing it somewhat, and regurgitating it in reasonable working condition. If you have free (or supervised) access to such an aid, some of the harder work can be avoided, as can some of the uncertainty of leaving the process to others.

When clay is just a little too soft after pugging (and only experience will tell you when this is), it can be stiffened by kneading on a plaster slab. This will homogenize it at the same time, and is not too demanding in terms of either effort or time. However, if the amount required is large, or if the clay is excessively soft, the pugmill can be a valuable asset.

Using a cutting wire to wedge larger lumps. Compare the foreground mix with the clay that has already been wedged.

Slamming down, ensuring the close joining of a curved to a flat surface, avoiding any entrapment of air. This process is usually used when processing larger amounts of clay – meaning lumps that can be held above head height and dropped down to impact with clay on the slab.

Use the pugmill as follows:

Step 1 Have readily at hand the soft clay, plus a small amount of stiffer clay.

Step 2 Add a golf-ball-sized lump of harder clay to a tennis-ball-sized lump of the softer clay, and feed the combined lump into the pugmill.

Step 3 Feed in the whole batch and check the consistency. Remember that a large vertical pugmill will contain upwards of a bag of clay *before* you put yours in, so do not expect the first extrusion to be perfect. Feed in plenty, to exclude the original contents, and repeat the process as necessary, adding softer or harder (but *not* dry) clay until the desired consistency is achieved.

Avoid using sloppy, almost liquid clay, or clay that is excessively hard – even a pugmill will have trouble digesting extremes, and by introducing such clay you will certainly not make things easier, in fact quite the contrary. Used intelligently, however, the pugmill will enable you to reconstitute clay in a relatively short time. Remember, though, that pugging is not a substitute for kneading, this being essential to ensure total de-airing and homogenization prior to throwing.

Odd Properties of Clay

- Clay does not absorb water readily. Subterranean layers of clay inhibit drainage; ponds lined with clay existed for ages in the days before butyl liners.

- Damp clay is less inclined to absorb water than is completely dry clay.

- Open, coarse bodies are marginally more inclined to absorb water than are fine, dense bodies.

- Dry clay in small, thin pieces will break down in water more readily than larger lumps. The latter appear soft and slimy on their surfaces, but inside remain dry.

Such properties can help or hinder the potter, particularly in recycling clay, or mixing slips or glazes.

Softening Up Hard Clay

Emphasis so far has been on stiffening excessively wet clay, but much of the foregoing could also apply if the opposite were required. Thus a pugmill could be used to mix softer clay to a stiff batch. Wedging would take a little longer; but where relatively modest amounts are required – sufficient for an evening class session on the wheel, for example – a simple and effective method can be used, that might be called 'slice and dice', a useful pre-kneading or wedging procedure (*see* photos).

Two lumps of clay to be thoroughly mixed, metaphors for sloppy and stiff, or different bodies.

Slice, using a potter's wire, and stack alternately.

Water cannot easily be added to clay, so if your lump seems too hard to prepare properly, the best recourse is to add soft *clay*. Knock hard clay into a block (like a loaf of bread), and then do this, more or less, with a supply of soft (this could be reclaim slops). By taking alternate slices of wet and stiff clays, build up a stratified pile, which, when all the clay has been used up, can be (carefully) pressed or knocked into another 'loaf' with horizontal strata. Turn the 'loaf' onto its side (the strata are now vertical), and slice and repeat as before, ensuring that each layer is placed at right angles to its predeces-

sor. Keep repeating, so that cross-sections of strata are patterned with little squares of different texture and/or colour. The now well mixed clay can be wedged and kneaded into a homogenized block, ready for use.

If no soft clay is available, there is no alternative but to resort to water. As has already been suggested, clay does not readily absorb water except on its surface, so where it is necessary that it should do so, as large a surface area as possible should be wetted. By making use of the slicing technique (above) and by keeping slices as thin as practical, it is

Cut again, laying subsequent layers at right angles.

The kneaded lump, cut to reveal a smooth colour and texture in cross-section with no air bubbles evident.

Further cutting and stacking dices up the layers even more.

If the mixed bodies are still too firm for easy kneading, add water via holes poked down through the layers, wetting as much surface area as possible. Knock into a consolidated lump, and repeat as necessary.
Note: This is a last resort, to be used only in the absence of more soft or sloppy clay.

possible to further increase the exposed surface areas by piercing the sliced lump with a thin stick or the long handle of an artist's paintbrush. Pour water gently over the clay, and this will percolate down through the vertical holes and out through horizontal cuts, wetting a considerable area.

This method produces very wet, slippery slices of clay which, when cut and turned in an attempt to wedge, become a soggy mass of diced-up cubes. These will be difficult to turn and press into a consolidated mass at first, but persevere. After a short period of apparent hopeless chaos, the clay will begin to form up into a reasonably manageable lump again, and by first wedging and then kneading, an improvement in overall condition will take place. The process may have to be repeated, and it might seem like a lot of work, but if it is the only way to get clay of the desired consistency, then it is well worth the effort. Ten or fifteen minutes spent preparing the clay will pay dividends later, in time saved and frustration avoided, when the clay is found to behave well, particularly if throwing.

Variations on these procedures can be used to blend different bodies and to introduce body stains, colouring oxides, sands or grogs, bearing in mind that dry ingredients will stiffen the body; so it is worth wetting any additive to be used in any significant quantity.

In Your Own Workshop

If you have your own workshop/studio, and have the monopoly as to which preparation systems will be used, some of the foregoing will seem superfluous. You will be able to keep reclamation down to a minimum by kneading up small quantities of clay as they build up, and you will be able to mix and soak harder clay with the slurry and trimmings from throwing. There will be little or no completely dry clay to cause hazardous dust, and you will be able to prepare reclaimed clay to your own requirements.

You will probably not be producing vast amounts of reclaim, and so it is unlikely that you will need a pugmill. Effective workshop practice will render such an item a waste of space in any case, to say nothing of expense. And like some kitchen gadgets, it could prove to be more of a hindrance than a help.

In Conclusion

Sometimes we are lucky enough to find that brand new bags of clay are in precisely the required condition. But if they are then stored inappropriately, we can expect less workable clay when the time comes to use it. Plastic bags, however well sealed, will inevitably allow moisture to escape, albeit slowly. So observe the following:

- Remember the importance of adequate storage. Air-tight containers are one answer; storage in non-drying conditions (cool, damp, away from draughts) is another.
- Always be prepared to re-knead clay after storage, even if this has only been overnight; the outer layer will almost certainly have stiffened, affecting the overall consistency.
- Protect prepared clay from drying out in the air while it awaits use. After all, you have worked to get it into condition, so don't now risk your effort by neglecting it.

Observe the above, and work to a system appropriate to yourself, and you will go a long way to overcoming some of the niggling problems you would otherwise encounter. As a bonus it will encourage the development of a deeper sympathy for the medium, and will transform the seemingly irksome task of preparation into an integral part of the craft process. You will be reassured in the knowledge that you can control and determine the outcome of your efforts, and you will then be freer to concentrate on the creative aspects of your work.

5 Design

Whereas the novice potter, and some books and courses, are rightly concerned with the practical problems of actually making artefacts, frequently little or no consideration is given to design. In some instances, the aesthetics of ceramics is discussed in esoteric eloquence, and this can be as confusing or unhelpful to the uninitiated as not discussing the subject at all. The simple and reassuring fact is that we cannot make anything without, in some way, considering design. In other words, it is not a case of being obliged to take design into account, but rather, it is impossible to make something *without* doing so. Design is implicit in the making process, and it is therefore included here, before methods are discussed, in an attempt to promote in you, the potter, a consciousness of it throughout any subsequent discussion of practical techniques.

Design Concepts

There are basically two approaches to design:

1. **Form**, which is concerned with the appearance of the end product. Is it elegant? Interesting? Does its form enhance it, or detract from it?
2. **Function**, where the prime concern is usage. What is it? What is it required to do? Is it capable of meeting that intended requirement?

In fact these design approaches apply to anything that is man made, and will be considered by a designer/maker in the context of client demand, if any, and personal predilections. They become the

Simple elegance: lidded milk jug, by Ray Finch. Nottingham Castle Museum & Art Gallery

primary, but not the only, factors in the design process, as may become clear if we look at a simple design brief.

Brief: To Make a Container for Liquid

What exactly is required here? Something to hold, or contain, liquid, suggesting a hollow form that has a base or floor with containing walls. It could be a mug, a cup or a bucket – even a reservoir. The brief as written is therefore not sufficiently specific, and leaves the designer unclear as to what is actually required. Further information would be necessary to clarify client needs and to enable a designer/maker to offer a solution. In the normal course of events, a client would provide sufficient information: either a pond was required, or a mug. Clearly, only one solution is acceptable, so both designer and customer have responsibilities to ensure clarification, where necessary. Consequently, it is usual to communicate precise requirements in a design brief.

One notable exception to this can be seen in the writing of some examination questions or briefs. Where evidence of a student's imagination and creative potential is significant, a somewhat 'open-ended' brief is more appropriate. Thus in the example above, there would be no constraints upon the student, encouraging wide-ranging exploration of perceived possibilities. Students would be expected to identify their own problems and solutions through research, and through the development and evidence of their own particular interests and skills, all contributing to a final solution or outcome. In such a circumstance one would expect a wide range of both problems – mug, pond or whatever – and solutions – the nature and appearance of the completed pieces. In this sort of situation, there is no more emphasis on *form* than on *function*; the design brief is itself designed to afford individuals complete creative freedom.

Fortunately, a studio potter (here to include students, and 'one-person' workshops, professional or amateur, regardless of 'status', all of whom are responsible for all stages of design and production) will usually be involved with projects rather more specific than the above, and will be required to address conventional design and production criteria. So, how can our original brief be better written? This obviously depends on what the customer wants.

Teapot, earthenware, Staffordshire, 1760–70.
Nottingham Castle Museum and Art Gallery

Equally fortunate for the potter is that most items likely to be requested have quite explicit specifications implied in their titles: mug, jug, teapot, and so on. Using 'teapot' as the subject here, we can consider precise function. What is required of a teapot?

- It has to contain hot liquid, hence volume.
- An aperture at the top is necessary for filling.
- The contents have to be poured out; a spout is the usual answer.
- It should be possible to pick it up, so a handle in some form is essential.
- A lid to contain heat and exclude dust is customary.

From experience, but not always from a cursory look at a particular article, we know that there are other factors to be taken into account. Dribbling spouts have been a constant challenge over the years. We usually take it for granted that a teapot can be filled to capacity without tea pouring from its spout before it is picked up. A lid that falls off when the pot is tilted could also be a problem. Numerous solutions to the latter have been applied, such as ingenious locking devices built into lid and pot, more suited to metal construction. These are often only short-term, however, due as much to the short memory of the user as to the fragile nature of the material. Probably one of the simplest solutions, for the studio potter, is to utilize the

Teapot, salt-glazed stoneware by
Walter Keeler, c. 1986. Nottingham Castle
Museum & Art Gallery

low centre of gravity principle to the lid, possibly with a retaining gallery thrown onto the pot (more of which later).

Factors Affecting Design

Materials and Processes

Designs for a specific item will differ, depending on the material selected for its production. Ceramic items have, by their very nature, a different characteristic to similar pieces fabricated in metal. In addition, as construction processes determine yet more characteristics, as seen in beaten, spun or cast metal, so different processes are reflected in a finished ceramic product. The form and 'character' of a piece are, to some extent, determined by the method of production, and so also have to be considered within the design process. A hollow ceramic cylinder, for example, could be made by several different methods, each having its merits and peculiar characteristics that would require consideration at the design stage.

Whether or not a particular process is actually possible will also have a bearing on the final outcome, if only in a negative way. That is to say, if a person who cannot throw wishes to make a teapot, he will be obliged to hand-build by some other technique, and the result will be very different from the originally conceived thrown pot.

The potter, of course, can normally ignore materials other than clay for the making process but, as has been remarked above, clays come in a wide range of body types and can have a significant effect upon what is, and is not possible in a given situation. Comparison of these two very different clay bodies will point up their basic characteristics, which in turn will dictate the designs that will suit them best:

Red earthenware
1. Smooth body.
2. Characteristic 'terracotta' colour, i.e. red-brown; the colour lightens after firing.
3. Matures at about 1100°C.

4. Overall shrinkage can be in the region of 15 per cent.
5. Generally among the cheaper bodies on offer.

Raku/Crank
1. Coarse, gritty body.
2. Usually grey, changing to a light biscuit colour after firing.
3. Matures above 1200°C.
4. Overall shrinkage could be as low as 8 or 10 per cent.
5. Blended specifically, but rather more expensive than the above.

1. In this first characteristic, the smooth body will be excellent for small pots and for most construction processes. It will take fine detail well, too. The coarse raku or crank clay will be ideal for larger, hand-built pieces, but will be rather uncomfortable to throw, though by no means impossible.
2. The difference here can affect subsequent glaze colour. Visual appearance of *unglazed* terracotta is quite acceptable; light biscuit colour is less so, and will require cosmetic modification.
3. There is significant difference in this third characteristic, with an important distinction between *earthenware* and *stoneware*, together with its implications for glazing and firing – more of both below.
4. Shrinkage occurs at two stages: when drying out, and during firing, more or less in equal amounts. When producing large sculptural pieces, particularly at higher temperatures, lower shrinkage rates reduce the risk of damage, and collapse during building.
5. The cost difference may or may not be a factor.

A Reminder

One of the prerequisites for a piece of ceramic is that it should be thin. In fact, it is more helpful to think 'even', so that there are no wild changes in thickness in a piece, and therefore less stress between thicker and thinner parts of the whole.

Construction

Form will be determined to a considerable extent by the selected method of construction: thus a wheel-formed pot will look very different to one built with flat slabs of clay. It is also sensible to take into account the changes and stresses imposed upon the material, and hence the structure, caused by drying and firing. Forces acting upon (if not against) your pot are **shrinkage**, both during the initial drying out, and when being fired; and **expansion**: when the temperature of a body is increased, the body expands. Furthermore, unique tensions develop when a clay body is obliged to both shrink and expand *at the same time*.

While your ware is undergoing these traumatic changes during firing, kiln furniture, such as shelving, is probably (although made of ceramic material) only expanding and contracting: any shrinkage will already have taken place during its manufacture. Nevertheless, any such movement is significant in that it will be different to that of the pot, and this is of particular import when the pieces being fired are heavy and/or flat, since they will then be subjected to considerable additional stress imposed by the conflicting rates of expansion and contraction. This is known as 'drag'.

Another problem, and possibly the cause of more angst, is that kiln shelves behave rather like storage heaters in that they tend to hold their heat rather more than do thin ceramic pieces, with the consequence that, again, conflict is inevitable. So to avoid damage to large, flat bases, either design the vessel 'out' as far as possible, avoiding expansive bottoms, or elevate the whole pot, supporting it on props or wads of clay, so that vessel and shelves may cool independently.

Beginners are often tempted to produce large, flat forms, firstly because it seems easy, and secondly because such vessels can be bought from mass-production outlets and are seen as role models. However, it should be remembered that industrial processes involve the use of inert 'pastes' specially developed for a specific firing schedule. We, as craft potters, use real clays, besides which we frequently operate in a freer environment that allows both compromise and happy accident.

Shapes

Although potters produce literally millions of subtly different shapes, all of these derive from just a basic three: the cylinder, the cone and the sphere. These are often combined to produce a composite form; however, let us examine them first in their simplest terms.

As potters, we work in three dimensions. However, our three-dimensional basic shapes can be reduced to two dimensions, giving three profile shapes:

3D	2D
Cylinder	Square or rectangle
Cone	Triangle
Sphere	Circle

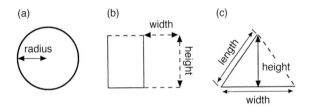

(a) The circle has only one dimension.
(b) The square and rectangle have two.
(c) The triangle has three.

This rather obvious idea can be applied to the design of pots in terms of structure and aesthetics. As the diagram illustrates, a circle has only one dimension, a square has only two, and, for the purposes of simplicity, so has the rectangle. A triangle has three dimensions. The latter is the most complex shape and is open to a vast number of permutations in terms of relative dimensions, whereas the circle, and indeed the sphere, has only one – the radius.

In ceramic terms, as elsewhere, the sphere is the perfect shape. Stresses on its form, either because of shrinkage, or expansion/contraction, will be evenly distributed given that, if made in ceramic, the thickness of the wall is even. Thus its dynamic tensions are in equilibrium. In a similar way, a cylindrical tube will be less prone to stress than one with a square section. Having only one dimension, the sphere is also aesthetically beyond reproach.

Unfortunately this 'perfect' ceramic form cannot be left in its perfect state and subjected to the fire, since air trapped inside would expand at a great rate when it was heated, exploding the form – if it had not already cracked as a result of the trapped air becoming compressed due to the initial shrinkage arising from its drying out. To avoid this, a hole of some sort is essential. This, of course, does not usually present a problem, because pots normally require apertures of some sort to fulfil function. However, the form will also require at least a modestly flattened foot in order to prevent it rolling about during firing, and later as a finished object. Glazing would also pose a problem; see the section on Glazes (page 00). Because of modification, the form that now suggests itself is a compromise between the ideal sphere and a flat-footed cylinder or cone. The degree of compromise will be determined by aesthetic and functional considerations:

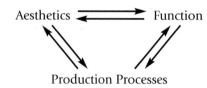

The simple model above indicates the interrelationship between these three areas or factors, and this significantly influences the design process.

Shape, Shrinkage and Stress

- The ideal form is the sphere; conversely, a large flat slab is probably the worst.

- Simple, consolidated forms will encounter less conflict than exaggerated shapes.

- Wide parts shrink more, pro rata, than small parts; this can result in distortion.

- Wide openings, e.g. lips of mugs, are unsupported, in contrast to their bases (feet).

The Perfect Shape?

So is there such a thing as a 'perfect' shape? As we have seen, different making techniques inevitably affect the appearance of the completed article: the thrown teapot will look very different from another built using flat slabs of clay. There is no reason to suggest that either method is better, and given that equal attention has been paid to the criteria of function, both would work equally well. The major difference would be of form: one would be based on a cylinder, the other on a rectilinear form.

As a result, one might appear more attractive than the other – though such a value judgement is probably more a question of personal preference, and is likely to differ from one person to another. In short, two completely different processes will produce two articles with very different visual appearances, but both may be equally well made, both are likely to work well, and both will be attractive to look at, as long as the maker has an awareness for design.

Design Skills

An awareness of, or instinct for, design evolves over years, in much the same way as production skills are developed and refined. The experienced potter will have experimented, unseen, with many possible solutions in order to achieve what seems like an easy, and ready, final solution. An elegant form thrown on the wheel is always marvellous to witness, and the seemingly casual way in which others assemble spontaneously complex, hand-built forms is deceptive. Underpinning these achievements is a wealth of experiment and experience.

One of the things not usually obvious to anyone other than the maker is that designs for each piece have probably been considered at some length before practical work commences. Many artists use sketches and working drawings to examine both the overall appearance of a piece, and aspects of detail. Others tend to work empirically, resolving problems along the way, possibly producing a range of completed items varying in appearance, selecting and discarding according to personal criteria. Any craftsperson who has made literally thousands of teapots or mugs over many years will have the dexterity and vision to produce acceptable examples, apparently with ease. If you lack such breadth of experience you will need to reflect on details of process and form, and might well make a number of false starts, either on paper or in clay. Thus if initial attempts to make a particular article seem unsuccessful you should not feel too disheartened, because everyone has experienced a similarly tentative start.

Before moving on from this topic it may be helpful – even if rather obvious – to remind the reader that technical ability will, in large measure, dictate form. That is to say, if you cannot command the skills required to produce other than rudimentary forms by the chosen means, the time you spend drawing amazing, complex ideas on paper might be better spent practising the technique. The resulting attempts will provide both increased expertise in the long run, and a range of forms you can actually produce. There is a correlation between, on the one hand, inexperience and overstatement or over-ambition in design, and on the other, experience, simplicity and appropriateness.

The best way forward, therefore, is probably to keep things simple. Certain shapes or forms are more readily made than others, given a particular production method. Build up a bank of experience (assisted by what follows below) by 'doing', experimenting with the various processes, and enjoying it all, and you will develop your own design instincts without excessive conscious effort. Experimentation leads to experience.

Keeping Things Simple

Simplifying and 'deconstructing' forms not only helps iron out problems of overstatement and over-ambition, it also clarifies working and building methods. If a form can be appreciated more simply at the design stage by being considered as a combination of basic shapes, it can probably be made more easily after similar consideration. Thus a straight cylinder can be developed during the throwing process into a form with a fatter 'belly', a 'waisted' neck or a widened 'lip', each change being

a logical step in the production process, achieved at an appropriate stage so as not to jeopardize the progress already made.

Alternatively, a piece could be visualized in sections, and then designed to be made in the same way, based on the 'deconstruction' of the envisaged finished piece. This would bring the seemingly impossible within the realms of the probable. For example, two bowl shapes attached rim to rim could provide a cylindrical belly form, or tall, elegant cones might provide upper or lower sections built into an otherwise impossibly difficult piece. Some of these possibilities will be examined in later chapters.

Let us return to the idea of keeping things simple. It can sometimes be helpful to think of pot forms in terms of basic two-dimensional shapes. That is to say, a cylinder is seen as a rectangle, a cone as a triangle, and a sphere as a circle. Designing a circle holds no terrors for anyone, since its single dimension will always guarantee a perfect shape. A square has only two dimensions: height and width or breadth, both the same; like the circle, there are no proportions to consider. A rectangle, however, has two different dimensions, so here we are obliged to consider abstract design factors. We are also confounded by the simple, age-old problem that has preoccupied artists and craftspeople, among others, over many centuries: how can a 'perfect' rectangle be constructed? In a mathematical context, how is it possible to produce two dimensions or lengths that have a 'perfect' relationship one to another? In a potter's terms, is there such a thing as the perfect cylinder?

Perfect Proportions

A square can be variously described as equal, balanced, perfectly formed, symmetrical, or the basis of a mandala symbol. It could also be described as boring. A rectangle, not being a square, could, therefore, be considered unbalanced, asymmetrical, disunited – or at least less boring than a square. The degree of disunity, inequilibrium, or plain tediousness thus rests with the relationship of the two dimensions: height/length and width/breadth.

Permutations of height and width are obviously

legion. Designing a 'good' rectangle therefore has almost limitless possibilities, as will the profile shape and proportion of a ceramic form based on a rectangle. It will also, to an extent at least, be determined by its intended use or function. Nevertheless, convention has determined some rectangular shapes as being 'better' or aesthetically more pleasing in appearance than others. Paper and book shapes are classic examples of acceptable convention. In the relatively recent past, it was possible to obtain paper in various sizes as well as in, more significantly, various proportions. Standardization has to an extent phased out alternatives; photocopiers and PC printers are designed to work only with the new 'A4' format. The consequent restriction of choice in this respect may be offset by financial convenience, and books may fit better on shelves. However, they may still not be everyone's idea of the perfect rectangle.

This elusive relationship of one measurement to another so preoccupied both artists and mathematicians during the pre-Renaissance period that eventually, at some time during the fifteenth or six-

teenth centuries, a mathematical formula, the 'golden mean rule', was established, or discovered, which enabled construction of the 'golden mean rectangle'. The extent of the formula's unique beauty is not within the brief of this book, but the 'recipe' for a basic golden mean rectangle can be: using a ratio of 8:5 as the relationship between height and width, a rather elegant rectangle can be constructed.

If a simple cylinder is made with a diameter of 5in (13cm) and a height of 8in (20cm), the result is a mug shape, which conforms to the golden mean rule. Such a cylinder has proportions very similar to mass-produced mugs, which are widely available as commemorative, tourist, feature or promotional items. The appearance of this particular shape and its subtle variations is obviously popular: it is clearly easy to produce, and relatively inexpensive. Its simple, clean shape and proportion is at least neutral; it seems not to offend one's sensibilities. And it is readily decorated using a range of techniques and specialized motifs, including transfer mug strips.

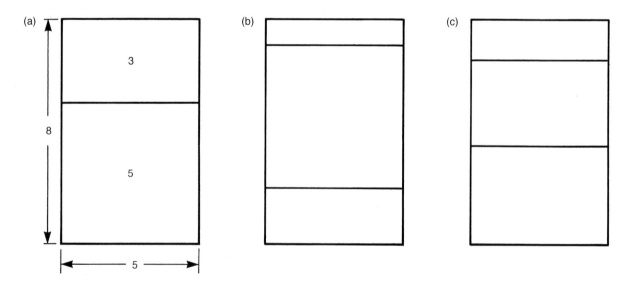

The 'golden mean' rectangle/cylinder in 'portrait' format, where (a) has a simple division into a square, plus a 'golden rectangle' based on the ratio 8:5; (b) the square now divides the rectangular 'balance', or what is left, into sub-divisions echoing the 8:5 idea; and (c) the 'golden rectangle' sub-divides the square according to the 'golden mean'. The decoration of a simple cylinder affords limitless permutations, achieved by contrasting rough/smooth, glazed/unglazed, light/dark and so on, and/or banding (painting: oxides, slips etc), dipping (slip, glaze), or double-dipping.

Varying Dimensions

A rectangle can also have one or other of two formats, as illustrated. When applied to a three-dimensional ceramic form, selection of format – i.e. portrait or landscape shape – will result in a tall cylinder or a short, squat one. Choice will depend on personal preference and intended use, and will almost certainly reflect utilitarian convention. The portrait profile, with an appended handle, is often chosen as a mug shape, and can be quite elegant. The landscape form, on the other hand, would probably feel 'unbalanced' if selected for the same purpose, as well as looking inappropriate in that context, to say nothing about its 'earthbound' and decidedly *in*elegant appearance.

The important message here is not that there is a uniquely beautiful and mathematically correct rectangle on which to base a cylinder, but rather that there are innumerable variations open to investigation in the quest for pleasing ceramic forms. In addition, in summing up the significance of the golden mean, it is reassuring to note that whether utilizing the 'classical' mathematical, or the empirical 'romantic' approach to design, there is surprising similarity between the two schools of thought, ranging across two and three-dimensional, fine and applied art and craft activities. In other words, there seems to be a consensus between those who 'know' something to be 'right', and others who instinctively 'feel' that it is so. This results in remarkably similar solutions to basic questions, such as how to decide upon a pleasing rectangle, or how, or where, to divide it. Just look at windows or mugs.

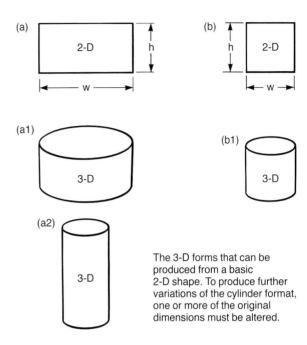

The 3-D forms that can be produced from a basic 2-D shape. To produce further variations of the cylinder format, one or more of the original dimensions must be altered.

Simple variations to the cylinder, illustrating (a1) 'landscape' and (a2) 'portrait' formats.

It is most unlikely that anyone would consider confining activities to the simple cylinder. And by adjusting one dimension – i.e. the top or bottom diameter – a cylinder is soon developed into the next basic shape, or form, namely the cone. If the possibilities of the cylinder are extensive and subtle, the possibilities of the cone are limitless. The reader will readily be able to imagine the implications of having three, rather than two variable dimensions with which to experiment. A conical form could either be stable or extremely unstable,

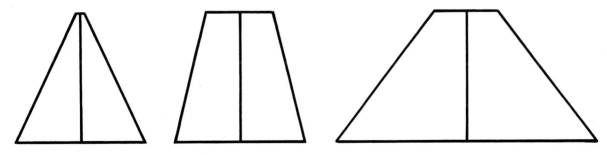

By changing one measurement/dimension at a time, the appearance of a cone is drastically altered; inverting the profile will also have a significant effect in terms of refinement, absurdity and so on.

Deconstruction of a traditional jug-form into composite parts: two cones and a sphere.

totally 'earthbound' or elegant, and refined or absurd.

'Function' can assist and clarify abstract design considerations to some extent; the visual appearance will also depend on aesthetic preferences. Thus one person's idea of an elegant jug form may be considered by another to be unstable and therefore completely impractical. And a jug blessed with a non-dripping spout might nonetheless seem unbalanced or '*lumpen*' to some users. The aim here, however, is not so much to match form with function as to indicate an approach to developing visually interesting and generally acceptable shapes. After all, no one wants to produce ugly, ill-formed pieces, however well they may be made, and however well they function.

It would, of course, be possible to restrict activity to the production of simple, single geometric forms while still achieving a high level of practicability. Straight cylindrical mugs, jugs or vases would no doubt 'work', and their appearance be attractive enough, but a creative potter would almost certainly find such constraints tedious. The challenge is likely to be to vary, modify and/or distort these basic shapes, while at the same time allowing them to grow naturally into each other, or to combine them to produce a composite 'whole'.

As will be found during the throwing process, some 'composite' forms develop naturally, while others will require encouragement through planning. In other words, it is helpful to know what you are trying to make, and the stages through which the piece has to progress; that is, how the end is to be achieved. Practical issues relating to *making* will be clarified through projects illustrated elsewhere in this book.

Developing Your Ideas

Bearing in mind the premise that simplicity is preferable to overstatement and over-ambition, an ideal way to start developing ideas is to use a sketchbook. 'Thumbnail' sketches employing profiles based on simple, basic geometric shapes can be of immense value. A wide range of ideas can be explored quickly and then refined for more detailed consideration. This could lead into 'artist's impressions', or visual realizations, of completed pieces, prototypes produced as a means of both exploring visual possibilities and potential processes, or perhaps a combination of the two approaches. The results will inevitably include interesting variations in shapes, together with indications of how best to proceed in practical terms. Analysis of a drawing will provide a breakdown of component (geometric) parts and, in some cases, an indication of how to prefabricate sections of the proposed piece.

Research

As already suggested, ideas for your work can be developed by, as it were, playing with basic shapes in the abstract. But there are other sources for your inspiration, all of which can be recorded in a sketchbook or an *ideas* folder. So if you are interested in, say, natural forms – for example, seedpods or beetle markings – you can document your observations, annotating as necessary, and building up a valuable resource for later use. Sketches, drawings (usually more developed, with attention to detail) and writing down your thoughts and ideas, can all be made from direct reference to chosen objects. Photographs (your own and those taken by others) and magazine illustrations, postcards or C.A.D. images can be collected, either in your sketchbook, or possibly in a shoebox if that's more convenient.

You can make notes and/or sketches by looking at the work of contemporary artist/craftspeople; and reference to historical and alternative cultural craftwork is a limitless resource for form, decoration and processes. The important thing is not to make your sketchbook a vehicle for drawing skills, but to record ideas and observations. Do not be precious about it: keep it informal, however messy, and informative. And whenever possible have visual references visible – pin up interesting material on a wall so that you can see it as you work. You will probably find that often ideas come from quite unlikely places, and will enable you to produce work that is characteristically your own.

Compromise

Throughout this book there are examples of how finished pieces can be designed, and of making processes that are planned to best suit assembly requirements. The reader will be encouraged to take full advantage of any creative ideas by working *within* the constraints imposed by technical ability or availability, rather than struggling against them. For example, not having a potter's wheel or a gas-fired kiln should not be seen as a disadvantage: instead, make the most of what *is* available or possible, and turn restriction to your advantage. If you cannot meet your objectives, change them! So, if you don't have access to a potter's wheel, or you cannot actually use one, build by other means, using the skills you *do* have, and making the best use of those tools available to you. There are a number of low-tech methods of making ceramics that will be illustrated in later sections of this book, one or other of which may well prove to be a challenging and rewarding alternative to wheel-work, or whatever else is simply not possible in a particular circumstance.

6 The Studio/ Workshop

Any potter who has moved house, and therefore workshop, will tell you that moving house is easy: it is the other bit that hurts. Any established workshop contains a mass of 'collected' articles, equipment and materials that the owner would find difficult to list, in spite of the fact that it is all considered essential to the production of work. This is due, in part at least, to our collecting things as we go along, appropriate to special needs and situations that we identify as we develop our own working methods.

As will be seen, however, there is no need for an elaborate array of expensive tools or equipment if you wish to work at home, whether in the kitchen or in a purpose-built or converted room, shed or out-building. Neither is it our intention to replicate a supplier's catalogue, but only to suggest basics. Some items are essential; some will become desirable or necessary in order to extend the range of possibilities within the activity; and other things may become embarrassingly expensive white elephants once purchased, and take up valuable space in the workshop. So start with the bare minimum, acquiring additional tools and equipment as and when they become necessary.

Whether the proposed workshop is to be used by only one person working at home, or is the foundation for a specialist provision in a school, basic requirements will include clay storage and preparation, a 'making' area, and the means by which to fire finished work. A potter's wheel would also be a likely requirement. A suitable work surface is necessary, as is a storage system for work in progress.

Clay

Because clay arrives in polythene bags, storing it presents no serious problem. Plastic or galvanized metal dustbins are useful; alternatively, the original bags could be stacked and/or double-wrapped until required. Once opened, however, rather more care should be exercised to prevent clay drying out, so it needs to be protected from air and heat. Store it in a cool, ideally damp place, away from the kiln, and keep it airtight. Kept in this way, clay will actually improve its plasticity.

Once the clay has been used, a system will have to be devised. A surprising amount of clay does not actually make it to the kiln. Some of this will be wet, some of it dried out, and some will have been handled so that it is no longer plastic enough to be re-used unless it is recycled. First, then, a plastic bowl, or just a plastic bag, will serve to gather up the reclaim. With care, the softer pieces could be put in with stiffer, but not dry clay so that it consolidates a little, ready to be kneaded up again. The harder clay is best allowed to dry out completely before recycling, so a second container will be necessary.

Where reclaim is kept to a minimum by the potter diligently attending to scraps as they occur, it should be relatively easy to avoid ending up with excessive heaps of reclaim later. Using a reasonably tight system as suggested, keeping accumulated reclaim to a minimum, it should be possible to keep on top of any recycling, even in a school where neither technician nor pug-mill is available to reduce the load.

View of workshop

In situations where reclaim inevitably builds up, storage becomes a bigger problem, requiring additional bins and space. In workshops used by numbers of different people, such as schools and colleges, there is likely to be contamination, even when appropriately marked lids are always used on reclaim bins. Foreign matter, dust, rubbish and tools can easily be lost within the depths of these, only to reappear again when built into the side of a pot, causing damage to someone's hand, or jamming a pug-mill. So, quite apart from the problems of 'inconvenience', there is also the wider issue of 'health and safety' to bear in mind.

Shelving

All the marvellous pots produced will need to be put on shelves where they can dry out slowly and safely, and be stored before and after firing. A damp cupboard is also useful for the storage of items that must be kept moist prior to completion later – though where there is not enough room for a special damp cupboard, wrapping the pots in plastic will serve the same purpose. Any cupboard space would be useful, either to help keep pots in the leather-hard state – as well as their plastic covering – or to protect their surface from dust.

Kilns

When pieces have completely dried out, there has to be some means of firing them. Different types of kiln and the techniques of firing them will be discussed in some depth in other chapters. Visits to local colleges or schools with good ceramics facilities might well be worthwhile, as would contact with local potters. The latter, in particular, are generally justifiably proud of their kilns, which they have often built themselves, and they will usually be quite prepared to discuss a kiln's merits, and also to indicate its drawbacks as experienced at first hand.

First, therefore, do some careful research; then obtain a kiln that suits your requirements.

If your only wish is to produce ceramic jewellery, your needs will be amply met by a small electric test-kiln requiring just a domestic 13-amp power supply. A small top-loading kiln of the same rating could be an alternative. On the other hand, if you intend to produce pots or sculptural pieces and hope to sell enough at least to break even on the cost of your hobby, it would be sensible to go for a larger kiln at the outset.

Your choice of kiln depends on what you want to do with it; what you can, or will be able to afford; where you are planning to site it; and what energy source is available to power it. Electric kilns are nowadays quick and clean firing; they are relatively easy to install, with professional help; and can be fitted with easy-to-use mechanical or microprocessor control units at very reasonable cost.

Gas-fired kilns are an obvious alternative. There are two types: models that consume normal domestic gas from the mains supply, and others designed to burn bottled liquid gas. The latter burns cleaner and does not create dangerous gaseous by-products requiring tall chimneys to exhaust them safely. On the other hand, piped-in gas is convenient once installed, and is likely to be less costly in the long term. Technical advice is always available from your local gas board, and should be sought well in advance of installation. Apart from the possible cost of getting a supply to the kiln site, it is wise to check with them what extra equipment may be required, and also the likely cost. If the conventional alternatives do not appeal, you may be tempted to consider building a wood-fired kiln. In some vicinities fuel may be both cheap and plentiful, but both construction and firing are labour-intensive. A first successful firing will probably be more than adequate reward for the expended effort; however, if reliable, consistent and economical firings are needed, a gas kiln is unlikely to prove the most viable option.

Choosing a Kiln

The entire ceramic process depends on firing, and so access to a kiln is obviously essential. The action of heat on clay, as we have seen, achieves a metamorphosis, changing the material into something quite different; it is also active in changing other materials into glazes. Both of these can affect our choice of kiln and are discussed fully in Chapter 13, Firing (page 197). Other considerations relate to type, size and volume of work, and are discussed in other sections of the book.

Wheels

Some sort of wheel is the other most basic requirement. Whether or not you actually need one again depends on what you intend to produce. Cost is also a very real consideration because, like kilns, there are wheels for all occasions. When purchasing a wheel it is worth remembering that it will have to be capable of working with you for however long you continue to produce wheel-thrown pots. The size of the wheel does not determine the size of the pot, but its price will often reflect its quality and design specifications. The chosen wheel may work well throughout its lifetime; but it will be a source of discomfort, frustration and irritation if it is simply not capable of doing the job required of it. Enrolment to an evening class should provide an opportunity to use different wheels; try them for personal 'fit', and to discover how well the different types function under load.

Other Essentials

In addition to the four items mentioned above – clay, shelving, kiln and wheel (is it really essential?) – there are other items that are essential either to the production of the wares themselves, or for the comfort, well-being and convenience of the potter. Thus a strong **workbench** is required for the production of hand-built pieces, and to accommodate a flat **plaster slab** for clay preparation. This extremely useful item can easily be made from plaster of Paris, or fine dental plaster in the same way as moulds, as described in Chapter 3, page 26 and Chapter 10, page 152. If space allows, a bench for each is an advantage: the plaster slab and any slop will then not hinder making and finishing, and there will be less likelihood of dry scraps of clay being accidentally mixed in with soak. A **sink and running water** are also very useful, although it is possible to manage without if they are available reasonably close to the workshop.

As long as you have access to clay, kiln and a workspace, you can make a start. As work progresses, a need for minor items will become apparent, and these can be acquired as and when they are required.

Personal Tools

The best tool for most ceramic processes is, of course, one's hands; the need for others will arise according to the job. There are, however, certain tools that form the basis for anyone's personal toolkit, and these are likely to prove essential both in the preparation process, and to assist in production. Some can be used for a number of different jobs, and it would perhaps be sensible to identify these in order to collect together a 'starter' kit.

Clay cutters: Can be home-made, using strong, thin nylon fishing line and two wooden toggles, buttons or pieces of clothes peg. They are used for cutting clay when wedging, kneading, preparing balls for throwing, and so on; they can also be used to cut slabs from blocks of clay. They are useful for trimming off uneven rims on thrown wares. Twisted metal wire (*see* diagram below) or nylon is used for removing thrown pots from a wheel.

Potter's knife: Has a very sharp, tapered point; its narrow blade does not 'drag' when used to trim plastic clay. It can be purchased or made from a ground-down kitchen or table knife; it is used for cutting out slabs, trimming, scoring, piercing and scraping at various stages of the production process. Sponges: Small natural sponges can be purchased

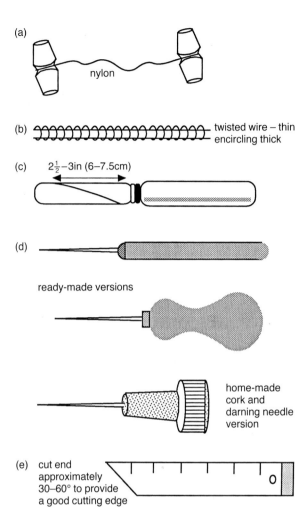

Some potter's tools: (a) nylon cutter; (b) twisted wire cutter; (c) DIY potter's knife; (d) potter's needles; (e) dog-ear tool.

from pottery suppliers or, more expensively, as make-up accessories. A small one would be about 2in (5cm) in diameter; larger ones are useful but not essential. They are used for cleaning up or 'softening' hard, cut edges, and for mopping out 'slurry' from thrown wares. For this work, natural sponge is preferable to synthetic, which tends to be hard and rather too abrasive; natural sponges also hold more moisture. A large bench sponge is useful for generally cleaning up wheel and work surfaces; synthetic sponges, as used for cleaning cars, are ideal for this.

Potter's needle: Easily made by inserting a darning needle, eye end first, into a wine-bottle cork or similar, and it floats. Bought versions tend to have rather thick needles and thin, dowel-rod handles, and they are not always easy to find in clay slurry or water. They are used for trimming uneven rims, for scoring, and for cutting thin slabs of clay.

Dogear tool: Easily made from a broken 12in (30cm) or a 6in (15cm) ruler. Cut one end at about 45 degrees (*see* diagram): this will serve to turn off excess thickness on thrown pots. It is possible to purchase boxwood modelling tools that will do the same job, but they are really too good, and too costly, to be subjected to abrasive contact with revolving clay and wheel-head. A flat ruler has the added advantage of being easy to grip.

Steel scrapers: Made from flexible blued steel, usually in the shape of a kidney, with one side flat, or straight. They are relatively cheap, so it is not really worth attempting to make your own. One of medium size would suffice. They are used to smooth or chamfer off leather-hard or dry wares; they could be used as throwing ribs; and are useful for cutting clay in the absence of a potter's knife. They are indispensable for refining the profile shapes of coiled pots, and for cleaning joins in slabbed pieces.

Turning tools: Stem turning tools look rather like paint scrapers, and can often be used in exactly the same way. Strip tools are basically hooped steel-cutting tools on stems and handles. These tools are used on leather-hard clay to remove unwanted thickness prior to firing; they therefore tend to wear away.

DIY metal one-piece turning tool: This can be made from hoop-iron strips, bent and hardened to provide a variety of cutting edges. Home-made versions can be so fashioned that they are rigid enough to avoid 'chatter':

- You will need a strip of mild steel about $7 \times \frac{3}{4} \times \frac{1}{12}$in ($18 \times 2 \times 0.2$cm).
- Cut the end to the profile required (see diagram).
- Heat the end of the metal until it is red hot.
- Seize it securely in a metal vice and bend to shape – hammer if necessary: the angle should be approximately 70–90 degrees (experience will show what the best angle should be to avoid 'chatter').
- Allow to cool, then grind or file off at about 30 degrees to produce the desired cutting edges. Various shapes can be made on different-sized shanks so that almost any turning job can be tackled.

DIY strip tool: Probably the easiest tool to make, and probably the most useful.

For a handle use a piece of planed wood, approximately $6 \times \frac{3}{4} \times \frac{1}{4}$in ($15 \times 2 \times 0.6$cm).

The cutting loop can be made from a piece of $\frac{1}{4}$in (0.6cm) blue-steel packing strip, cut to length, and fastened to the handle using short nails or screws. The join can be covered, using self-adhesive (insulation) tape, or whipped with string, to ensure that the loop is secure and any rough edges to the metal are covered up.

Wooden handles of different widths can be used, and old, broken 'junior' hacksaw blades: these have the advantage of teeth on one side, producing a

(a)

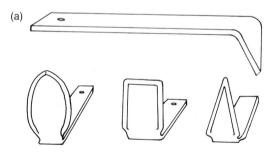

(a) One-piece turning tools provide a variety of cutting edges; (b) making a turning tool.

(b) to make a turning tool

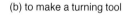

heat to dull red

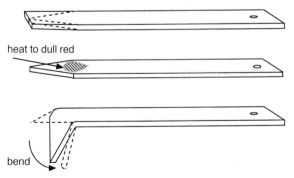

bend

An assortment of bought and home-made turning and looped modelling tools.

Old hacksaw blade attached to a wooden handle.

multi-functional tool. Take care when bending these blades, particularly when manipulating them into small, tight loops. Nor is attaching the blade to a handle easy, relying on taping or whipping – nails and screws not being an option when using tempered steel. For convenience, holes can be drilled in the handles, so the tools may be hung on cup-hooks or nails on a board.

Sponge stick: Can be purchased, or home-made using a length of dowel rod, to one end of which is fastened a piece of sponge, preferably natural. It is used for mopping out water or slurry from the insides of tall and narrow pots during and after throwing.

Modelling tools: A wide range of boxwood, forged steel, plastic, and steel wire, looped modelling tools are available from pottery or sculpture suppliers. The better quality versions tend to be expensive, but are much more pleasant to use, as well as being more effective. It is probably sensible to obtain only one or two to start with, rather than investing in a whole range of items that may never actually be used.

Extending the Basics

Gather together the above tools, augmenting them with a collection of miscellaneous items that will be useful in some way or another. This could include old forks, spoons, combs, toothbrushes,

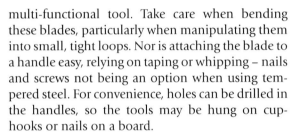

'Whipping': a loop of string is over-laid, starting at the cutter end. The short end is kept clear (top).

Draw the last coil through the loop (right), pull on the short end (left) to drag tail and loop back under the coils. Cut off the excess.

discarded saw blades of varying coarseness, and almost anything else you think could be used to impress, scratch, scrape, cut, pat, paddle or otherwise mark or manipulate clay. You will then have an ample toolkit.

Workshop Tools

The following list describes a selection of items that will either add to a personal kit or are necessary for the establishment of a workshop. They would not normally be considered the sort of items that students attending courses in established studio/ workshops would be expected to provide.

Rolling pin: Wooden ones are the best; clay tends not to stick to them to the same extent as it does to non-porous materials. Used for rolling out clay slabs. Longer ones are the most versatile: 20in (50cm) long, and 2in or 3in (5 to 7.5cm) diameter would be good; kitchen rollers are usually a little on the short side. A towel roller generally does a good job. Alternatively, lengths of metal or plastic pipe can be used, though again, sticking can be a problem.

Rolling guides: These are wooden laths used in pairs of varying depth so that slabs of different thickness may be rolled out to regulate the thickness of rolled slabs. A suggested length might be 18–20in (46–51cm) and about 1in (2.5cm) wide by $\frac{1}{4}$ to $\frac{1}{2}$in (6 to 13mm) thick, depending on the required thickness of the slabs.

Mould frame: A useful gadget for casting moulds or slabs of plaster. These can be purchased ready-made, or made up from four lengths of planed timber approximately $24–30 \times 6 \times 1$in ($61–76 \times 15 \times 2.5$cm) plus four right-angle brackets which hold the frame's sides and allow the casting area to be adjusted as required. Old floorboards and some house bricks can be used to provide an effective alternative.

Harp: Used when cutting successive slabs of the same thickness from a block of clay. Pragmatists will prefer to use either notched dowels in conjunction with a cutting wire with rings attached at each end; or better still, the well tried and tested rolling pin and laths.

Hole cutters: Available in a range of sizes, these work like an apple corer, cutting and removing the central core cleanly. Cutters with a semi-circular cross-section clog less than tubular cutters.

Callipers: These are offered for sale made in wood, plastic, Perspex or metal, and are used for checking and comparing measurements, for example when making lids to fit containers. For occasional, one-off jobs, either use a pair of oil-painting brushes or a couple of pieces of dowel rod held by an elastic band to form a V-shape adjusted to the measurement to be checked. A single dowel can also be used in some situations (*see* photos in the chapter on Throwing).

Lawns and cup sieves: Lawns are usually constructed with wooden sides and stainless-steel mesh, and are used for preparing working quantities of glaze or slip. They are available in mesh sizes from 30s (coarse) to 120s (fine), and usually about 8in or 10in (20 and 25cm) diameter. 'Cup lawns', as the name suggests, are smaller versions, and used for sieving test batches.

Sorting tools: These are used like a cold chisel, for cleaning up kiln furniture, and sometimes pots, after glaze firing. Discarded stone- or wood-carving chisels can be used, although without tungsten carbide tips they will not be effective for long.

Tile cutters: Available from pottery suppliers for cutting uniformly shaped square, circular or hexagonal tiles from rolled slabs.

Sgraffito tools: It is possible to purchase double-ended tools with which to scrape away areas of pigment or slip, or to engrave or inlay. Potters' knives and needles can be used, as could almost any sharp tool that can be handled comfortably and conveniently.

Decorating brushes: A wide range of brushes is available, some for general use, others for specific jobs. Collect together a few, including household paintbrushes, and see what can be done with them. Purchase two or three, specifically for (ceramic) art-work as you find a need. Consult with, or borrow from other people, to discover the merits and dis-advantages of different types of brush, before spending good money on expensive items that might not be of use to you.

Slip trailers: Usually a soft plastic or rubber bulb fitted with a removable plastic nozzle. Used for trailing slips or glazes, to decorate in a similar way to cake icing. For preference obtain several, so that a range of colours can be used at the same time. Squeezy bottles can be a cheap alternative, though they are sometimes rather difficult to handle with dexterity.

And More ...

A glance through one of the glossy catalogues pro-vided by suppliers will show the extensive variety and range of tools available. There is no doubt that having such items readily at hand is convenient, and can often cultivate and extend the range of per-sonal freedom, technically and aesthetically. And anything that assists in broadening the creative experience is worth considering. As an example, a clay gun can be used to extrude fine sections of clay in a wide range of cross-section shapes. It works rather like a hypodermic syringe, forcing clay through interchangeable dies.

Similar effects can be obtained using a garlic press, or by pushing clay through a kitchen sieve. Arguably these could be seen as gimmicks, remov-ing from the maker the need to be imaginative or inventive. But such tools can also stimulate ideas, and could be seen as creatively beneficial. The morality of using such tools should therefore not be an issue; on the other hand, cost might.

Tool Checklist

When considering the possible purchase of tools, check that they are functional, worth the outlay, and potentially able to repay the cost in some way. What maintenance is required? Are there any fiddly or crucial parts, the loss or damage to which renders the piece useless?

Can you manage perfectly well without that particular item? What is absolutely essential in order to carry out the proposed work?

There *is* no definitive list, either for personal use or for setting up a studio or workshop; the foregoing included. Personal experience will suggest the need for any other items in additional to those listed above – or the exclusion of others. What really matters is that you discover for yourself what is right for you, what you feel comfortable using, and what you can easily manage without.

Layout

How the work area is laid out is worth serious con-sideration. If you are starting completely from scratch, such things as power points, lighting, sink and even windows can be installed for maximum convenience. Where some existing facilities are to be utilized without alteration, the way equipment is eventually arranged will be determined to a lesser or greater extent by these factors. That is to say, a power point will determine the position of a wheel perhaps; a window might be crucial in the placing of a work surface, light being one of the factors in any working area. Try to arrange things so that nat-ural daylight is available, particularly for detailed work. A good source of light helps to highlight tex-ture, pattern and form, as well as lessening poten-tial eyestrain.

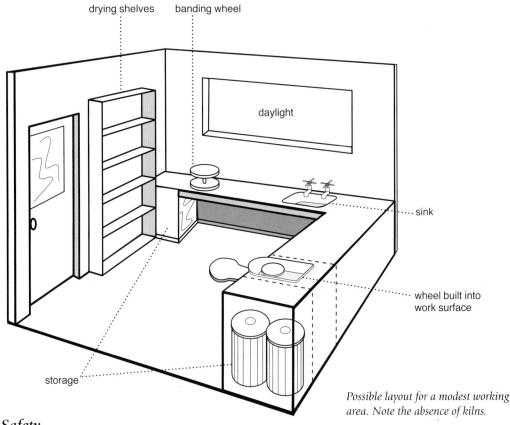

Possible layout for a modest working area. Note the absence of kilns.

Health and Safety

Give serious thought to the positioning of electric light switches and power points. First, ensure that electric sockets and switches are *at least* just *over* an arms-span away from a sink – in other words, far enough apart to make it impossible to have one hand in water, and the other on a switch! The usual convention, that light switches are best located immediately inside doorways, avoids the risk of stumbling across an unlit workshop in search of a light.

Inhalation of silica, in the form of clay dust, is a serious health hazard. Wherever possible, avoid dropping or spilling of clay or glaze. Do not tread it into dust, and clean it up before it dries out. Damp sand, brushed across the floor, picks up clay without raising dust. Always 'damp clean' work surfaces and floors, rinsing to avoid residues of dried clay after drying.

Clothing should be clean. Do not allow dried deposits of clay to build up; body movement, and patting or shaking, will all create undesirable and potentially lethal dust clouds.

In the diagram can be seen an illustration of a workshop area based loosely on our own. The kilns are best sited, and most materials stored, in the area beyond the door, which can be conveniently ventilated without affecting working conditions in the well-insulated studio, where frost-damage to pots is avoided, and the working area is a more attractive proposition to use on a cold winter's evening. A small top-loading or test kiln using a 13 amp power point can be used in a working area, as long as ventilation is adequate. If used at night on economy rate power, it will provide a good substitute for a storage heater, in addition to firing your work economically. Most sheds, garages or other out-houses tend to be less than ideal in terms of comfort, and in our experience, a little time and energy spent on draught-proofing and insulation is highly worthwhile.

7 Hand-Building Techniques

Pinching

One of the properties of plastic clay is that it can be pinched and stretched into almost any shape. The simplest way of producing hollow ware is consequently the 'pinching' or 'thumb' method. Although often considered somewhat lacking in ceramic dignity – perhaps because sometimes it serves as an introduction for beginners, and the results are therefore somewhat lacklustre – it is an excellent way of exploring the aesthetic and tactile potential; in other words, of developing a feeling for the medium. The beginner, in particular, will benefit from such close, intimate contact with clay, better realizing its character and potential.

Pinching a Two-Piece Pot, with Step-by-Step Illustrations

- Take enough prepared clay to make a golf-ball sized ball, rolled between both hands.
- Place the ball of clay in the palm of one hand, and
- While slowly turning the clay, gently but firmly press the thumb of the opposite hand into the ball.
- Work around the clay, opening it up, developing *depth* first;
- Retain some extra thickness at the rim or neck.
- Continue pinching, working always *around* the form, aiming to achieve a semi-spherical (or deeper) bowl shape. Work inside the form, avoiding too much pinching at the rim.

Hand-building (coiling)

Initial opening, turning the ball all the time to ensure even thickness.

Checking the diameter.

Developing the hollow form.

Use a potter's knife or needle to score the rim, and (left) apply slip.

- Still retain some thickness at the rim; ignore minor cracking.
- Gently place the completed bowl shape onto a flat wooden or plaster surface to allow a narrow foot to be depressed into its base.
- Repeat to produce a second, similar bowl.
- Use callipers (a ruler or pencil will do equally well) to check diameters for 'fit'.
- Allow both forms to stiffen up to 'leather-hard' so that they are no longer floppy.

Joining

This part of the process is fundamental, and applicable to all ceramics situations. To achieve adhesion, use 'potter's glue', usually referred to as 'slip': this is made by adding excess water to plastic clay to reduce it to slurry of creamy consistency. Just poke a hole into a small lump of clay (the same clay as the parts to be joined), add water using an artist's hog-hair brush, and stir.

All contact surfaces need to be 'scored' well: use a potter's knife or needle to roughen them.

- Add a generous coating of slip.
- Bring the parts into contact, using gentle wriggling/jiggling pressure to squeeze and weld the joint, getting rid of excess slip and ensuring precise positioning.
- Give the join time to consolidate, then clean it up using a metal kidney tool, working diagonally around the form to achieve a unified outline shape.
- Finish off by adding any appendages/detail …
- … and burnish (if required), before the clay has dried out, while still of a firm leather consistency. Useful tools might include the back of a spoon, plastic pens, smooth pebbles; finish by polishing with a piece of chamois leather. If chamois is not available, use dry, clean fingers lightly to achieve the same effect.

Add a soft coil to one rim.

Modelling over the coil to effect a good join.

Fettling: cleaning up the surface. Use modelling tools and metal kidneys to scrape off surplus slip or undulations.

Scoring and slipping to affix an appendage.

Tapping down to level the rim.

A wooden modelling tool being used to clean up the inside join.

Cleaning up and burnishing the join.

Pinching Tips

- Use relatively soft clay; remember that it will dry out quickly when in contact with warm hands.

- Keep the clay on the move to prevent excessive warming up, applying even pressure throughout. Ensure that all parts are evenly pinched. Try not looking at the clay as you work it, relying mainly on touch.

- Avoid over-enthusiastic, hard pinching in one part, and the temptation to speed. Rather, enjoy the relaxed, tactile experience of manipulating and controlling the form as it emerges from the humble lump.

- Parts to be joined must be 'leather-hard', and as near as possible of the same consistency; in other words, one should not be stiffer than the other. The same applies when attaching foot-rings if making bowls, and in any event should be observed whenever joining any clay components, however made.

- Make a whole series of shapes and sizes, and try different combinations to build 'composite' forms.

- Time spent cleaning up the joins, scraping off undulations, and generally attending to cosmetics will add considerably to the overall effect.

Slab-Building

As the name suggests, this process makes use of flattened slabs of clay. All that is required is a rolling pin, a couple of laths (to ensure even thickness), and a cloth (a lightweight canvas or other material which will not stretch out of shape is best). The latter prevents the slab from sticking to the work surface, and can be useful as a support when moving the rolled-out clay, and particularly when lowering a slab into a mould.

Rolling out Slabs

Proceed as follows:

- Knock (hit, bash, thump) a lump of homogenous clay into a flattish pancake about 1in (2.5cm) thick; do this on the canvas.
- Turn the pancake over, and use the rolling pin to reduce thickness and stretch and flatten the clay out, working from the centre. Do not attempt to force the thickness down to the level of the laths at this stage.
- Frequent inverting, and altering the direction of the rolling, will greatly assist in achieving a consistent, even thickness, particularly when rolling out large slabs.
- Continue rolling, pressing down firmly on the rolling pin until resistance is felt as it comes in contact with the laths.

The resulting slab can now be turned into a mould or allowed to stiffen up to leather-hard before cutting into suitably sized and shaped pieces for assembly.

Roughly flattened, using the heels of the hands to even out the thickness.

Guiding laths used to determine even thickness. Roll out until the laths are felt to be in contact with the rolling pin. Allow slabs to stiffen up by laying them out on an absorbent surface (in background).

Carefully release slab from canvas to avoid distortion.

Making a Simple Lidded Box

This project involves the basic principles and techniques necessary to any hand-building project, however modest or ambitious. It is intended as a starting point, indicating the 'how to' rather than the 'what', and allowing the reader the opportunity to customize the concept and/or outcome in any way that seems appropriate.

The completed piece will be (more or less) cubic. The supporting illustrations show how a tile cutter can be used to cut out the four side pieces, then the walls are assembled, and the base and top attached. An alternative method is to make paper or card templates first, incidentally introducing the element of design, and using them to mark out or cut around the component parts. This is also a useful method of visualizing the eventual outcome and adjusting proportions if necessary. The ideal tools for cutting slabs are a potter's knife and a steel rule.

At risk of stating the obvious, remember that clay slabs will have thickness, and that this can add to the overall dimensions; it accounts for the procedure employed above, which ensures adequate size for the base and top.

Use flat boards of asbestos substitute (sometimes called Superlux) on which to stiffen up the slabs: doing this allows the clay to dry evenly, avoiding curled-up corners. Off-cuts can sometimes be purchased from builders, and are worth their weight in gold. In their absence, turn the slabs frequently to avoid one surface being exposed to the drying properties of air and warmth and so

A tile cutter is used to cut out slabs of equal size. Notice the slab is stiff enough to maintain its flatness.

The joined slabs support each other as assembly progresses.

Each surface to be joined is scored, slipped and cleaned up before the next join is made.

The fourth inside join is tidied up. Use a hog's-hair paintbrush as a combination sponge/modelling tool.

The top and base can be made from uncut slabs. After scoring and slipping all the appropriate surfaces, lower the four joined sides (open box) into place, pressing firmly, and trim roughly to size.

A steel rule and potter's knife used to trim to final size.

Clean edges with a metal kidney. Use the rule again to obtain a 'clean' edge.

Cut off a suitably interesting lid.

'Sharp' edges can now be softened, using a finger to gently rub off excess.

The eccentric cut helps to locate the correct fit.

shrinking in advance of the other side, thereby pulling and distorting the slab.

Allow the slabs to stiffen to leather-hard *before* cutting out; this enables cleaner cutting, and no sticky clay pulling on the knife to distort the shape. Clay shrinks as it dries, so by cutting later, the maximum finished size is assured; although this might not seem very significant, particularly on a modest scale.

Test for stiffness by carefully lifting one corner or edge of a slab: if the whole slab tends to lift and seems able to support itself without undue sagging, it is probably about ready for trimming. *After* cutting, a 4in (10cm) square tile should barely bend, maintaining its flatness. Larger slabs of the same thickness will tend to move a little more. Do *not* allow to dry out completely, as dry clay pieces cannot be joined adequately: a join may appear to hold, but it will not survive firing even if it survives for a short time as the slip dries out.

Assembling and Joining

Always ensure that all pieces to be joined are of the same consistency of leather-hardness. Eventual shrinkage will then be even throughout, reducing stress and distortion.

Score (roughen up) both surfaces to be joined, and apply a generous coating of slip to each. Bring both together firmly, using a 'jiggly' movement to squeeze out excess slip and locate the parts accurately. Sometimes a thin coil of clay can be modelled into the corner of the join as additional strengthening, as well as to look cosmetically enhancing, particularly on larger, more open forms.

In this particular project, air is initially trapped inside the cube prior to releasing the lid. If, after assembly, the box is allowed to dry out a little before cutting, shrinkage will compress the air locked inside, and this will help to maintain the cubic form, and prevent the flat surfaces from becoming slightly concave.

Coiling

This method is sometimes considered to be either primitive and/or childish, and is even dismissed as not 'proper' pottery. This is in curious contradiction to the history of the craft as it has evolved over several thousands of years; indeed, as a means of making, it is versatile, dependable and often extremely sophisticated. The first advantage it offers is *freedom*, since forms are not restricted to the circular, or to symmetry. Another is *pace*, as the maker has remarkable control over growth and form, allowing time for reflection. But perhaps the most important is that of *scale*. Coiling has frequently been used on a modest scale, as the Bronze Age food vessel indicates, but it is also eminently suited to larger work, as exemplified by the large Nigerian jar, made for food or drink (*see* photos).

Cylindrical Forms

The accompanying photos and captions illustrate the procedure required to produce cylindrical forms. The intent here is to clearly indicate the method of construction, building a vertical form.

As can be seen in the photos, added width is achieved by increasing the lengths of the coils. To reduce the diameter and thereby narrow the form, simply reduce the length of the coil. To change from the circular, or to start from an eccentric base, just place the coils appropriately, and allow the form to develop in the way you want it. The main thing is to plan ahead. Have a reasonably clear idea of what you want to build.

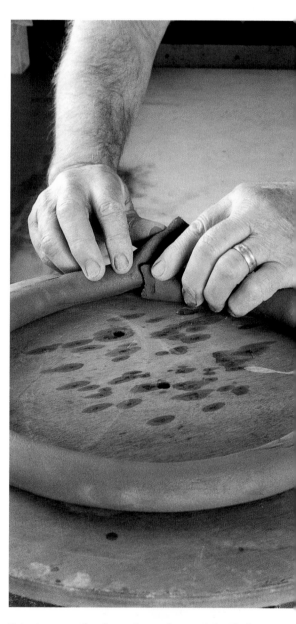

Bringing two coil ends together, to form a circle. If a base or foot is necessary, proceed as illustrated in the above series.

Modelling in the second coil.

After a lengthy break coils will have stiffened somewhat. To recommence building, score and slip.

Pots can be covered, excluding as much air as possible, when work is temporarily stopped.

When the form has stiffened a little, model down on the outside. Finger- or tool-marks can be left as integral decoration, over part or the whole of the form. Think design.

Coils should be deliberately lowered into place.

Coiling an Open Form

Before commencing, ensure that the clay is prepared properly, i.e. kneaded, or homogenized by other means. Usually clay out of the bag, fresh from the supplier, is ready for use in this context. Using it is a test in itself: too soft, and the clay will stick to the work-surface; too hard and it will not roll, or it will crack and dry out quickly in the hands. Basically, it will soon be obvious if it is not right (*see* the accompanying photos and captions).

Roll out a coil, using the fingers to fan out and stretch the clay evenly.

Ball in place centrally on a bat.

Pressing out a disc-shaped base.

Gain length in advance of rolling by squeezing into a sausage.

Placing the first coil. Score and slip to ensure a good 'weld'.

Model down the inside of the coil to attach to the base. The outside can be left at this stage. When the clay stiffens a little it will be less inclined to distort – so do only enough modelling to get the form growing in the intended way.

Carefully place each subsequent coil, as a single ring, checking for even 'growth'.

Examine from over the top, and from the side elevation, turning it on a banding wheel. At this stage leave the modelling texture/pattern. When the coil is suitably positioned it can be moulded into the previous one, while steadying with the other hand. Use a thumb on the far side; it is easy to see what you are doing.

After stiffening, the inside surface can be smoothed using a wooden 'rib'…

…or beat gently to achieve an even, parabolic (as in egg-shell) inside curve, using the back of a spoon, a wooden screw-driver handle or similar. Support the outside with the other hand.

The outside coils can be moulded together in stages, as the form stiffens. Invert the pot on a bat. Place this on top of the pot, lift from below the bottom bat, then quickly turn over.

Use a serrated metal kidney or scraper to clean up the outer surface.

A smooth metal kidney tool finishes off the job.

Pebble pot, coiled; decorated with engobes and glaze. Stoneware, by the author.

Coiling Tips

- To begin with, attempt to keep forms simple. Try to ensure that upper layers are reasonably supported from below, either by stiffening or by avoiding exaggerated changes in direction. Or both. In short, do not try to defy gravity.

- Work slowly and methodically. Avoid the temptation to make a pile of coils in advance of building, as they will probably harden too much before you get the chance to use them.

- Bear in mind that the time it takes to roll out each coil gives the previous ones just a little more time to stiffen, and, more important, gives *you* time to think about where the whole thing is going: pace, and contemplation.

- Patting, poking or generally over-working the clay at this stage actually seems to make it more plastic – and floppy. Therefore handle it as little as possible.

- If the form does become 'floppy', and/or time is at a premium, speed up drying by using a hair-drier or electric paint-stripper to apply heat – though take care to apply it evenly, and do not over-dry.

8 The Potter's Wheel

The action of making pots on some form of potter's wheel is known as 'throwing', and any witness to this process cannot fail to be impressed by the apparent ease with which all manner of variations on the simple cylindrical vase shape can be achieved.

Anyone attempting to throw for the first time will also have been struck by the apparent waywardness of the clay, and the difficulty of controlling a lump of totally inert material that seems suddenly to have taken on a life of its own. Initial efforts may well be frustrating and, for some people, can be totally negative, giving them the impression that they should simply give up, considering wheelwork to be beyond their capabilities. However, with time, and an increasing understanding of the process, it should be possible for anyone to develop the skills necessary to manage the potter's wheel. So let us look at the three basic factors in the equation: a wheel, the clay, and you.

The Wheel

As mentioned elsewhere, there are various types of wheel, but initially it is probably easier to learn to throw on a powered wheel. If you have the choice, you will find that a good quality electric wheel that operates smoothly with a reserve of power, rather than just excessive top speed, will allow you to

concentrate on the other problems you face, instead of worrying about how to peddle the wheel and manipulate the clay at the same time.

Personal fit is also important, and you should be able to reach the controls comfortably, without disruption to your working position. Where an adjustable seat is fitted, try different positions to determine the best height for back comfort and foot control. If there is no seat and you are obliged to stand on one leg, you may possibly find a stool makes life easier. In any event, try to find a wheel that is comfortable and which you find easy to operate.

The Clay

The clay's consistency must be totally homogeneous: it should have no harder or softer areas, no air or water pockets, and no foreign bodies such as small pieces of sponge or chips of plaster. Young children sometimes pick up drawing pins and pencil sharpenings in their clay; cleaners and caretakers confuse soak-bins with rubbish bins, and even experienced potters misplace pieces of chamois or sponge.

Most importantly of all, the clay should be of a suitably soft consistency. Preparation is very important here: if you can knead it you can probably throw it. It is really something each potter has to decide for him- or herself, based on personal experience. After a relatively short time you will get the feel for what is best for you; but whatever you do, avoid stiff clay.

Opposite *Wheel work.*

Learning to Throw

There are probably three ways of learning to throw:

- Watch an experienced potter – endlessly if possible.
- Practise, with an experienced thrower providing one-to-one advice and encouragement.
- Practise on your own until you get it right.

The best way is probably to proceed through the above points, falling back a stage as necessary. A fourth way to learn might be to read appropriate books, though as a sole means of acquiring experience, this method falls very short of adequate; but a book can nonetheless offer some unique support. To begin with, reading and examining photographs can provide initial impetus, while the book can also provide a sort of stationary action-replay, allowing the reader to examine, at his/her leisure, actions that otherwise happen too quickly to be analysed to any extent. It can also have a diagnostic role, in that comparing methods can identify helpful alternatives.

Making a Start

To ensure the best possible chance of success, be well prepared. Just watching a tutor throw the body of a jug, even though he might be explaining step-by-step exactly what is going on, is not really enough. It can be inspiring and motivating, but it is not really preparation: as in most things, learning by doing works well, and pottery is no exception. Nevertheless, having said that, an understanding of what you are trying to do is certainly necessary, and this can be obtained in some measure in advance of your first practical attempts on the wheel. Reading books can help; photographs and explanations can make sense, coupled with watching demonstrations by experts. My own view is that to start with, watching is the greatest help. If you can spare the time to watch a potter constantly in action at the wheel, you will sooner or later feel a genuine urge either to emulate or improve on his/her example.

An understanding of the various stages will develop, so that you will start to feel that you could do a little better. You will be impatient to have a go yourself, and confident that in some measure you have grasped the basic stages in the process.

Having watched a craftsperson at work you will have noticed several things. The clay will have been thoroughly prepared in sufficient quantity to ensure a working rhythm. Balls of clay will have been measured out, and protected from the air and subsequent drying. The potter will have organized the working area so that tools are readily available; water is at hand in the wheel tray; and there is something available with which to wipe off his hands. Balls of clay will be stored within easy reach.

You will soon become aware of a deliberate, systematic approach to the task, where the potter's actions are considered and methodical, and the overall process of throwing a hollow vessel has been broken down into a series of stages, which may appear to flow together or may stand apart as obvious distinct steps. Whether you watch practising potters or read books, it will be useful, if not imperative, to identify these stages, as each determines logically how to proceed with ease to the next.

The attempts of an unprepared beginner, on the other hand, will show no such calm purposeful approach: the process will appear to be a struggle between the would-be potter and the material upon which that person attempts to impose his or her will, and the results will rarely be successful.

The overall process can be broken down into the following stages:

1. Centring the clay on the wheel-head.
2. Making a solid cone.
3. Making a solid cylinder.
4. Opening the clay.
5. Pulling up into a hollow cylinder.
6. Forming this into the desired shape.

Before this, of course, must come 'preparation', without which centring will be virtually impossible. These stages can be examined individually to see how each step dictates the success or otherwise of the next.

The Tools you will Need

Essentials

- Bowl of water, placed readily at hand in the wheel-tray or on a board at the rear of the tray.
- Sponge: small 'elephant-ear', natural.
- An old or broken piece of ruler approximately 6in (15cm) long, with one end cut off diagonally to a dog-ear shape, at an angle of about 30–45 degrees.
- Cutting wire – twisted wire or nylon, easily home made.

Non-Essentials

- Potter's needle, for trimming uneven rims.
- Small sponge on a stick for mopping out tall pots too narrow to get your hand or fingers inside. It need not be of natural sponge.
- Potter's ribs, for shaping walls, turning down rims, smoothing bases of plates.
- Assorted modelling tools. Used as ruler above, for marking and impressing to emphasize rims, etc.

Lastly, a reminder that the clay must be homogeneous and of the right consistency if you are to be successful.

Be prepared: clay, kneaded and covered to prevent uneven drying. Have water, tools and sponges ready.

Throwing a Pot on the Wheel: Step-by-Step Procedure

Step 1

Centring is the process of distributing the mass of clay equally about the centre of the wheel. If clay is first made up into balls that are then placed in the middle of the wheel-head, there should be fewer problems with shaping the clay. When cubes or uneven lumps of clay are plonked on randomly, a great deal of luck and brute force will be required to persuade the clay to distribute itself evenly about the axis of the wheel.

Novices will find that it is best to place the ball of clay gently on to a dry wheel-head, using dry hands, directly over the centre. Holding your hands directly above the wheel helps you to judge the centre. Use the concentric rings marked on the wheel-head to guide you, and when satisfied that the ball is central, depress it a little onto the head. Turn the wheel using your hands, and firmly slap the clay as it turns, forcing it down onto the wheel-head into a cone shape so that it is stuck firmly. Use dry hands for this also, because if either the wheel-head or the

Slapping down a ball of clay, to fix it firmly and centrally to the wheel-head. Look down from directly above.

The ball, now roughly 'coned' and centred.

Water, to lubricate, applied to the revolving clay.

ball of clay is wet, the water or slurry will cause the clay to skid off the wheel. When you have hand-centred and fixed the clay you can proceed to the 'fun' part.

Step 2

Set the wheel in motion at a reasonably high speed. It spins anticlockwise, so that the clay is travelling towards your left side and hand, and away from you on your right. This is important to note,

because the next stage is to completely centralize the clay by persuading any protruding lumps to move inwards and upwards so that they appear to disappear at the top of a spiral movement. To effect this, these lumps are met by an immovable object (your left hand) as they travel round towards you (*see* below).

Lubricate the lump of clay with water by gently squeezing a small wetted sponge over the top of the clay. Merely dipping your hands in water will probably be insufficient; drenching the clay, on the other hand, simply causes slurry to fly everywhere.

The left hand, held immovably, forces the lump towards the centre, the right hand and fingers guiding. Use medium/ quick wheel-speed.

Reduce the height, applying pressure from above.

Squeezing up, into a tall(ish) cone, bringing 'wobbles' upwards, to disappear at the top of the spiral.

Flattening the cone further.

Start at the bottom of the cone, allowing the protrusions to 'bump' into the heel of your hand, rather than pushing hard yourself into the side of the clay. The lumps will be obliged to move inwards and upwards as long as your hand remains firm, and provided you are not 'fighting' excessive non-conformities. Remember to work in small steps, little by little, and to lubricate with water before each movement. Clay has to be coaxed gently but firmly, so be patient, and you will soon be rewarded with a perfectly centred cone.

There are numerous ways of actually holding your hands against the clay; at this stage the left hand has to do the major part of the work, and the right hand can only support it. Arms and body form a rigid triangular structure resistant to the force inflicted by mobile protuberances of clay. This position can be made even stronger by keeping the elbows in to the body, and/or by placing the arms firmly on to the thighs or the top edge of the wheel-tray; the wheel and body then combine to form one solid structure, the intention being that you can cause the clay to move by small degrees.

The clay should not be moving *you*, and if it is, either you have not locked your hands firmly enough, or the clay is rather too firm. Another possibility is that you are trying to move too much clay in one attempt, pushing excessively with the heel of your left hand so that, after initial pressure has moved the clay further off-centre, the momentum of the eccentric clay is just too much for your arm to resist.

Having centred a cone of clay, you will have overcome the main difficulty in the whole process. It is this centring that usually causes the greatest heartache to most beginners, so it is well worth overstating the probable causes of failure:

- Ensure that the clay is adequately prepared.
- Be careful to have a dry wheel-head, hands and ball of clay before attempting to stick the ball onto the wheel-head.
- Coax the clay to move in modest steps, so do not force it too far in one go. If your first attempt fails, remember the above points, particularly the need for a dry wheel-head and clay ball, and resist the temptation to return a soggy dollop of used clay to the wheel. Just put the used clay to

one side to await recycling later, either via the soak-bin, or preferably by kneading it up with any other used clay at the end of the session ready to be stored for re-use, and then have another attempt.

Step 3

The centred cone will now require flattening from the top to produce a solid cylinder. Use the thumb of the left hand to depress the point of the cone

Flatten into a solid cylinder, or …

… draw up again to further 'centre' the clay.

gently but firmly, steadying the clay with the right hand. It will not be necessary to have quite such a fast wheel speed here, so reduce it a little, and co-ordinate hand movement with the speed of the wheel. This should present no difficulties, and even if things go slightly wrong, all you need do is return to Step 2, coning, and then restart. The solid cylinder should be thrown into a form having a square profile.

Step 4

Like Step 1, Step 4 is rather critical. A few simple if obvious pointers are listed below, which will smooth the way towards a satisfactory outcome.

- To make a hole at the centre of the clay it is essential that the clay is first centred on the wheelhead.
- At any given motor speed the peripheral speed will be greater than the speed nearer the centre of the wheel.
- A granule of clay travelling one revolution on the outside of a lump of clay will travel further than a granule nearer the centre.
- Granules of clay piled up along the axis of the clay will not travel; they will simply revolve upon themselves.

To open the clay, downward pressure is applied to the centre of the top of the cylinder. As central wheel speed is virtually nil, a moderately fast speed

A grip for flattening the cone.

Opening the clay. Alternatively the left thumb, or both, can also be used. Work from directly over the clay, lock hands, arms and body to form a rigid 'tool', obliging the clay to move, not yourself.

can be applied. Keep your eyes right over the centre, and pour all your concentration, as well as your left thumb, into the centre of the revolving clay. Imagine the molecules of clay piled up along the clay's axis. You are trying to press them downwards as they rotate. Support the thumb with your right hand to maintain pressure at the exact centre, and open up the clay firmly and carefully, pushing the topmost centre molecule down into the body of the clay until the end of your thumb is about $\frac{1}{4}$in (0.6cm), or finger thickness, above the wheel-head.

As you become more experienced at judging depth, you will instinctively know just how far to press without obtaining a beginner's flowerpot with an accidental drainage hole! A useful means of measuring inside depth against outside height is to take, say, two pencils or similar, then lay one across the top of the cylinder, and place the other at 90 degrees to it: you can then compare the outside and inside measurements downward from the horizontal pencil.

Although actually measuring the initial opening is not essential, it can be reassuring to know you have left neither too thick a foot, nor one so thin that when the pot is cut from the wheel there will be a hole in the bottom. In the early stages you will find it useful to check again when you have opened the clay further, as described below.

Step 5

Having opened the clay with a thumb (or use both, or any other combination you feel comfortable and have success with), you will now be ready to expand the opening widthways, while preparing to stretch the clay vertically upwards. From a solid, perfectly centred cylinder as can be seen on page 86, you will have produced a hollow cylinder with thick, even walls.

Using your right middle finger (it's longer and stronger than the other) pinch the lower wall, applying pressure on the inside, meanwhile using your left hand to support and maintain the outside shape. Leave a fat collar or flange of clay above.

This opening-up at the foot of the pot can be a critical step. Bearing in mind the principle of wheel and clay speed, any movement at, and away from,

Use the right-hand fingers to pinch against left-hand pressure, further opening the inside bottom.

the centre will have to proceed very slowly to compensate for the slow rotation of the clay. As the point of contact spirals outwards, the clay's speed will increase so that hand movement can be speeded up in direct relation to it. Co-ordination of hand and wheel speed is always necessary, but at this particular stage a movement made too quickly from the centre outwards could produce a cylinder with walls of uneven thickness.

The thick collar will be stretched or 'unrolled' vertically upwards by a pulling action imposed from inside. Use the fingers of the right hand, clawing or pinching, and maintain the overall width of the cylinder. As the clay stretches between the two pressure points, both hands move smoothly upwards, drawing the wall of the pot up into a more thinly walled cylinder.

When centring the clay it is important to use the left hand in much the same way as in Step 1. It gently but firmly maintains the outside shape, deepening the wall vertically by preventing outward expansion caused by centrifugal forces acting on the clay. These forces become more pronounced both as wheel speed and diameter increase. Remember, peripheral speed is greater. This could be seen as a negative action as compared to the

Mopping out slurry, using a small natural sponge.

Another 'pull' upwards, increasing height again.

Gaining height, restricting outward growth with the left hand.

A watcher's eye view of the grip.

positive action of the right hand's fingers, which squeeze or coax the clay upwards, ultimately forming a rather thick pot of uniform thickness, and then thinning to complete the process. This 'negative force' – the clay being 'thrown' outwards from the centre – is the essential principle underlying the process, and the one the potter aims to control.

So far, all the action has taken place on your left hand's side, with the clay travelling *towards* the points of contact. From here on, however, all the forming, shaping and refining of the form will be carried out on the right-hand side, with the clay moving *away* from the points of contact.

Step 6

The walls of the pot have now been made relatively thin. The clay has been frequently lubricated with water, and although a vertical form will easily stand up by itself, the friction imposed by hands and finger, and further shaping (and excessive water) can cause distortion to the form. The pinching action could also impose some 'braking' on the revolving form, particularly at the top. It is there-fore necessary to use minimum contact – a knuckle or a fingertip rather than the whole palm of the hand – and to do the drawing up and shaping in gentle stages.

Apart from the foregoing, this step is both easy and very exciting. First examine the photograph illustrating a good way of making a pincer action using both hands: thus the left hand will work on the inside of the pot, tending to act outwards; the right hand, in the main the knuckle of either first or second finger, will act on the outside, opposite the left finger, producing a gentle squeezing pincer action.

As with previous steps, each movement or squeezing action starts at the foot of the pot and moves steadily upwards, creating the characteristic spiral markings on the vessel. It is lubricated to avoid friction, and is continued to the top lid of the pot and beyond. Note that the hands must not be snatched away, but pressure released gradually, so as to maintain and ensure even thickness of the pot wall. The upward spiralling action should, as in the foot or base of the pot, apply equal pressure to all parts of the clay. A quick action upwards,

The throwing 'pincer' grip demonstrated, making a bridge between both hands.

Commencing the throwing movement, on the right-hand side of pot and potter.

The pincer movement, drawing up the wall, maintaining a rim.

Consolidating the rim or lip.

Alternative view of the 'opening up' grip (see photo on page 89).

Flange of clay left at the foot requires trimming off using a dog-ear tool (cut-off ruler) or rib.

unco-ordinated to wheel speed, will squeeze only a part of the whole, and alternating thin and thick spirals will give a corkscrew shape to the pot that will be difficult or impossible to correct in subsequent movements.

If the hollow form achieved at the end of Step 5 is reasonably thin, Stage 6 will be easy and direct. To produce a simple but well thrown cylinder you will only need to make one or two pinching movements, followed by a little trimming from the outside foot; then cut the finished pot from the wheel-head.

Complete throwing, and then clean up the pot using a squeezed-out damp sponge, mopping out the slurry from inside and out. This cleaning up not only enhances the visual appearance of the pot, but also removes any residual water – the lubricating agent – that could now at best delay stiffening up, and at worst cause splitting if left on the pot. If you examine the lower outside wall you will probably find that the wall of the pot slopes outwards and downwards onto the wheel-head, leaving a rather untidy rim-like flange. This can be cut away from the foot using a dog-ear turning tool: hold it rather as you would a pen, preferably in the left hand, then work on your right-hand side so the clay travels away from you, steadying the tool with the right hand, and cutting down so the trimming twists outwards from the pot.

Cut downwards, peeling off a strip of unwanted clay.

Using a rib, cut from an old credit card, to form a rim.

Step 7

The finished cylinder must now be removed from the wheel and allowed to dry out slowly. Obviously the clay is very soft at this stage, so any handling must be done with care to avoid distortion or damage to the form. There are two variations on one method for doing this, both of which

have their particular merits. Both are outlined below.

The pot is released from the wheel by cutting with a taut wire or nylon line, then removed bodily on to something like a wooden tile. The cutting tool is easily made out of a length of fairly strong nylon fishing line or wire about 12–14in (30–35cm) long, with a button, or a duffel-type peg, or just a

Releasing the pot.

To check the cross-section, cut the pot vertically down (held short, horizontally, uneven rims can be trimmed off, level) …

Sliding the pot onto a wetted bat.

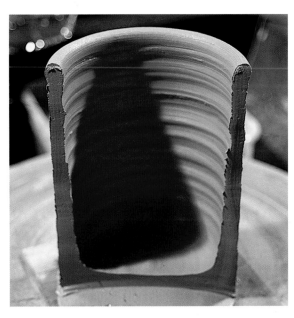

… to reveal a reasonably even thickness – or otherwise.

piece of dowel rod attached at each end. Cutting wires that use a metal ring at each end can be purchased, but these obviously do not float, and are therefore harder to find if they fall into a wheel-tray awash with slurry and wet clay trimmings.

Variation A

1. Have a tile or wooden bat at the ready.
2. Wet its upper surface well.
3. Flood the wheel-head with water.
4. Keeping the wire taut and firmly down on the wheel-head, cut off the pot, allowing the wheel to turn as the wire is dragged or pushed across beneath the pot. This both releases the pot and allows a film of water to be drawn under the foot so that it can be gently slid across the wheel-head.
5. Using the outside edges of the hands, or as many fingertips as can be brought to bear, gently turn and slide the pot towards the edge of the wheel. At first it may not move, but it will soon slide easily. Apply pressure at the foot of the pot where the base can support its walls.
6. Hold the wet bat against the side of the wheel and slide the pot across on to it. Mop off water from the bat with a small sponge and leave the pot safely on one side to stiffen up.

Variation B

1. Have a *dry* bat or board ready to receive the pot. *Do not wet* the wheel-head.
2. Preferably using a twisted wire cutter, cut under the foot, as described in 4 above.
3. Make sure your hands are clean and dry.
4. Tilt and lift the pot upwards, using both hands cupped around it, with most lifting being done by the little fingers and the outside edges of the hands where the base of the pot gives support to the walls. The rest of the fingers and palms give added support, but care must be taken not to squeeze the pot out of shape. A slight twisting action will help to release the pot, which, even once it has been cut off the wheel-head, may be slightly reluctant to leave its birthplace.

Very smooth-bodied clays can sometimes split across the base having been wetted for removal by variation A. Some minor denting of the foot is almost inevitable, requiring turning to trim the foot finally. The main advantage of A is that everything is wet anyway, and once the pot begins to move it is sometimes more convenient for clearing up than B. Where the pot has been trimmed satisfactorily, however, B provides a clean and rather unique foot, requiring no further attention other than a wipe over with a slightly damp sponge when it is leather hard. Like most potters, you will no doubt use a particular method for a particular job; though on the other hand, you may always prefer to use just one.

Both the above techniques work perfectly well for small pots, relatively vertical or upright pots, and for smaller bowl shapes. Attempting to lift off larger plates or bowls can, however, lead to losses, which is at the least distressing. If it is your intention to throw large pots, your best course of action is to throw on bats – circular pieces of marine-grade plywood that either fix on to specially modified wheel-heads, or can be stuck on using clay.

Simplicity is Best

College and school ceramics workshops will provide varying facilities for wheel-work generally, and also specific specialist tools and equipment such as modified wheel-heads and bats. As to the merits of the systems available, suffice it to say that simplicity is usually best. Bats held in place using clay as the adhesive have been known to slip off centre: but at least there can be no serious mechanical loss or failure, and moreover no real cost is involved, and the wheel-heads revert to normal very easily.

Generally, irrespective of the specific system used, there is little difference between using bats or not, except that larger and broader-based pots can be removed more easily. However, when using wooden bats it is usual to slightly dampen the upper surface before attempting to stick clay to the head. Being porous, the bat has a tendency to dry out clay immediately in contact with it, absorbing moisture and reducing adhesion. Experience will soon show you just how much dampening is required when using bats made of a particular material.

It is also worth remembering that the pot requires releasing from the bat before being left to stiffen. Because it is so easy to lift bat and pot off the wheel, cutting off can sometimes be forgotten, and tension building up in the clay due to uneven drying and shrinkage could then cause splitting or warping in the pot; so do make a point of cutting through with the wire before removing it from the wheel.

A Handy Alternative

If the use of bats seems rather excessive, try using newspaper. Proceed as follows: before attempting to remove the pot, gently place a sheet of paper across the top of the lip/rim. Lightly rub the paper down to stick to the top, sealing air inside: the weight of the newsprint on its own will almost be sufficient. This 'drum skin' prevents distortion of the circular lip as the pot is removed, and the trapped air helps support the potentially saggy form.

More Adventurous Shapes

A technique for throwing simple vertical pots has been described in some detail. The next step is to attempt to form the vessel into a slightly more exotic shape. Most traditional vase and jug shapes are based on an S-curve, simplified or exaggerated to produce what the potter considers to be an acceptable profile shape.

To draw up clay into a cylinder once it has been opened, equal pressure is applied at the same level using the pinching technique, drawing clay up from the foot to the lip of the pot. To widen the form, the inner pressure point (the fingertip, or tips, of the left hand) should be slightly higher than the outside point (the right hand). To narrow the form, contact points are reversed so that the outer contact is now higher. If an S-shaped profile is required – for instance, a vase shape – the movement should again be reversed.

If you make a 'pinch' tool with your hands, you

Forming a neck.

can adjust contact between left fingers and right knuckle to achieve outward or inward pressure. By again using the triangular structure, with elbows in and down so that the hands are locked together at the apex of the triangle, you will have a firmly held pincer tool. The distance away from the axis of the pot can be changed slightly to follow the shape of the pot and to control its development by slightly turning your whole upper body, to move the apex inwards or outwards as necessary.

To begin with, keep the profile shape subdued, a little understated, only gradually developing the curves, a little more with each upward movement. Do not attempt to change a form from straight cylinder to an exaggerated curve in one movement, as this will cause too much stress, particularly on the over-thinned and over-stretched lower regions. A wobble would then develop, which could quickly become uncontrollable, and the lower part of the pot would simply collapse. Experience will soon indicate the extent to which you can modify shape in one movement using a particular body prepared to your own liking.

The basic throwing technique can be used, with variations, for the production of most wheel-formed pieces. If, for example, outward pressure is imposed upon the cylinder, a simple open bowl shape will develop. When a bowl is intended, however, it would be preferable to open the solid cylinder into a V-shape from the start so that form develops logically.

Work with the left hand supporting the clay, as in centring. From the final V-shape, the change to working on the right-hand side can be made, drawing up and out to refine the clay into the desired bowl shape (*see* photographs). Try to maintain a parabolic curve on the inside of the bowl, with no bump or indentation at its centre.

Another grip for reducing the neck.

Mopping out slurry.

Forming a foot-ring using a plastic 'rib'.

Pinching a lip: carefully squeeze and pull up.

Pinch in the throat.

Use the index finger against the finger and thumb of the other hand.

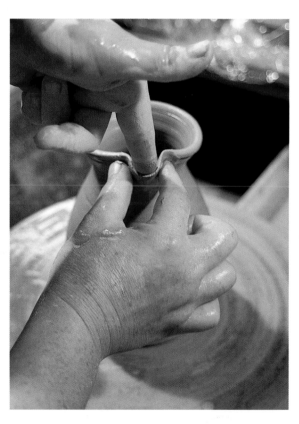

Supporting the lip inside and out to form the required shape.

A 'strangle-hold' grip, used to reduce or completely close up a neck.

Right *A modelling tool used to strip off excess clay at the foot; banding with red iron oxide slip to start the decoration.*

Opening the clay.

Tidying the rim.

Drawing up the wall.

Mopping out slurry, to reveal a parabolic internal curve.

Repetition Throwing

The apparent ability to produce exactly similar wares is an excellent sales pitch. Unquestionably there are craft skills involved, but as a street-wise potter yourself, remember that you can actually throw a dozen items or more from which to pick your matching set. So do not be intimidated by the idea of repetition throwing – just make sure you have no audience.

A couple of basic factors assist greatly in achieving similar end products. Obviously you must start with the same sized lumps of clay: with smaller items such as cereal bowls, accuracy in weighing out is very important – if one ball is 2–3oz (57–85g) heavier than another when the desired weight is only 8–10oz (227–283g), there will be a possible excess of 25 per cent, and this will be reflected in the eventual size.

Secondly, to repeat forms successfully it also helps to get a rhythm, so plan to throw a reasonable batch, and if necessary write off the one or two early, less successful attempts that you are bound to make before you have achieved it.

Mechanical Aids

- Callipers
- Adjustable markers
- Gauge post

Callipers are useful for measuring diameter or height, though in their absence a paintbrush handle or straight stick serves just as well. Unless you plan numerous repetition runs, and want professional-looking equipment to support that, the DIY adjustable marker system illustrated will be quite adequate. Basic dimensions can be set up, based on the first pot thrown, or to a pre-conceived design. A lump of clay and a few bits of dowel rod or old hog's-hair paintbrush handles, are cheap, easy to use, and require minimum storage if not used.

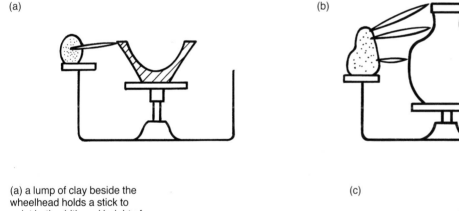

(a)

(b)

(c)

(a) a lump of clay beside the wheelhead holds a stick to point both width and height of an intended bowl.
(b) several sticks could be used to set dimensions of a more complex form.
(c) a commercially produced alternative.

adjustable pointers

weighted base

Gauge post and DIY versions.

The Etceteras

Most bowls have turned feet, so either leave plenty of thickness at the base, or, if the bowl is fairly small, trim off the excess flange at its foot, cut off with a twisted wire, and clean up with a sponge. Soup or cereal bowls can be finished effectively without the need for turned feet. A variation on the bowl can be turned and inverted to produce a simple lid.

An alternative lid can be thrown, based on a combination of bowl and plate (see diagram). Restrict the thickness of the base so that by cutting off with a twisted wire there will be no need to turn the lid. If this is not possible, then the lid should be turned down to an appropriate thickness, and lightened in the process.

Most novices experience the problem of walls ending up uneven in height, particularly on pots that have been narrowed in at the top. This usually arises from inadequate preparation, centring, or uneven opening of the clay, leaving perhaps only a very slight increase in thickness somewhere around the cylinder. This lump may have been successfully thrown, upward, undetected, only to arrive at the lip as an unwanted wave spoiling the finished line of the pot. It can, however, be easily trimmed off. Use a needle held at an appropriate height and gently pushed through the wall of the revolving pot until it comes into contact (gently) with a supporting finger held inside, opposite the point of entry. The released rim of clay can then be lifted carefully away while the pot is still turning, leaving a clean-cut edge that now requires softening or rounding off using a damp sponge or wet fingers.

As clay-covered cork-handled needles can inadvertently become lost in clay and only reappear when stuck into fingers, it may be worthwhile to try an alternative method, making the needle obsolete. Use a nylon cutting wire, held very short between two hands in such a way as to stretch the line taut between the ends of the thumbs. Using what has effectively become a miniature potter's harp, the offending bulge can be trimmed off by carefully cutting down from the lip as the pot revolves, levelling the cut at the appropriate height and thus trimming horizontally completely around the top of the pots.

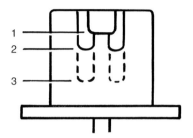

(a) open the clay to produce a central protruberance from which to form the knob.

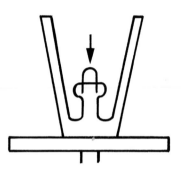

(b) gently depress centre. Use a rib or 6in ruler inside rim to broaden.

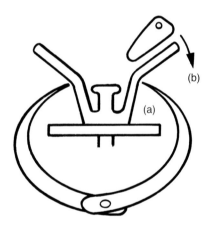

(c) do not overflatten. A gentle transition from (a) to (b) will give tolerance to the fit. Measure with callipers to match sizes of rim and lid.

Throwing a lid.

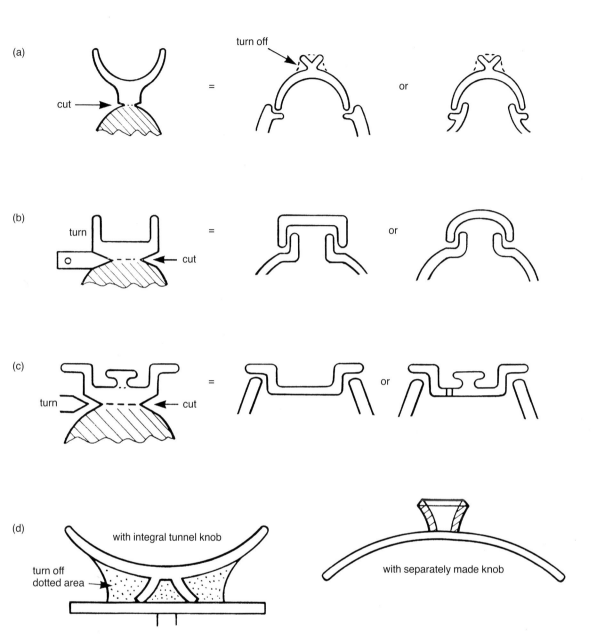

Some suggestions: (a) a simple lid thrown and cut off the hump, knob turned; (b) without knob; (c) teapot or storage jar lids; (d) shallow bowl shape with integral turned knob, or turned flat to receive a separately made knob later.

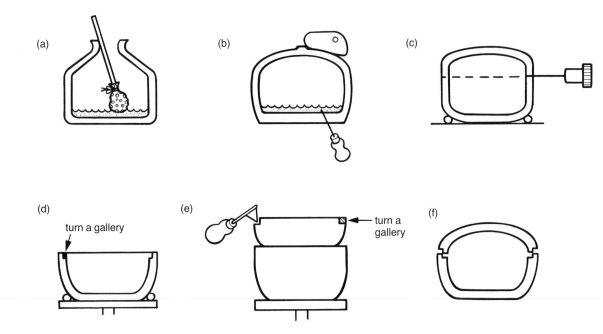

Throw a lidded bowl – a suggested project. (a) Remove slurry/water with a sponge prior to closing up. (b) depress with rib, ruler or hands to close in the top, or throw it up into a knob; use a needle to drain off trapped water – the hole will re-seal. (c) Release the top section. (d), and (e) turn interlocking galleries. (f) Cross-section view of galleries.

Throwing a Plate

Apart from mugs, jugs and cups, the most familiar ceramic object is probably the plate. However, our familiarity is probably with mass-produced plates that are both very light and usually decorated with sterile glazes and screen-printed transfers. Bearing in mind that the character of hand-thrown plates is essentially different to their factory-made cousins, and that hand-making matching sets of anything is not always a precise science, let us look at the technique of hand-thrown plate making.

As always, clay must be centred, coned, and for plates, formed into a squat, solid cylinder. The clay is opened in much the same way as in any other situation, except that the opening can be made wider. A rib can be used (as illustrated) to obtain a smooth, flat base as well as to turn down the rim.

It is actually remarkably easy to produce plates in theory, but in practice there are several things that should be borne in mind. First, the plate, regardless of size, will be virtually impossible to lift from the wheel in a plastic state. Throw the plate on a bat, allowing safe early removal, freeing the wheel for other use. When turning down the rim, avoid the absolute horizontal, as the weight of the clay, particularly on very wet plates, will cause the rim to sag. Leave the rim sloping slightly up and outward to avoid this.

A major problem with plates is that, although it is desirable to stiffen the whole object quickly to 'fix' the shape, the rim will dry more quickly than the base. This can happen because first, it has air almost all around it; and second, it is not resting on a damp, moisture-retaining bat. This can cause the rim to pull in and upward again, losing the intended 'plate' shape. Slow, even drying, away from draughts and sources of heat, will help to alleviate this. Damp cupboards can be used, although a plastic bag from a dry-cleaner's, very thin and light, can be floated down over the plate so it can be left somewhere safely out of harm's way.

It is usual to attach a bat to the wheel-head. So first throw a disc and cut grooves to aid adhesion …

… and centre a bat onto it, and firmly press or thump it down to secure it to the wheel-head.

A rib is used to level the inside.

Opening and flattening simultaneously.

Throw a low wall.

Trim the foot.

Neaten the rim.

Ease the wall outwards, by throwing …

… and using a rib to smooth it off.

Apply slip, if required, by banding on with a suitable brush.

A Summary of Throwing

Any description of throwing techniques is bound to be long and somewhat involved, so the overall process is reviewed here in order to clarify and focus on the most essential factors. The stages are, in order:

1. Preparation – clay, tools, equipment, including storage.
2. Centring the clay on the wheel-head.
3. Opening up the clay – work on the left (the clay is travelling towards your left hand).
4. Shaping and refining the form – work on your right, with the clay travelling away from the points of contact.
5. Removal and storage.

Three main factors determine a successful outcome:

(a) The clay must be homogeneous.
(b) It must be 'centred' on the wheel-head.
(c) It must be 'opened' in such a way as not to build in an exaggerated spiral and/or walls of uneven thickness.

Provided care is taken at each stage, (a) will assist in securing success with (b). In turn, (c) depends on (b) and on wheel and hand speed. In short, the process can be divided up into the steps above, which also fall into the two categories of working on your left hand and on your right. A skilled craftsperson may well appear to allow each step to flow naturally into the next, but the steps are nevertheless there to guide and aid you through the process.

'Preparation, practise, perseverance': follow these tenets, and you may be sure that adherence to the principles contained therein will be richly rewarded.

Turning

Throw a bowl with an over-thick base. Allow it to stiffen and, when ready, gauge the thickness in the base and lower walls by measuring (plumb the depth). Measure the walls by gently pinching with fingers inside and thumb outside the pot, to get a feel of the thickness. Use your thumbnail to scratch the outside walls where thickness is excessive; as their depth is reduced by turning, these scratch marks will help to indicate the amount of clay that still needs to be removed.

In short, before turning a pot, get to know it thoroughly.

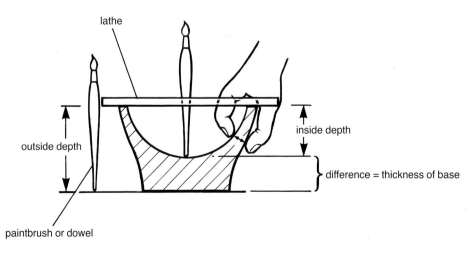

Use the finger and thumb to 'feel' the thickness of the walls; use brushes or dowel rods to measure inside and outside depths.

Centre, and secure with slugs of clay.

Hold the tool firmly to reduce the risk of 'chattering'.

Turn out inside ...

... and outside the foot-ring, and burnish the surface with a dry finger to consolidate the surface.

Complete the job by applying your potter's stamp, or mark, pressed directly into the foot, or into a small disc of clay applied specially for the purpose.

Bowls requiring turning can be inverted directly onto a potter's wheel, centred, and held in place with short coils, or slugs, of clay. Taller pieces will require careful attachment to the wheel-head, and a sensitive application to the tools to avoid accidentally pushing the piece off-centre and off the wheel-head. Pots with narrow lips/necks will need to be supported on the wheel-head in some kind of chuck – it may be possible to make use of an upturned bowl as shown.

Step 1 If necessary, turn the base of the bowl or chuck to ensure level centring.
Step 2 Make absolutely sure that the chuck is properly centred and affixed to the wheel; use soft plugs of clay to stick it in place.
Step 3 Invert the pot into the chuck, and fix it to the rim using soft clay as on the wheel-head if necessary.
Step 4 Turn off excess thickness.
Step 5 Carefully release the pot and chuck, removing the soft pads of clay.

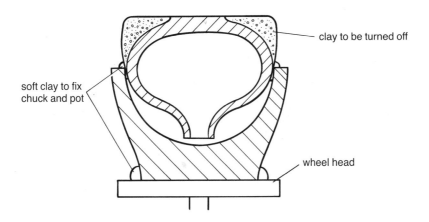

clay to be turned off

soft clay to fix chuck and pot

wheel head

Chuck or bowl used to secure a narrow-necked vessel for turning.

Custom-made clay chucks can be thrown directly on to the wheel-head. They should be allowed to stiffen before use. After, they can be recycled before they become too firm. If it is intended to turn long runs of repetition-thrown pots, biscuit-fired chucks would be more durable. Other alternatives include plaster-cast and turned chucks, and bought-in chuck-heads that fit some potter's wheels, both these probably being inappropriate for most studio potters.

Advanced Throwing

Most experienced potters would prefer to throw blindfold than attempt to define the word 'advanced' in this context. But where one person might struggle for an hour or more to throw a modest bowl, another might dash off a dozen in the same time; and someone else's impressively large vases might look amateurish when seen beside another's wonderful little gem of a bowl. In other words, techniques or methods that might appear advanced to some, will inevitably appear basic or obvious to others. Nevertheless, two factors seem to impress the layman and novice alike: the ability to produce large thrown wares; and the ability to produce sets of similar-looking pots (repetition throwing – see page 99). But rather than suggesting either of these as an advanced technique or otherwise, we should consider the basic element that divides the beginner from the expert. An experienced craftsperson works *with* material and equipment, while the novice often struggles against them. Getting every-

thing right is not finicky; it is to your advantage to have everything prepared or arranged to your liking; it also enhances confidence.

Before You Start

PREPARATION

The clay body must be homogenous and of a consistency you can handle. Thus a body that is too stiff will be difficult to centre; and although very soft clay will 'grow' easily, it will be incapable of supporting its own weight in anything other than simple, probably vertical shapes.

QUANTITY

Students often expect clay to stretch somehow beyond its volume. If large vessels are the aim, sufficient clay must be available (*see* below).

Limitations

This relates partially to consistency: a grogged body will support itself more readily than an extremely plastic, smooth body. Porcelain and some smooth earthenware bodies will therefore require rather thick throwing with considerable turning later. Similarly, exaggerated shapes will require extra thickness for support prior to stiffening, and then turning down to the required shape.

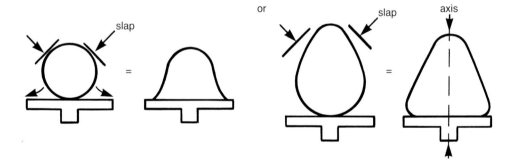

Slapping clay down onto the wheel-head.

Summary

- Work with the material by having it prepared exactly for the job in hand.
- Avoid handicapping yourself by using inappropriate or insufficient material.
- Do not expect to make a ready-to-use product without recognizing all the limitations -- of the materials, the processes and your own abilities. Careful consideration should always be given to the basic properties of the clay.

Throwing Large Vessels

As suggested above, size is dictated in part by quantity. The first problem when throwing a large pot is to make up balls of clay larger than would normally seem manageable: psychologically, it seems, larger lumps are somewhat threatening at first. If you find this is the case, build up in modest steps to start with, developing more confidence as your success increases. Keep to vertical forms in early practice sessions, gradually increasing your repertoire to include wider, more open shapes.

Throwing Tall Pieces

Whether it is large or small in real terms, a tall pot must have height relative to width. To gain height, clay has to be elevated from the wheel-head. This involves applying pressure inwards and upwards at the base, some of this before the clay has been opened, and (indeed, usually most) after opening but before serious shaping.

When throwing small- and medium-sized lumps of, say, 1–7lb (0.5–3kg) in weight, balls of clay can be centred without too much difficulty. Either slam the clay down firmly on top of a slow-turning dry wheel-head, or place it carefully into position over the centre of the similarly dry wheel, turn it, and simultaneously slap the ball down into a cone shape using both hands.

Larger lumps can be pre-formed like a pear, and then slapped down. The aim is to centre the mass of clay above the axis of the wheel so that it requires only a minimum of 'fine tuning' once the wheel is set in motion. This reduces the need to fight bumps as they revolve, and so the more centring that can be done by slapping, the less is required by throwing.

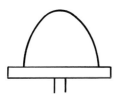

(a) centre a cone or beehive shape.

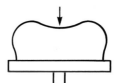

(b) flatten and depress.

(c) open – use a fist to punch down as wheel revolves slowly

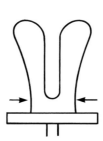

(d) add collar to gain height.

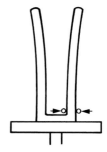

(e) pressure applied from bottom upwards to gain extra height with each movement – as in the photos on page 91.

Punching down.

Throwing in Stages

The perfect scenario does not exist as far as throwing is concerned. That is to say, if the clay is soft enough to centre easily, it might well be too soft to support height and weight; conversely, when it is firm enough to support its own weight, it may not be easy, or even possible, to centre the larger amount necessary to achieve the desired height. As in so many situations, a compromise has to be reached.

Compromising with time can be one way forward. Use the soft body to centre, open and collar easily, then when a reasonable start has been made, leave the clay to firm up prior to final shaping and cleaning. This could take a considerable time, depending on conditions in the workplace, and it also ties up a wheel. However, you can further compromise on sensitivity to material and traditional craftsmanship, speeding up the stiffening process by applying the hot air from a hair dryer or electric paint-stripper – though take care not to cause uneven drying or to dry the piece too rapidly. If the pot is turned slowly on the wheel and the warm air applied to the areas that need to be stiffened, both inside and out, the piece will soon be ready for further thinning and shaping.

It is sometimes a good idea to part-throw a piece before lunch, the break being sufficient to enable further work later on. Whole pots can be left for longer periods, such as overnight, again depending on the working environment. If the piece is partially covered (particularly the upper part) with a plastic bag, the remaining exposed, lower parts will firm up while the upper areas will remain workable. Remember that it has taken millions of years for the clay to become the plastic material we use today, so a little extra time spent transforming it into something else is as nothing against such a backdrop.

Building as You Throw

An interesting variation on the above method is to throw, say, a vessel to half the required height (possibly 14–16in (36–41cm), or to your best possible height), keeping its section reasonably thick.

Allow the piece to stiffen until the top is firm enough to be scored. Apply slip, and then a thick coil of soft clay. Model and/or throw some of the new clay down over the join to ensure maximum adhesion, then draw/throw the additional clay upwards to form the next part of the vessel. Add further coils as conditions allow until the vessel is complete.

In order to consolidate and compress the joins, and to disguise the same if desirable, use a wooden rib or metal kidneys inside and out. Turning (when leather-hard) will also remove uncomfortable undulations in the profile shape; but be careful not to turn away too much in these areas, as joins may become exposed and weakened.

Wobbles when Centring

When centring small lumps of clay it is important to ensure that no wobbles exist. The profile of the centred beehive or solid cylinder shape should appear to have no movement (wobble) as the wheel revolves. With large lumps, the accuracy is less critical: a slight wobble at the upper extremity will be thrown out as the piece develops. In fact, if a large lump is opened by literally punching down its axis as it revolves, the resulting open cylinder will seem decidedly uneven as the clay revolves slowly; but as soon as the drawing-up pressures have been applied once or twice from the bottom upwards, most, if not all irregularities will have been evened out.

Tips

- It is better to have too much, rather than too little clay.

- Concentrate on gaining (early) height; worry about shape later.

- Remember to increase thickness *pro rata* with height; don't try to throw a pot that is too thin.

- Excess clay can be turned off later; err on the thick side.

The ability to manage large lumps on the wheel comes with practice, and with having, or at any rate developing, confidence in your ability. Remember, you are doing the throwing, the clay is not throwing *you*!

Throwing 'Off the Hump'

The centring of small balls of clay (anything less than 2lb/1kg in weight) becomes progressively more difficult as size diminishes, for it is both easier and quicker to centre one large lump than it is to centre a number of small balls. The idea with throwing off the hump is to capitalize on the convenience of having only one large ball to centre upon the wheel, using only the top of the lump or hump to produce small pots, one after the other. The main mass of clay remains centred firmly on the wheel-head, and only the top part requires re-coning after removal of the previous pot. The protuberance at the top can then be thrown in the usual way.

Finishing and Removing

Pots thrown in this way obviously cannot be removed from the wheel in quite the same way as direct throwing permits. Finish the pot in the usual way, using a sponge and/or chamois inside and out to remove slurry. Turn off any little excess weight, particularly at the foot, using a wooden dog-ear tool and cutting as narrow a foot as is practicable. Cut precisely horizontally to release the pot, using a twisted wire (but no water). Lift the piece gently from well in at the foot, and place it on a dry board.

This technique is particularly useful for the production of small, open forms such as eggcups, mustard pots and little bowls. It is possible to throw a lid off the same lump as used later to throw the body of its parent jar or teapot. It is also possible to throw a series of lids, knobs or spouts, again without the need to centre more than one piece of clay.

Note that the base may also require turning. If it has been thrown well, and cut off carefully with a twisted wire, it may not need anything other than a perfunctory trim to clean up the foot. Functional or

decorative handles, knobs or other appendages can be added while the piece is still leather hard. A simple, impressed decoration might also be suitable (*see* Chapter 6).

Project: Make a Teapot, the Conventional Way

A teapot is a more or less cylindrical pot with the following additions: a spout (a), thrown off the hump as above, modelled or pinched; a lid (b), possibly thrown as a shallow bowl as above; and a handle (c) which could be pulled in the traditional way, rolled and cut or modelled, depending on the overall design. Alternatively, the handle might be made of cane and attached to lugs on the shoulder of the pot.

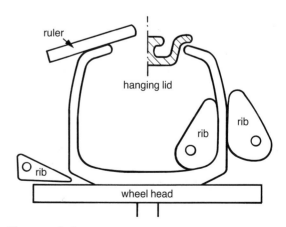

The teapot body.

The Body

Step 1 Prepare a supply of clay. Weigh out two or three balls, each weighing 3–6lb (1.5–3kg). Throw these to form the bodies of the teapots. Keep the forms simple, and a little taller than you think is perhaps appropriate. Try to leave only enough thickness at the lower (foot) part to support the rest of the body; this can be removed before the pots are cut off, thereby reducing or eliminating the need for turning.

Step 2 Use a rib, ruler or modelling tool to narrow the shoulder. Aim to throw the rim so that it will take well to a hanging lid.

Step 3 Use ribs to shape and trim the profile, both inside and outside as necessary.

Step 4 Release the pot using a very tight nylon-wire cutter and water, sliding it off onto a bat or board. Sponge away any water before leaving the pot to stiffen. You might also try throwing directly onto a wooden bat to prevent the risk of distortion when removing the body from the wheel. Additionally, the use of a twisted wire to cut the base, coupled with the application of a sheet of newspaper across the rim of the teapot body, will prevent distortion during removal.

'Pulling' a handle: it is stretched and tapered, then allowed to stiffen while formed into the desired shape.

The Lid

Step 1 Measure the first teapot lid with a calliper and endeavour to throw subsequent pots to the same size – the lids should be interchangeable.

Step 2 Throw the lid off the hump or individually, whichever is found to be easiest. Make the initial shapes taller and more V-shaped than inclination might suggest.

Step 3 Make several spare lids so that the best looking and fitting can be selected for use with each pot.

The Spout

You will probably prefer to throw the spout off the hump, as above. Aim to produce tall, narrow shapes, collared up and in by the 'strangulation' method. Make at least three spouts per pot to allow choice of shape, and wastage when cutting and shaping them to fit.

The Handle

While the thrown components are stiffening up to leather hard, a start can be made on the handle. The traditional 'pulling' method will require both adequate spare to allow for wastage, and time to pre-form and stiffen prior to attachment. If cane handles are appropriate and available, only their lugs will need to be made. The simplest lugs are

Alternatively a 'slug' can be attached, and pulled in situ.

Drawn out to sufficient length …

… by drawing the clay downwards.

Bending into position.

Cutting …

… and joining, by scoring and slipping, 'thumbing' to create a neat conclusion, and modelling into the form – an appropriate place to locate a potter's mark.

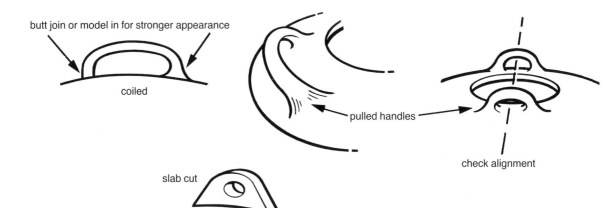

Coiled, pulled or slabbed lugs can be attached to receive cane handles.

created from coils of appropriate length and thickness, these being attached to the shoulder of the parent pot.

It is important that both the handle and pot surfaces to be joined are of similar consistency, and that both sides of the join are well scored and slipped. Maximum strength is required for any handle; small contact areas leave no room for weaknesses. Such joins can be vulnerable to tensions caused by uneven shrinkage during the drying-out process: long, slow drying is better than quick, uneven drying.

Hot-air strippers or hair-dryers used to speed up drying require careful handling. Their use will undoubtedly enable quicker assembly, a convenience most potters welcome, but take care not to overdo the application of heat, particularly to appendages. When the teapot is complete, allow it to dry out slowly with the appropriate lid in place, either in a damp cupboard or inside a plastic bag. Remember: slow, careful drying is essential for all complex forms.

9 Decoration

The decoration of clay vessels is evident in even the earliest and most primitive of ceramic forms. One might speculate that decoration began as a means of differentiation between domestic and ritual or ceremonial wares, or that potters might have chosen to mark their wares with symbols identifiable to themselves. For whatever reason, it appears to have become an inescapable, or integral, part of the making process, and plays a significant role in contemporary ceramics.

Obviously many more methods, techniques and materials are available to contemporary potters

Above *Cypriot earthenware vessel, c. 900 B.C. Nottingham Castle Museum & Art Gallery*

Left *Jug of lead-glazed earthenware, decorated with applied bosses; made in Nottingham in the fourteenth century. It was found in Parliament Street during excavations for Victoria Station in 1895. Nottingham Castle Museum & Art Gallery*

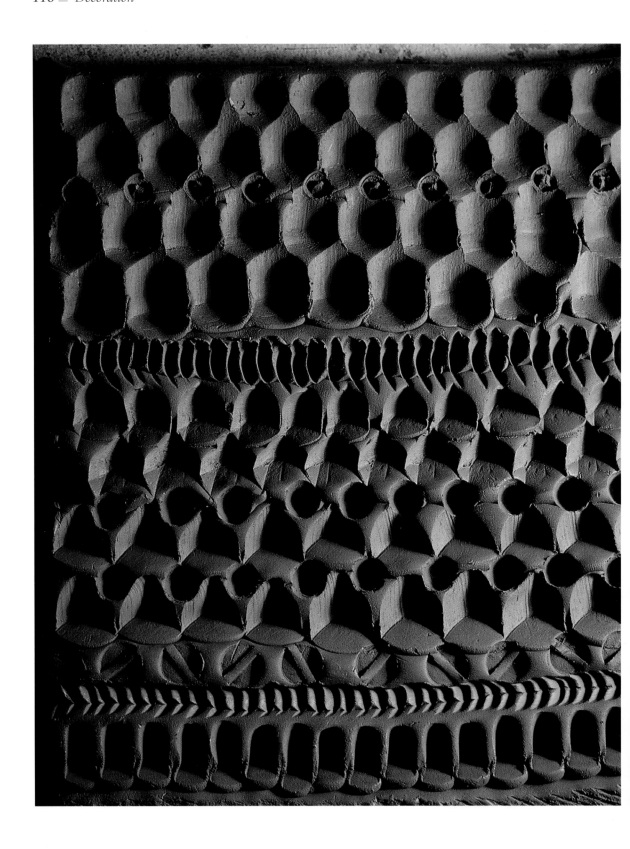

than to potters in the distant past. The making and firing of wares has become more reliable, and decoration has developed alongside these advances. Certainly the spectrum of ceramic colours alone has increased the possibilities open to both amateur and professional alike.

This is all great, but it is important that we do not lose sight of ceramic form. An important point to make here is that careful consideration must be made to ensure that the decoration and form complement one another – an ornate form that is overly dressed may at best look inappropriate, and at worst downright silly. Sometimes it is best to let the form stand for itself, with perhaps just a simple glaze.

If, on the other hand, you wish to have a free hand when it comes to the decorated surface, simple forms with clean lines and strong rims might provide a more satisfying and aesthetic solution. It has been argued for some time that there have been good pots and great decoration, but that the two rarely occur together. This view may be overstated, but an awareness of the argument may go some way towards resolving ill-conceived, overworked and unattractive pots.

Having said all that, it would be useful to have both a shape and appropriate surface treatment in mind when you begin on a pot. So many people make the mistake of building up a form without first giving consideration to shape, size, scale or proportion. Simple sketching is very useful because it gives you a chance to investigate all the possibilities for shape, and also because it tests the appropriateness of proposed decoration as applied to your conceived form.

Furthermore, if you consider decoration at the start of the building process, you will not make unavailable to you those decorative techniques that must be done before the pot is fired – for example, slip decoration or sgraffito, both done at the leather-hard stage. Thus decoration does not have to be a compromise if it is considered at the beginning, and not as an afterthought. Decorative techniques can be tried and experimented with

Opposite *Patterns created in the process of joining coils, using fingers and/or tools to mould and/or impress.*

before you commit your pot to an irretrievable process.

Techniques such as brush- or stencilwork may be tried out on sheets of newspaper, and test tiles or thumb pots also offer another quick method of trying out many of the techniques available to you. Experimentation, coupled with careful recording, will help you to build up a library of techniques, which can be drawn upon in any given situation.

Decorative processes must necessarily be ceramic: they must be capable of surviving some sort of firing process, both to integrate with the ware and to endure. They seem, therefore, to fall into two distinct categories: 'in' and 'on'. The 'in' process refers to marks made in the clay itself or modelled onto it, and the 'on' process applies to colour.

'In' Decoration

Within the 'in' category can be included surface patterns or textures that reflect the nature of the building process (throwing marks) and the material (coarse or smooth clay). An extensively quoted example of this is the basket-weave texture, thought to have originated accidentally. The basket, a very early craft form, had its drawbacks as a container for small objects such as grain. In an attempt to overcome its shortcomings, clay was used to line the basket. When the basket perished it was placed on the fire as fuel. It has been suggested that this may have been an early discovery of pottery, as the clay would have baked in the fire. As pottery became more developed, the basket-weave pattern remained as a decorative reminder of the past.

'Accidental' decoration can include vigorous throwing marks, and patterns created by the action of fingers and tools as an essential part of the 'making' process. Applied decorative detail such as relief modelling, non-functional spouts, handles and sprigging also fall into this category. Remember that robustly built and structured pieces will require perhaps no more than a simple glaze to render them suitable for their intended function, while at the same time not detracting from the inherent surface qualities.

Slip

The earliest forms of pottery from Asia Minor and Mesopotamia (c500BC) relied on white liquid clays painted onto red bodies for decoration. This form of slip-decorated ware has emerged in many cultures throughout history, and is still produced by some cultures today. A modern example is the superb pottery produced by the Pueblo Indians of North America by strong, simple forms and bold geometric designs of coloured slips painted directly onto the pots, these being allowed to dry, and then burnished with the aid of a smooth pebble or the back of a spoon. Burnishing the surface compresses the small, fine surface particles of clay, hence producing a shine. This ware is unglazed, and has good form and pattern, the contrasts between clay body and/or slips forming a major part in the success of the ware.

Slips are very versatile: they may be sprayed, poured, painted or trailed onto clay surfaces, or a combination of all of these can be used; the consistency will vary according to the type of process used. In addition, you may like to experiment with colour. A basic white slip that uses 100 per cent white earthenware clay can be changed with the addition of varying percentages of metal oxides or body stains. Your experiments might produce ten different blues, greens or pinks. Please note, however, that you must avoid using copper carbonate or copper oxide slips on internal surfaces of containers that will be used for food (bowls and plates) if they are to be covered with a fritted lead glaze.

Slips should be applied directly onto soft to leather-hard clays. If you wish to paint patterns, sketch your ideas roughly on paper first; a complex pattern will need patience and persistence. A simple but effective starting point could come from geometric shapes such as squares, circles or triangles. See how many permutations you can discover.

Once you have some idea of pattern, you may begin painting slips onto the surface of your pot (apply two layers). You might find it helpful to mark lightly a few boundary lines to make your job easier. Once the pot and slip become leather hard, you might leave the piece to finish drying out completely, or burnish it with the back of a teaspoon: rub the teaspoon lightly over the surface in a circular motion, taking care not to smear the slip.

Two-handled cup, slipware inscribed 'Daniel Steel Mead ME 1712', made in Staffordshire. Nottingham Castle Museum & Art Gallery

SLIP TRAILING

Slip can also be trailed onto damp or leather-hard clay. Examples of English slipware can be seen in many museums, perhaps the most important being the large platters created by the Toft family during the eighteenth century.

Slip trailing requires a steady hand, confidence and a bit of practice – try using sheets of newspaper before committing your ideas to clay. The more important tip for success in slip trailing lies in getting the slip to the correct consistency: too runny and your pattern will spread, too thick and the slip will not flow easily out of the slip trailer and will stand too proud on the surface. Don't be afraid to experiment.

CHARACTERISTIC PROPERTIES OF SLIP

As slips are usually applied to relatively soft, raw clay, there is an immediacy, spontaneity and liveliness inherent in most processes involving the use of slips. Trailed marks or gestures will lend vitality and variety to the decoration, while the studied mixing and control of precise colour provide a complementary stability to the whole. It is virtually impossible, and undesirable, to create mathematically precise marks and patterns. 'Happy accidents' and 'artistic licence' are synonymous with slip decoration, as is the consistency of colour.

Trailing into a ground of slip of a contrasting colour probably allows for the most attractive finished result. The trailed slip tends to settle down into the wet surface, avoiding uncomfortable raised surfaces where they might not be suitable – as on plates. *Gentle* tapping (of the whole piece onto a bench, for example) encourages this settling-in of the slip or slips. There are, however, at least a couple of potential problems with this method.

First, an excess of water contained in the slip can cause the recipient vessel to split or sag. Teapots, jugs and mugs would be at risk where the weight of spouts and handles imposes a downward pull on soggy bodies. Where it is necessary to apply slip to the inside of a piece, pouring usually gives the smoothest result. This must be done quickly to prevent sagging, allowing little or no time for moisture

Staffordshire charger, slipware, late seventeenth century. Nottingham Castle Museum & Art Gallery

to affect the leather-hard clay. Similarly, for exterior applications dip the piece quickly, and if necessary apply heat and draught to avoid over-wetting. In fact, a hair-dryer or electric paint-stripper can be used to stiffen up suspect areas quickly, including handles and spouts, and can be used to hasten the drying of wet slip before further colour is applied. This can prevent the over-familiar sight of collapsed pots, soggy, detached handles and other associated disasters that can confront you on your return from a well-earned coffee break. Much the same is true when applying glaze prior to once-firing, so a similar ordered procedure is required.

It will also be found that different application processes will demand different slip consistencies. A rather runny, single-cream mix that is suitable for dipping or perhaps painting will probably be too liquid to be trailed successfully. For trailing, the consistency will need to be more akin to double cream: thick enough not to spread out excessively, but mobile enough to be used in a slip trailer as mentioned above. To these minor practical problems there are no pat answers, but by trial and error you will soon develop expertise appropriate to your circumstances, finding your own solutions and being rewarded in the knowledge that you did it your way.

The major argument for using slip is its inherent control of colour. Adding known and recorded amounts of oxides to known amounts of dry clay powder will produce consistently predictable results. The same applies to colouring glazes, while other means of applying oxides to wares are less precise, relying much more on feel and experience. The only requirement for slip is that it is applied evenly; a smooth, rich covering will be achieved, this being further enriched by a transparent, honey or 'iron spangles' glaze.

Conventional and Unconventional Treatments

What follows is an attempt to indicate the traditional usage of slip, and ways in which the medium can be used in a more relaxed manner. Similar approaches are suggested for other techniques so that you can become familiar with a wide range of possibilities, which can be used discreetly or in combination. The resulting freedom from convention will allow full rein for creative expression based on traditional expertise and knowledge of the skills involved.

Trailing is possible using squeezy bottles, slip-filled balloons fitted with glass pipettes and secured at their throats with rubber bands, or – more usually – standard slip trailers bought from any potter's supply shop. The latter come in a range of shapes and sizes, although you may find the smaller slip trailers are sufficient and more comfortable in the hand. Different trailers will have slightly differing nozzle apertures. Should you require a smaller trailed line, a glass pipette can be inserted into the hole of a slip trailer with a removable nozzle, or you can try using the insulation casing from electrical wire as this seems to fit well into the tip of most trailers. As stated earlier, the thickness of trailed lines is also determined to some extent by the consistency of the slip.

Before you begin any slip-trailed pattern, you must ensure that your trailers are full. To do this, expel all the air within the bulb, push the tip into the slip and let go: slip will be slowly drawn up into the body of the trailer. When the bulb is completely filled, extract the tip from the slip, and gently squeeze out the excess air until the slip appears at the nozzle, holding the trailer with nozzle upwards. Many pots are ruined because a slip trailer half full of air has been used, and this causes slip to be splattered out, rather than expelled smoothly. Care must be taken not to let air back into the trailer during the decorating process if unwanted splattering is to be avoided. Gentle, steady pressure and a more or

Playing with coloured slips, trailing and dotting freely.

Levering-off the platter and bat.

less vertical slip trailer will help the whole process along.

A simple feathered pattern is a good exercise to begin with: you may wish to try it out on a tile or scrap of clay first. Begin by either spraying, pouring or painting on a base slip, then trail two different colours alternately across the surface. Draw the tip of a needle or feather through the lines in one direction, then the other. All that remains is to give the dish a gentle tap or two to allow the slips to flatten and merge into the still wet base slip.

You may wish to experiment in order to develop your own patterns, or be guided initially by historical influences. Research the trailing techniques of the slipware potters of Staffordshire (1600–1700), in addition to those of other cultures, to discover the range of possibilities open to you.

Marbling

A simple but extremely effective technique is that of marbling, which is particularly effective when combined with press-moulding, as the mould ensures

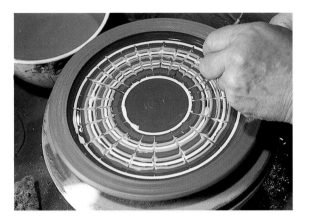

Above *After banding on with different coloured slips, drag a feather or pull a pin carefully across to create a 'feathered' effect.*

Below *Add further free-trailed decoration until the desired result is achieved.*

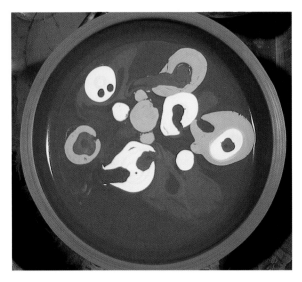

Commence 'marbling' by applying blobs of slips onto a wet undercoat of a contrasting colour.

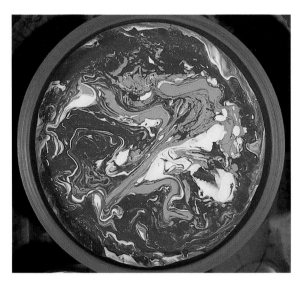

Carefully lift and tilt the plate or dish (supported on a bat or in a mould), allowing the slips to merge and intermingle in swirls.

that the dish is well supported throughout the process.

The slab of clay is pressed into a suitable mould, and two to three different coloured slips are then poured onto a base coat applied to the whole surface. Take care not to use excessive amounts of slip for three reasons: first, it can make the dish over-soft, causing it to dislodge itself from the mould when the surplus is poured off. Second, it can be difficult to get rid of enough slip, thereby causing the clay to become over-wet and so crack in the mould during the drying process. This is a waste of materials, as the eventual mixture of two to three slips has to be thrown away. (As you gain experience you will be able to gauge the amounts to use, to the point that little or no surplus remains on completion of the process.)

The slips are then swirled and jiggled into patterns by rolling and turning the mould around until an acceptable 'marbled' pattern is created. The excess slip is then poured out, and the rim wiped clear. If the result is not acceptable, wipe off all the slip using a large sponge, allow the pressed dish to firm up again after its wetting, and have another attempt.

This simple technique offers endless possibilities, as no two dishes are ever the same, especially

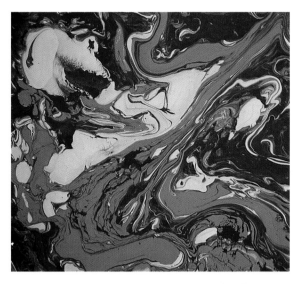

Close-up detail. Note the subdued colour, which will come to life after glaze firing.

as the possible colour variations are virtually endless, with both oxide and body-stained slips. The technique is also possible on thrown ware, as illustrated, and on the flat inner/upper surfaces of plates, platters, and so on – although it requires more skill and practice to apply only enough slip to these, to achieve the desired effect without the need to pour off any excess. After biscuit firing, surface and decoration are enhanced and protected by the application of a transparent or honey glaze fired to 1060–1100°C.

Engobes

The term 'engobe' is often used interchangeably with slip. Basically they are similar and are used in similar ways, but there are differences in their composition, in that slips are mainly composed of clay, whereas an engobe will contain materials normally found in glazes. In this way engobes lie somewhere between a slip and a glaze. They provide a vitreous surface – not at all like the 'dry' feel of unglazed slipware – which can partly or completely obscure the colour of the original clay body.

As with the slips mentioned above, the colour range of engobes is seemingly endless, with the addition of body stains and oxides. Engobes can be made to suit a range of wares and firing temperatures. The recipe given below for white engobe works well at both earthenware and stoneware temperatures, and can be applied to leather-hard clay. Engobes can be dipped, sprayed or painted, or the three techniques can be combined.

If the pieces are to be dipped, the consistency of the engobe should be that of a thick glaze, whereas a thicker mix (yoghurt consistency) will be necessary for painting. You will find brushing with engobe easier than with a purely clay-based slip, as the engobe seems to 'catch' on the pot, sticking to it quite easily. This is particularly noticeable on a highly grogged clay, where the engobe is a joy to use.

USING ENGOBES WITH BRUSHES

If you intend to use the engobe as a base on which to decorate further with engobes (or oxides), you may wish to spray or dip the piece first. That said, engobes brush on just as well, and usually cover in two coats with little trouble. Large, flat, Japanese hake brushes hold good quantities of colour and are ideal for the job.

Painting with a 'hake'.

Slip-trailer used to build up a varied decoration.

When painting engobes, wax out any areas you wish to remain clear – this is useful if you wish to avoid wiping splashes off foot-rings and the like. Charge your brush fully and paint; when the brush begins to drag, recharge and paint again. Once you have a full base coat, wait for it to become matt before applying a second coat. You may wish to apply more than one colour at either stage; interesting effects can be achieved if different colours are brushed on over each other to create soft, overlapping edges. When the engobe dries to leather hard, you could then introduce sgraffito, or brush oxides finely onto the surface to introduce further depth.

Sgraffito

The common approach to sgraffito is to coat a red earthenware body with white slip. This can be achieved by painting on about three coats of slip, allowing each coat to dry partially (wait until the shiny wet surface has gone matt) before applying

Scratching (Sgraffito, above and opposite) through slip, revealing the colour of the underlying body.

the next, brushing at right angles to the previous coat to avoid obvious brushmarks later. Alternatively, take advantage of the chance to lay down a variegated textural surface by being freer with your brush technique. The white coating is then scratched or carved through, revealing the warm red body beneath.

Experiment with coats at different stages of the drying-out process to discover the specific characteristics of different tools and techniques. While the applied coat is still wet (shiny), combing can be effected by dragging appropriate tools lightly through the slip to break the surface. Bold, spontaneous marks can be made using two or three fingers in unison to wave and zigzag into the wet surface. You could also try using bristles from a sweeping brush or the spreader from ceramic-tile adhesive.

As the surface stiffens, decoration becomes more studied. Clay removed from the coating and, possibly, from the body has to be lifted clear of the tacky surface to prevent unwanted swarf building up or dropping into the pristine surface pattern. Various tools are useful: wooden modelling tools; wire-hooped sculptor's tools; hair- grips, possibly attached to pieces of dowel or old paintbrush handles. Take care not to allow a build-up of scrap to clog the tool or spoil the decoration.

If the coating of slip is allowed to dry thoroughly with its parent body, it can be sgraffitoed in the truest sense, literally by *scratching*. While some spontaneity may be lost at this stage, there is ample opportunity for control and fine detail – although there is a tendency for the slip to chip, so cut rather than scratch, and use sharp tools. Previously prepared surface-pattern designs can be applied directly from detail or tracing paper onto the dry surface, or can be drawn straight onto the white surface using charcoal or a soft pencil. Light washes of vegetable pigment (coloured inks) could alternatively be brushed on to guide your sgraffito tool in cutting away the final design.

Sgraffito tools can, of course, be purchased, and usually come in the form of double-ended weapons: a sharp point at one end, complemented by a broad but sharp blade at the other. You may, however, find that you can make use of anything as a substitute, from nails ground down into appropriate tools to the misappropriation of lino-cutters

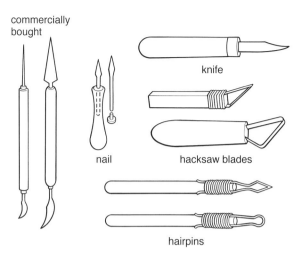

commercially
bought

knife

nail

hacksaw blades

hairpins

Sgraffito tools can be home-made by modifying everyday items.

or scalpels. The most important feature is that the tools are sharp; a comfortable grip will also be most welcome if a lot of slip needs to be cut away.

Dust and waste should be cleared away regularly from the work surface to keep a clear view of the overall design. It is very tempting to blow away the debris, but as this will only make more cleaning work later, carefully tip the waste into a suitable receptacle. Any remaining pencil or wash guide-lines will burn away in the biscuit firing.

An extra dimension can be added to sgraffito by a subsequent addition of oxides and/or body stains. Depending on the exact effect desired, dry stains in powder form can be dusted, brushed, dabbed on with a powder puff, sprinkled or sponged onto and into the surface of the slip coat-ing, either before or after sgraffito, or in combina-tions.

Oxides can be applied raw, where they are applied dry or as water-based washes. On damp surfaces, possibly disturbed by the process of apply-ing oxides, there will normally be a blending with the receiving surface. On a completely dry surface, however, it is advisable to mix up a simple under-glaze 'paint' which will assist in binding the oxide to the surface. An addition of a small amount of glaze will provide both vehicle and adhesive, and also ensure good bonding with body and glaze when fired later.

'On' Decoration

'On' decoration, utilizing colour, can be further subdivided into 'in' and 'on' categories. These sub-divisions refer to whether colouring agents are (a) added to the clay before building, or (b) applied directly to the surface of a finished piece. Naturally occurring clays with different body colours (for example, terracotta and porcelain) can be applied in this way to contrast with, or complement the body colour of the ware. Bear in mind that it is usual to check for 'fit', and frequently necessary to modify slip composition to ensure adhesion to the body, particularly after firing. Metal oxides can be used directly as pigments, painted on or under glazes, or to provide colour to otherwise lacklustre slips. A range of oxides are also used in the produc-tion of lustres.

Traditionally, decorative colour techniques have been seen as discreet processes – for example, early English slipware (in), majolica-ware and the high-fired stoneware of the Far East (on). In Faenza, northern Italy, the original faience techniques, first

William and Mary charger, Lambeth delftware (copper, cobalt, manganese and iron oxides painted on) c. 1690. Nottingham Castle Museum & Art Gallery

Blue and white Chinese baluster vase, late nineteenth century. Dragon decoration, cobalt oxide, bands (impressed) painted with manganese and iron oxides. Photo: courtesy of the Trustees, Weston Park, Shropshire

introduced in the fourteenth century and some-times referred to as majolica-ware, are still being taught today.

On-Glaze Painting

This technique, including faience and majolica, involves painting metal oxides on top of a glaze. It has been developed to a high level in both loca-tions, reflecting the brilliance and excellence of both the colour response and the brushwork possi-ble when using simple oxides.

After thorough drying and biscuit firing, wares are coated with (usually) an opaque white glaze.

Decoration is then applied directly to the unfired surface of the glaze, building up the design using bold brush strokes to suggest, rather than slavishly to copy or repeat natural forms and patterns.

As the popularity of on-glazed earthenware expanded in Europe, the character of the original faience techniques changed to include modelled decoration, as on stoneware. More fluid glazes were then combined with smooth and low relief sur-faces, and matt glazes were used alongside shiny ones, these often being blended together. Rutile and titanium oxide were used widely in addition to tin oxide so that the original nature of the faience tended to get lost; illustrating both the tendency towards innovation on the one hand, and the need to conserve the best traditions on the other.

The Importance of Design

Decoration can be built up step by step, making intuitive responses to what has already been done, relating marks or areas of one colour to that of another. Alternatively, a design can be developed

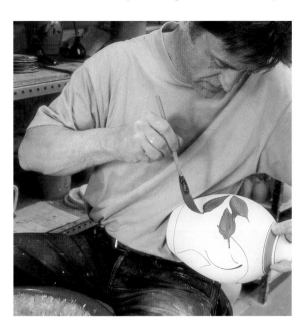

On-glaze decoration by Mike Powers of Nottingham Pottery, painting with a well charged Chinese brush. Pigment can be applied raw, in the form of 'watercolour', or in a glaze.

on paper, and transferred to the pot later. The problem here is that what seems possible using a pencil, eraser and/or paint on paper will not always work in the same way on a pot, particularly when covered with unfired glaze. So whatever means are used to plan the original idea, it then has to be translated into 'on-glaze'.

There are four basic oxides/colours available, which can be applied as thin or thicker washes to exploit tonal ranges. Brushes, and other means by which colour can be applied, each with its own characteristic qualities, offer a wide range of possibilities. The following may be helpful as a general guide to individual experimentation:

Manganese dioxide: Dark browns, purplish with alkaline glazes. Use first in thin, pencilled lines to establish the structure of the design. Used as a 'clothes line' upon which to hang the rest of the decoration.

Red iron oxide: Red-browns down to pale yellow ochre when applied thinly. Can be used boldly, and is more powerful than others, so its thickness is not critical.

Cobalt oxide/carbonate: Blues. Very strong – use thinly; carbonate slightly less so. Very effective when used monochromatically (as per Willow Pattern).

Copper oxide/carbonate: Greens. Very strong, also volatile – tends to 'bleed out', blurring the edges. It can affect the colour of adjacent pots in a kiln. It can also cause glaze to run on vertical surfaces, so avoid broad bands or large areas of pattern near the foot of the pot.

For more information, see the Table of Oxides, in Chapter 11, Glaze.

Technically, on-glaze painting can be tricky. The dry, powdery surface dictates that pigment should be applied in a lively and spontaneous manner to avoid dragging off glaze, or over-loading with colour. Which begs the question, how thick should the pigment be applied? There is no precise answer to this, except to say that variations in colour intensity are a characteristic of the technique. Experience helps, as does the following test. Paint a brush stroke of pigment mixed with water onto old newspaper – if it is possible to read the print through the

Coloured glaze applied via a slip trailer.

Further detail added to build up the decoration.

oxide it is probably not too thick. At best this is only a rough and ready guide, and has to be matched with the particular oxide (see comments above concerning strength), and – inevitably – experiment and experience.

Practise First

Painting on a powdery surface means that mistakes cannot be erased: the only option is to wash everything off and start again, after the pot has dried out sufficiently to accept glaze again. It can be helpful, therefore, to practise first, using blotting paper. This is almost as difficult to work on, and it offers an opportunity to develop a vocabulary of 'one-stroke' brush, sponged and 'printed' marks so that the design can be built up in stages. Use blotting paper or newspaper, painting with red iron oxide (cheap) or red clay slip (cheaper).

An Alternative Practice

Subjecting the pot to a 'hardening-on' firing can solve the problem of 'surface'. Pots to be on-glaze decorated are biscuit-fired, glazed and re-fired to a temperature high enough to harden the surface of a glaze without causing it to melt. Depending on the type of glaze, this would probably be in the region of 950–1000°C. The resulting surface is hard but still porous, and very much easier to decorate, although mistakes are still irrevocable; and washing off is not an option. A major drawback is the additional cost of the extra firing, coupled with additional handling and the almost inevitable loss of 'spoilt' pots. This practice is usually restricted to commercial mass-producers, who have to balance 'seconds' against losses.

As most studio potters produce one-offs, or a range of relatively simply decorated repetition domestic ware, the tendency is to work with, and respond to, limitations (and probably mistakes, too), rather than to eradicate them. In this respect, potters will refer to qualities such as 'lively', 'spontaneous' and 'exciting' rather than 'precise', 'identical' or 'consistent'.

'On-glaze' is a method that can be applied to any

Bowl with underglaze colours on a white body, with transparent glaze. Maker: Jude Wensley

type of ware. Academic considerations apart, the intention is simply to apply oxides on top of an unfired glaze. Colour response will be at its brightest at the lower end of the temperature range, and when used on a white ground as in majolica ware (opaque white tin glaze). Colour will become more muted as temperatures become higher, and will be increasingly influenced by the background body colour, in the same way that washes of watercolour paint are less vibrant when applied to dark-toned papers.

Underglaze

Underglaze decoration has a wetted-out look, enhancing colour quality and rendering it entirely permanent, protected by the glaze, and is usually applied to biscuit-ware prior to glazing. Underglaze works particularly well at earthenware temperatures, where colour response is especially bright. This is also true of metal oxides used as on-glaze. It is also worth pointing out that the range of commercial colours available to the potter at earthenware temperature is more extensive than for stoneware temperatures.

Once biscuit-fired, decoration can then be applied with underglaze colours, these being mixed with water to a watercolour consistency. Surfaces could be further developed by overlaying or

Medium jars, thrown, slabbed and decorated with underglaze colours in engobes. Maker: Jude Wensley

scratching through the colour before glazing. In addition, the underglaze painting technique works well on a ground of white slip with (or without) the sgraffitoed line, combining the soft fluidity of the colours contrasting with the clean line. Transparent glaze is then applied to the whole piece by dipping, pouring or spraying, and firing takes place again. Although it is usual to apply underglaze colour to biscuit-ware, it may also be applied to 'green-ware' – but care must be taken when placing the work in the kiln so as not to smudge the surface.

Detail of brushing out.

Some Additional Techniques

Some years ago a visiting oriental potter developed a technique of throwing simple cylinders that were then covered, while still wet on the wheel, with a 'white powder' (i.e. feldspar, whiting, china clay) of ceramic origin. Forms were then transformed from a cylindrical to a spherical body using a padded rib on a stick, rather like a boxing glove (*see* Ruthann Tudball's throwing sequence, page 143). This was used to widen the vessel from within, leaving the outside untouched. As the wet clay stretched, it caused the dry outer layer to craze, giving the form a remarkably fractured surface texture, echoing internal tension.

Variations on Printing Principles

By experimenting with oxides, body stains and rough surfaces, colour and texture can be applied to slabs before they are pressed into or over moulds or formers. Pigment dusted (avoid inhalation) lightly and arbitrarily onto a flat surface (usually a dry wooden board) can be picked up by the clay. A partially flattened lump of clay can be rolled out to the desired thickness so that oxides or body stains (or both) adhere to the clay, and then, after stretching, break to create 'chance' texture and colour staining. Reverse texture can similarly be impressed into slabs from a wide range of surfaces; try rough-sawn wood, bricks, plastic or rubber matting.

OFF-SET PRINTING

In a similar but more controlled way, pigment can be printed 'off-setting' onto the clay surface:

Step 1: A design is painted onto old newspaper using coloured slips or engobes, supported on a drawing board or similar.
Step 2: A slab is rolled out to almost the desired thickness on a separate cloth.

Step 3: The slab and cloth supporting it are then inverted onto the wet design and newspaper.
Step 4: After removing the cloth, the slab is rolled out to the desired thickness.
Step 5: Another board is placed over the slab, and both boards are then picked up with the clay and paper sandwiched between them.
Step 6: The board and newspaper are removed, to reveal a printed image offset on to the slab.
Step 7: After stiffening, the slab can then be built into the piece as required. If any newspaper remains on the surface of the slab, leave it in situ as it will burn away in the biscuit firing. Sugar paper or cartridge paper could be used if a more durable support is required.

The above will not produce a high-definition image and final statement; rather it will provide an under-painting and texture, and a starting point for further action at different stages in the development of the ware. At best it can act as a springboard; at worst it could be sponged or scraped off.

MONOPRINTING

A more sophisticated result is often possible by making use of the monoprinting technique, or rather a slight variation on it. The basic principle is similar to that of carbon paper:

Step 1: Coat newsprint or old newspaper with heavily stained slip; one or more colours can be used.
Step 2: When the slip surface has become matt, invert the sheet onto the pot so that the slipped surface is in contact with the clay. Now, by drawing on the paper, slip will be deposited onto the slab.
Step 3: Carefully lift the paper to reveal the design printed, or 'off-set' onto the clay. Do allow the paper to dry out, or the slip will begin to flake off – possibly onto the pot, and certainly onto your work surface.
Step 4: Dispose of any unused paper before it dries as to avoid the health and safety hazard of spreading flaking, dusty slip.

Applying a base coat of slip.

Applying slip to a sheet of newspaper.

Drawing through newspaper to 'offset' the line onto the base.

Carefully removing the 'carbon paper', in this instance using a transparent plastic base.

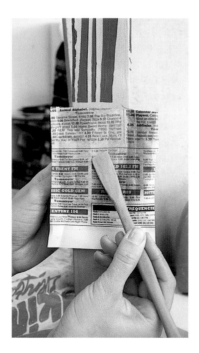

Burnishing to lay down solid colour.

Completed work by Phaedra Cozier.

Designs can be prepared on detail or tracing paper prior to printing. From the original artwork, the printing can be carried out in two alternative ways:

Method A

Step 1: Prepare the pot and 'carbon paper' as above.
Step 2: Lay the artwork on top of the blank, upper side of the newsprint.
Step 3: Trace over the original. A little more pressure will be needed to obtain a clean print, which may in any case not be quite as crisp as the direct approach above.

Method B

Step 1: Transfer the design on to newsprint *before* coating the reverse side with slip.
Step 2: When the newsprint is then placed *in situ* on the slab, your design can simply be redrawn on to the pot.

The resulting line-drawing, which has been transferred onto the clay, may be sufficient as a decoration. It can also provide a useful 'clothesline' on which to build up richer, more complex designs by brushing or spraying on further slips or underglaze colours. With care, it is also possible to superimpose further monoprints, but consideration must be given to the problems of offsetting (lifting off some of the work that has already been done) and the drying-out process.

Note: When monoprinting, avoid impressing marks into the clay by tracing just firmly enough to deposit slip onto the surface of the slab. Try not to have contact of any other sort with the 'carbon paper' or tracing otherwise unwanted marks will appear on the slab. As the slip coating dries out completely, it will no longer be usable. Dispose of it carefully to prevent unnecessary dust in the workshop as the dry slip flakes off.

Slip and Wax

As stated earlier, patterns can be created by painting slips directly onto wet or leather-hard clay surfaces. A negative effect to this can be obtained by painting wax or wax emulsion directly onto the leather-hard surface and then spraying or brushing slip over this. The wax will reject the slip, leaving the background slipped and the pattern as bare clay. This could be further enhanced by an occasional well-placed slip-trailed dot or line to give the design a second dimension. A word of warning: if wax emulsion is used, wait until it dries on the surface of the clay (this applies to biscuit pots too) as the slip or glaze will stick to the wet emulsion, thereby eliminating your design.

This technique can be used on both earthenware and stoneware pots (providing the slip will go up to stoneware temperatures). Particularly effective is a blue slip on a stoneware clay fired and covered with a dolomite or gloss-white glaze.

Glaze and Wax

Wax will resist glaze and slip in the same way, thereby affording further opportunity to create interesting surface patterns. Where wax is brushed onto biscuit-ware, that part of the surface will remain unglazed after firing. This is, therefore, not a good choice at earthenware temperatures, because of the porous nature of the body, but is particularly effective on vitrified stoneware bodies.

Glazing by double-dipping method is suitable for both earthenware and stoneware. The piece is fully glazed with a first glaze. Wax is then used to apply decoration to the dry surface of the glaze, either in bold brush strokes, or splashed on. A second contrasting glaze is then applied. The colour of the first glaze will be evident in the waxed areas after firing, while the remaining areas will be a combination of both glazes. This technique is also suitable for spray application of the glaze.

An interesting alternative to this method is to use a latex rubber-based adhesive such as Copydex or artists' masking fluid. This can be applied in the same way as wax, with a brush, or it can be trailed or dribbled, but it can be peeled off carefully later on. With ingenuity and advanced planning it is possible to maximize on both permutations of colour and texture when creative combinations of these techniques are exploited.

Pressing leaves into the leather-hard surface as stencils.

Spraying slip: wearing a protective face mask is good practice, even outdoors. Potter: Chris Marsden

Note: The resist/rejection principle is often used by potters who wish to prevent glaze taking on parts of a piece likely to be in contact with either the kiln bat, or other components such as lids. Apply a protective coating of wax emulsion to avoid the need for cleaning off glaze later.

Stencils

These can be used in conjunction with other processes, or independently to mask out areas that are to remain free of colour. Either a positive or negative image can be made by cutting or tearing paper. Both outer and inner paper shapes can be used as masks, or the two can be combined to create random superimpositions, patterns and textures.

Stencils can be used with various application techniques. Slip, underglaze colours or any other ceramic decoration material can be stippled, painted, sprayed, spattered (with a toothbrush), sponged or printed onto the surface, at any stage of the overall ceramic process. At an early stage, oxides could be sprayed or painted onto wet clay, while at a late stage enamels or lustres could be applied after the glaze firing.

Look out for novel material to use as stencils; the

ubiquitous leaf serves to illustrate the idea. Remember that, in all probability, the first application of colour will be only a start, a foundation on which to build further with varied applications and techniques. So, if a piece of plastic netting, previously used as a container for fruit or vegetables, seems somewhat prosaic, bare in mind that it is what happens later that turns it into poetry. Experiment with paper doilies, lace curtains, or anything else that will provide a protective mask and give rise to an interesting visual result.

Large stencils of a complex nature are only suitable for one-offs as they will inevitably become sodden and unmanageable after use. Acetate sheets offer a washable and reusable alternative. Smaller versions could be used on a scale suitable for short runs of tiles, particularly if stencil material is carefully matched to the decorating medium – a thick paper or card will not be reduced to a soggy apology too soon if used with a relatively stiff slip. Further, simple shapes with no fiddly, thin apertures will be easier to handle than extremely detailed cutouts; on a small scale, and if a simple motif is to be used, it might be acceptable to make several identical stencils to increase the number of prints possible. However, if the task in hand is worth the effort, why not attempt silk-screen printing instead?

Silk-Screen Printing

This can only be carried out on a flat surface, which restricts opportunities to the following:

- Printing directly onto clay.
- Printing directly onto glaze (fired or not).
- Indirect printing via transfers.

The process, as its name implies, makes use of silk as a support for a stencil. Silk, or one of the numerous specialist man-made fibres available, is stretched across a rectangular frame to form a tympan, in much the same way that a canvas is stretched prior to painting. The nature of the material will allow paint or ink to pass through. A stencil attached to the back of the screen will prevent the passage of ink except where silk is exposed – in other words, not blocked by the stencil. In this way the colouring medium can be forced repeatedly through the mesh to leave a printed image on numerous individual pieces, depending only on the type of stencil used.

It is not intended here to give in-depth technical details of specialist silk-screen processes, as simple paper stencils will usually suffice for basic ceramic situations. However, where a more detailed or long-lasting stencil is required, it would be best to paint out the silk as described below.

MAKING AND PREPARING A SCREEN

You can either make a screen for use on tiles from recycled material (for example, a picture frame or small window frame minus the glass), or create a custom-designed and built item from 1 × 1in (2.5 × 2.5cm) planed timber. The screen may be constructed from either softwood or hardwood, and can be 6 × 6in (15 × 15cm) or 6 × 8in (15 × 20cm). Note the following:

- Joints should be neat, and the frame should rest completely flat when laid on a work surface.
- The outer edges should be chamfered off to allow the material to stretch around the screen frame without snagging.

Now stretch a piece of silk over the frame. The type you choose will depend on the chosen printing medium: thus printing with slip will require a coarser weave than for on-glaze enamels. It may be helpful to consult a silk-screen printing supplier to ensure that all your materials are compatible. Then proceed as follows:

Step 1: Lay the material flat on a smooth, clean surface.
Step 2: Place the frame on top of the material so that there is at least 2in (5cm) spare for wrapping around the timber.
Step 3: Tack one side of the material to the tip of the frame, then pull gently but firmly at the opposite side at right angles to the frame, ensuring that the pressure is directly along the warp or weft. Work on the length first if it is rectangular.
Step 4: Next, stretch the material across the width in the same way – at the half-way point.
Step 5: Using a sides-to-middle system, fasten the material down at the quarter-way points, taking care to apply some diagonal outward pull in order to avoid built-in slackness when fixing the other sides.
Step 6: The corners can be eased outwards and up, forming a neat fold that is fastened down when the material is seen to be flat and straight.
Step 7: Fasten down at midpoints in any gaps, easing out any minor sagginess without over-stressing the material. Final fastenings will need to be about 1in (2.5cm) apart.
Step 8: The screen should now be perfectly flat, with little or no movement when pressed gently; in fact, it should be almost as tight as a drumskin.

On the suggested scale you will probably have little difficulty getting a good screen stretched at your first attempt. However, larger screens tend to be a little more difficult. You may find that drawing pins can be used initially to set the material more or less in place, removing them and applying a little extra tension before final fixing with either drawing-pins or am impact staple gun. The completed screen is now ready to receive its stencil.

Fabric under tension is obviously prone to damage. If care is taken to avoid this and the screen is cleaned thoroughly after use, it will last for years. If only simple paper cutout stencils are used, the screen need only ever have contact with the squeegee, some sort of paint (slip and the like) and water when washed. If a stencil is made by painting out parts of the fabric (to block off areas) it will have to be either cleaned off with an appropriate solvent, or discarded.

PREPARING THE STENCIL

This is very straightforward in theory, although in practice there may be one or two minor problems.

If a hole is cut in a sheet of newsprint, and the paper supported by the screen, then there is no problem. But if part of the stencil is cut completely from its parent piece, it will have to be positioned carefully prior to attachment to the screen. It would not be difficult to do so on a simple template, but with a complex design containing a great many unattached pieces it might be very time-consuming, if not almost impossible to get the pieces into place. Do not forget that random designs, picking up arbitrarily scattered pieces, might be an interesting alternative to a considered, complex and formal design.

A reasonable solution to the difficulty illustrated can be reached by compromise. The design can be modified to give support to otherwise loose elements, and the stencil cut accordingly as follows:

SILK SCREENING – VIA STENCIL

Step 1: When the outline design is drawn or transferred onto the thin paper, the stencil can be cut out using a scalpel or craft knife. Support the paper on a sheet of thick card or hardboard to protect the work surface, and carefully cut away unwanted paper. Before cutting, make sure that the paper stencil is large enough to allow the excess to be folded up and taped to the outside of the frame.

Step 2: Lay the screen down onto the stencil, fold up and tape in place. The design should be more or less centred within the frame with some masked borders all round, but particularly at two opposite ends.

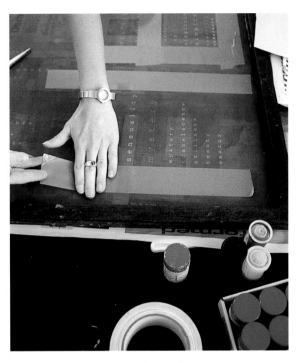

Packing tape used to mask off parts of the screen.

Step 3: Place the screen in place upon a slab of clay, and add the printing medium (slip, etc.) across the space left at one end of the screen.

Step 4: Use a squeegee to draw slip across the design to the opposite end of the screen, lift the squeegee over the slip and return, again dragging the slip to its original side. (Slip used for screen printing has to be very fine: at least 120-mesh sieve will be needed to prepare the slip.)

Step 5: Lift the frame, with slip and squeegee *in situ*, off the slab, placing it down with the slip-containing end slightly lower than its opposite side/end. Support the raised end with a piece of 2 × 1in (50 × 25mm) off-cut. This will prevent slip from running back to drip through the screen.

The paper stencil should now be well attached to the screen, the slip acting as adhesive; it will be good for at least a dozen or so pulls.

The original design should now have been printed off on the leather-hard slab. Check that the consistency is right: too runny and it will bleed back under the stencil; too thick and it will not pass easily through the screen.

Ready-prepared slabs can now be printed either pre-cut, or they can be trimmed after. Consideration needs to be given to register: that is, ensuring that positioning is reasonably precise – some form of locating system for tile and frame might be useful. As long as the position of the tile and screen is constant, the stencil can be located on the screen to suit. If you choose to print onto untrimmed slabs, the precise registering is of no account: you will be able to cut the tile to centre the design as required.

If a large screen is available it is possible to print a free, non-figurative surface pattern, having picked up onto the screen assorted shapes, as suggested above. With care it is possible to superimpose a second, or even a third colour, provided that each is allowed to lose its shine and stiffen sufficiently so that it is not smudged by subsequent contact with the screen. A tile-cutter can then be used to make the most of the decorated slabs, each tile having a unique pattern with intriguing variations while maintaining a unified whole.

A brief note on squeegees. Professionally made items can be purchased, but home-made versions are relatively simple to construct. Where it is intended only to work at about 4–16in (10–15cm) width, you may well find that either a window cleaner's squeegee (possibly reduced in length), or even a piece of stiff cardboard or rigid plastic will be adequate. For short runs and/or when using expensive oxides, it might be more convenient to sponge the pigment through the stencil, or to brush or stipple it. The main aim is to repeat the print; if you are not sticking to orthodox silk-screen rules it really does not matter.

Printing onto Fired Ware – Via Transfers

These are on-glaze decorations applied indirectly. Ceramic colour motifs are printed onto ceramic transfer paper, from which they are transferred onto the surface of the pot. The printing process involved in making the transfer is the same as that described above. Simple transfers can be made as follows:

Step 1: Use ceramic transfer paper for the paper base.

Step 2: The design can be either silk-screen printed,

Retrieving the printed transfer sheet.

or hand painted directly onto the surface of the transfer paper using ceramic on-glaze enamels mixed with a suitable medium (ask your supplier about the range available). Enamels can be mixed to achieve a variety of colours, but ensure that firing temperatures are compatible.

Step 3: Allow to dry in a dust-free environment for at least twenty-four hours.

Step 4: The completed motif will now require a support, holding all the disparate colours in their correct places. Covercoat, bought from suppliers, will provide this support; it will require about twenty-four hours' drying time before application.

Step 5: When the completed transfer is immersed in warm, but not hot, water the adhesive on the paper base dissolves. This allows the applied transfer to be slid off its base carefully and placed in position on the pot to be decorated. Considerable care is needed to ensure that no air bubbles are trapped under the transfer. If one corner or edge is positioned first, with the remaining skin curving away from the pot's surface, the whole can be lowered progressively so that air is excluded as the transfer is brought into contact with the surface. A sponge, squeegee or rubber kidney can sometimes be used to assist the process.

Transfer (Base) Paper

This can be purchased from specialist suppliers in sheet form in a variety of sizes and grade/weight. Surface pattern can be applied to the base paper by a wide variety of means, including painting, spray-

Applying the transfer to a white factory 'blank'.

The image is covered with 'cover-coat', poured onto the surface …

… and carefully spread into an even film. A rubber 'kidney' is ideal.

A rubber kidney can be used to exclude air and avoid wrinkles.

Soaking to release the image from its supporting base paper.

Patting gently so as to flatten completely, to expel air bubbles, and dry off excess water.

ing, stencilling, silk-screen printing, spongeing, splattering and so on. Large surface areas can be decorated so that the paper can later be cut up to size. By such means interesting colour, pattern and textural effects can be developed and applied in transfer form to any suitable ceramic surface.

Colouring Pigments

These usually fall into three categories:

- Underglaze
- Glaze and body-stains
- On-glaze

Underglaze colours are purchased in powder form for application to either pre-biscuit clay (green-ware) or biscuit-ware after being mixed into a paint using water or an appropriate medium purchased from the same supplier, available in oil-based and water-soluble forms. Both medium and pigment must be blended together thoroughly, this being best achieved by using a palette knife to rub the two together on a flat, smooth surface – a glazed tile or piece of plate glass is ideal. With the addition of 30 per cent or a little more of transparent glaze or frit, these colours can then be applied on raw glaze in the manner of majolica-ware, then – confusingly – becoming an on-glaze technique.

A finished piece by Chris Sayers.

The normal means of using glaze or body stains is by addition to glazes (5–8 per cent) or slips (10–18 per cent), passing the whole through a 120-mesh sieve later on. As above, glazes and body stains can be used on raw glaze or as underglaze colours if prepared as suggested. However, be sure to check that colours/stains are capable of surviving intended firing temperatures. Manufacturers indicate firing ranges, usually highlighting either those not suited for high temperatures, or those that are.

Colours and stains can, of course, be added directly to a clay body, either sieved into the body at slip consistency to produce an even colouring, or wedged as dry powder to plastic clay to variegate or speckle the body. Alternatively wet down the body stain with a small amount of boiling water, sieve this mix, and then knead it carefully into the base clay. Used in porcelain or T-material, clean, positive colours can be obtained, enabling a wide range of marbled, inlaid, laminated and agate-ware effects to be created. Sculptural pieces built by the author involve the use of stained clays integrated with others that have been textured and mottled by picking up loose, dry stains during the rolling-out processes.

More formal pattern and decoration would

Chris Sayers painting underglaze colours and frits onto a base white glaze.

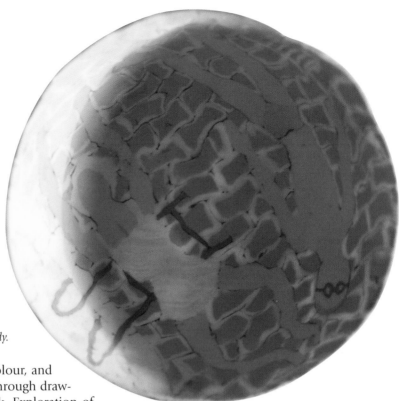

'Swimmers' bowl'; body-stained, and showing translucency of the porcelain body.

involve careful trials to test for colour, and extensive development of ideas through drawing and painting in a sketchbook. Exploration of geometric patterns based on chequer or square units, triangular motifs or more complex interlocking forms would be a good starting point. Conversely, free-formed designs might be developed from drawings, as illustrated in the laminated bowl with swimming figures.

Project: Laminated Bowl

This would appear to be essentially a building project, but its success depends largely on its integrated decoration. The first requirement is a suitable plaster mould; alternatively make use of a biscuit-fired bowl. Next, prepare a limited range of body-stained colour clays using one basic body. First attempts will be based on a white earthenware body, which will not be prone to slumping when fired. T-material or porcelain can be used, and in the latter case the form will require props or other support structures when fired to high temperatures. These coloured bodies can be used individually, laid into the mould as pre-cut shapes, or can be worked into

rolls or stratified slabs before being cut and arranged in formal patterns.

Step 1: Line the mould or biscuit-fired bowl with a very thin slab or sheet of white clay.

Step 2: Use dividers or a compass to mark out guidelines for the proposed design (see table below). Horizontal bands will provide a guideline grid on which to build geometric patterns. Verticals will help divide the circular area into equal slices or segments.

Step 3: Begin to apply slices and thin coils (possibly flattened by a rolling pin after hand rolling) to build up the desired design. Use a soft watercolour brush to apply slip when attaching pieces.

Step 4: When the building process is completed, allow the whole to stiffen until leather hard or even drier. Use a metal kidney to scrape away bumps; this will both ensure a smooth surface and will reveal clean, sharp resolutions to the coloured clays incorporated into the structure.

Step 5: After removing the piece from its supporting mould, the white clay can now be scraped away carefully using a razor blade or steel kidney to reveal the design below, this being accentuated by the remaining incursions of white clay between coloured bodies. Take care to avoid dust inhalation.

As an alternative method to the above you could again use a plaster mould, this time inlaying an arbitrary design using strips of white body and incorporating coloured images as appropriate. Some superimposition, possibly suggesting interwoven strips, will provide relief surface and additional strength to the piece. Completed vessels will have a relatively uniform outside surface, with an irregular relief pattern on the inside where the clay is not directly in contact with the supporting mould.

Firing

When porcelain is used in this way to produce bowl shapes, fire them up to 1280°C, unglazed and placed in an unglazed stoneware-fired bowl containing fine dry white sand, inside and out, to act as a supporting cushion. The bodies, being vitrified, have a satin appearance and are characteristically translucent if finely constructed.

Geometry

Creating designs within a circle can appear complicated. If divisions are to be more interesting than quarters and eighths, calculations based on radius and circumference appear to dampen enthusiasm.

1. First colour slabbed and rolled out into a thin coil.

2. Second colour wrapped around first colour.

3. Third colour similarly slabbed and rolled.

4. Carefully slice thinly with a razor.

OR sandwich rolls between two slabs of different coloured clays, either retaining their round shape or compressing them into squares.

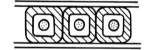

1. Slabs of different coloured clays layered and then sliced.

2. Use slices to build up patterns with or without additional coils between.

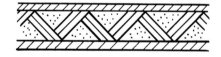

Thin rolls of coloured clay can be used to link and contain slices, thus unifying a design.

Making pre-formed modules for lamination or other uses.

So, if a division into five, seven or nine segments seems preferable to four or eight segments, the following may be of use to you if you have a simple protractor to hand:

Number of divisions	Size in degrees (°)
1	360°
2	180°
3*	120°
4	90°
5*	72°
6*	60°
7*	51°
8	45°
9*	40°
*visually more interesting divisions	

When a protractor is not readily to hand, use a length of string instead:

Step 1: Cut the string to the length required for it to wrap round the circle that is to be divided – in other words, around the belly or rim.

An indication of the colour range and the decorative possibilities in earthenware and stoneware.

K'ang-hsi Dish, powder blue – detail of the reserves. The Trustees, Weston Park

Step 2: With a little patience, this string can now be folded into the required number of equal lengths. Use the folded length of string, or set the compass or dividers to mark out the divisions.

To mark out circles to indicate bands on the inside of the vessel, use either a compass or band in guidelines with a brush, having centred the vessel in its mould on a wheel, in the same way as one would decorate the outside of a thrown pot.

10 Unconventional Methods

This chapter briefly outlines some variations on conventional processes, and a few unconventional procedures that do not fall easily into any of the categories covered elsewhere in this book. These may suggest others to you, which, although seeming to contradict conventional craft practices, will in fact extend the boundaries of your ceramics experience. Advice and/or instructions for some procedures have been reduced to a minimum, allowing the pictures to speak for themselves. Others have a brief mention in case they might suggest likely areas for further experimentation.

Making a Teapot – the 'Holistic' way

The following sequence of photos encorporates several processes, personalized and demonstrated here by Ruthann Tudball. The 'whole' grows naturally out of a single lump of clay, one action flowing into the next, including throwing off the hump, pulling and twisting handles, applying detail, decoration and finishing.

Above *Throwing a spout 'off the hump'.*

Opposite *Lifting off a thrown pot.*

Gentle contact controls the form. Cut off with a twisted wire, or reduce the diameter at the base, and use a pointed modelling tool to cut in.

The thumbs here determine the beginnings of the lid.

Narrowing the under-side.

Using callipers to check the diameter – note the completed handle.

Forming a gallery.

Releasing pressure having formed the rim and central extended knob.

Opening the body.

DIY cutting tool used to create surface texture.

Twisting the pulled knob to form a handle.

Drawing it up.

Fine-tuning the gallery.

Applying pressure to the inside to expand the form, using a home-made tool, with a padded end like a miniature boxing glove.

Pinched off …

A modelling tool, or the padded stick, used to apply pressure to internal joins.

Pinching up the rim …

… and fixed to the opposite side with slip or slurry.

The tool or stick used in a similar way, inside the spout.

… to attach a pulled handle.

Trimming the spout to size, using a twisted wire.

The cut and re-formed spout modelled into place.

Releasing the pot from the wheel using a twisted wire cutter.

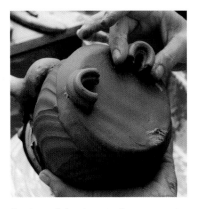

Sections of the ring, cut into appropriate lengths, and attached as feet.

Dipping the lid in glaze.

Carefully lifting the pot, using the fingertips in contact with the foot.

Adding impressed decoration.

Ensuring that small holes are not blocked with glaze.

A ring, thrown, to form feet.

Glaze, poured in and immediately poured off again, ready for a once-firing.

Painting on a 'resist' to reject glaze (or slip) as part of the decoration process. Use a 'Copydex'-type latex glue.

Richard Godfrey, easing a soft leather slab into a plaster press-mould. Photos in this sequence by the artist, Richard Godfrey

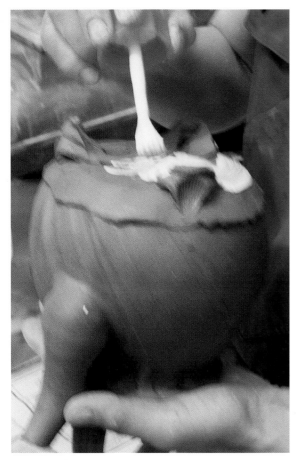

Again, used to protect feet from glaze. This resist is easily peeled off after glazing, leaving a clean, unglazed surface.

Using a rubber kidney, or a plastic credit card, cut into shape.

Prefabricating – Extending the Possibilities of Slabbing

Continuing the teapot theme, this sequence illustrates Richard Godfrey's method of combining what are, basically, two pressed dishes to form the body of a teapot. A similar technique follows, showing Sarah Hillman building a sculptural form. Do not be restricted by convention, either: slabs can be pre-formed on or in almost anything that will allow easy release later, from mini hammocks to sandbags. Just 'play your way' in.

Trimming corners to force clay in using a plastic ruler or credit card.

Leather-hard T-pot halves are scored with a hacksaw blade.

Richard Godfrey, bringing the scored and slipped halves together.

The pot rested on a cushion, showing slip pressed out from the joins.

Refining the form and cleaning edges; use a metal kidney or credit card.

Separate coils are joined together to form a handle. Photos in this sequence by the artist, Richard Godfrey

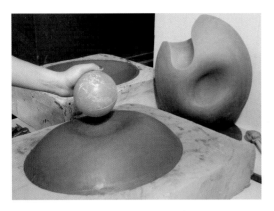

Sarah Hillman using a plastic ball-cock to indent the pre-formed, leather-hard, press-moulded form.

Lifting away the cut-away section.

All surfaces to be joined are scored and slipped.

Right *Sections are brought carefully into contact.*

Below *Internal joins are aligned and compressed for maximum adhesion.*

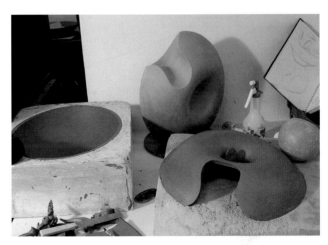

A block of foam rubber supporting sections while stiffening.

Assemblage – A First Step

Throw an assortment of simple shapes and, when leather-hard, try placing them one on top of the other, as in the diagram, until an acceptable permutation is established. The same principle can be applied to slabbed forms, or combinations of various techniques. An important consideration is that all sections should be at the same consistency of leather hardness. Another is aesthetics: it would be easy to get carried away at the expense of overall appearance. A sketchbook is invaluable here, as a means of 'trying out' and identifying sculptural and practical problems.

Soft clay is pressed into the sprig mould …

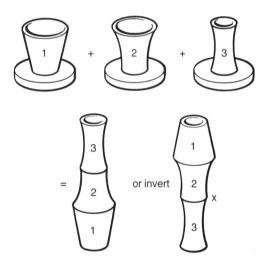

Allow sections to stiffen; turn, score and slip; then assemble.

… and levelled off using a plastic ruler, credit card or similar tool.

Sprigs

These are solid relief, decorative forms made in a similar manner to pressed dishes, for example the halves of tomatoes being the 'originals' (*see* project, Introducing the Ceramic Process, page 28), but on a much reduced scale and depth. It is possible to use all manner of objects in this respect. Alternatively, first model a clay 'original' on a flat board, then cover it with plaster to cast a 'female' mould. In the photo sequence, different coloured clays were used to illustrate the process (ensure that these are compatible for firing).

Sprig, still intact, awaiting positioning on the leather-hard tile or other surface in need of decoration.

Press a ball of soft clay onto the sprig …

Pat it down into place with a damp sponge, having scored and slipped the surfaces.

… and lift it clear of the mould.

Build up an overall decoration, possibly with a variety of shapes.

A selection of sprigs and patterned plaster surfaces.

Casting

Usually regarded by studio potters to be 'commercial', this method is increasingly used in innovative ways to produce items impossible to make by other means.

Adjustable shuttering, sealed with plastic clay, ready for casting. Corner brackets are used to hook over the walls, securing the structure ...

Filling plaster moulds with casting slip.

... or use clay. The object for casting located within the walls. Building bricks propped against the walls will give extra support when the plaster is poured in later.

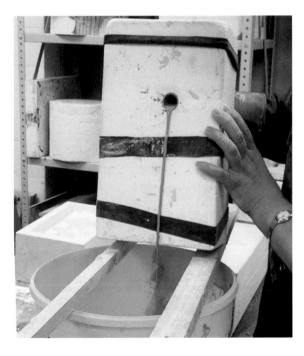

Slip being poured out, leaving a deposit behind, forming a cast/wall of stiffer slip conforming to the inside shape of the mould.

Karen Lyons pouring plaster around the lathe spindle to cast a block for turning.

Hand-carving an asymmetric form.

Above *Turning the cylindrical block into the required profile.*

Right *Complex moulds are needed to produce 'double-cast' pieces.*

Modroc

The product name for a type of bandage impregnated with plaster powder. It is cut into conveniently sized pieces (usually strips), dipped quickly into water, gently smoothed out between thumb and finger to consolidate the surface, then carefully placed upon the surface of an object, building up to two or three layers, and allowed to harden. Its main advantage is its lightness as a cast; and it is quick, and very accurately replicates surface. Use it in conjunction with release agents: baby oil on skin; mixtures of oil and slip for porous (plaster) surfaces.

Alginate

Used normally by dental technicians, this is extremely quick drying, and, like Modroc, can be used directly, applied thinly to a suitably prepared surface without the need for shuttering, or used to receive impressed objects (remember 'biting down'?). It requires accurate mixing (with water – read the instructions carefully), is likely to be too expensive for large-scale use and, because of its rapid hardening, is less universally useful than Modroc. However, it is 'clean', good for reproducing fine detail, and yet another alternative.

Variations

'Drawing' with Clay

'Chance' surface pattern and, to a lesser extent, development of form, dictated by the arbitrary use of slabs, coils and lumps, built up by the author.

Right *'Chance' building. Doug Wensley using 'T' material.*

'Inflation'

Thrown pots are sometimes expanded/fattened up by blowing. Roger Lewis here inflates slab-formed pieces.

Roger Lewis inflating a slabbed 'cushion'.

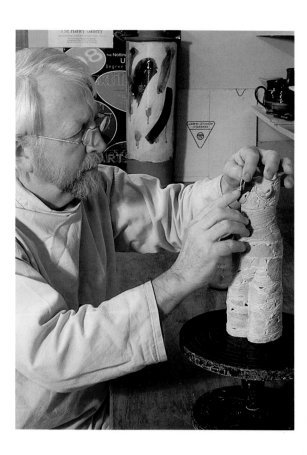

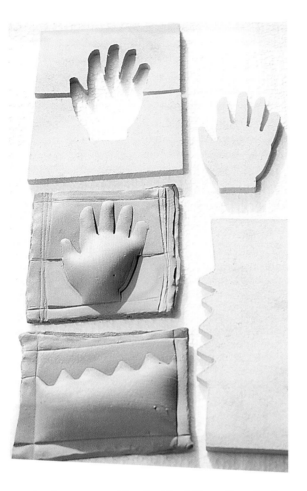

Wooden formers, pressed into 'cushions'. Photo: Roger Lewis

Peter Ilsley removing the 'catcher' with a needle-flame blow-torch.

Glaze

'Torching'

A mini blow-torch is used to release the 'catcher' from the pot – heat used as a tool. (*see* also John Wheeldon, Firing.)

Some unconventional ingredients can be added to glazes, usually after sieving so as not to remove them again, which creates interesting surface effects. Additions of iron oxide 'spangles', rutile or silicon carbide, used independently or in combinations, will provide almost limitless experimental

(left) Post-fired pot on catcher, (right) pre-fired pot and catcher.

permutations (*see* Emmanuel Cooper's bowls). Interestingly, common brick clays often contain impurities that burn up through a glaze to 'spoil' it, with spots and speckles of arbitrary colour and texture.

Slip

If exciting, accidental or arbitrary texture and pattern are required at the leather-hard stage, try soaking pieces of open-weave material such as sackcloth in slip. All vegetable matter (in this case the cloth) will burn away during firing, leaving the character and image imprinted on the surface. Similarly, strings and wool can be used to build up applied textural patterns that are impossible to achieve by other means. Similarly, these and other materials, such as lace, can be used as 'stencils' to glaze, slip or oxides, and so on.

Absorbent materials can also be used to 'carry' or support clays at the building as well as the decorating stages. The possibilities here are virtually limitless – for example, lacy patterns can be applied by laying suitably soaked material onto press-moulded slab dishes, or directly into moulds. Casting slip can be absorbed and allowed to dry out in garments so that after biscuit-firing one is left with, for example, a ceramic T-shirt. As an end in itself, this idea may have little to offer, but as a means of achieving something of significance, the potential is evident. If it suggests an avenue for exploration it is certainly worth mentioning.

Clay

As mentioned above, clay can be stained. If red clay is an impure clay acceptable for its colour, then local clays containing mineral particles, and so similarly impure, could be described as speckled. Additions of appropriate coarse oxides, metals or refractory substances can be added to bland clay bodies to render them textured or speckled after firing and glazing. Iron filings, stone dust, ceramic or glass chips, and all manner of other likely material

can be added to enhance the visual appearance of fired bodies, cutting, grinding and/or polishing revealing hidden qualities. Sand-blasting can create innovative modifications to a surface.

Some impurities simply add extra colour or texture, while others melt in the fire, giving rise to eruptions and bursts of colour on the surface of the clay and/or glaze. Careful testing and handling must be undertaken when carrying out such work: there are health and safety and manufacturing implications inherent in these procedures, so assess their potential, as mistakes can be disastrous. Testing is always advisable.

In the recent past, combustible matter has also been added to clay. This served the dual purpose of adding textural interest and lightening the fired piece. Sawdust, rice, pasta and sugar have all been ingredients, while additions of nylon and glass fibre have also been used. More recently, a more humble ingredient, paper, has been employed.

Paper Clay

This is simply a mixture of paper in pulp form, and any clay; it has been found to produce a raw material with surprising properties of considerable interest to potters.

Cellulose fibre, a hollow, tube-like structure, is a basic ingredient in plant matter, and is therefore a major constituent of paper pulp; it is readily available to potters in the form of paper, waste or otherwise. Tissue paper and newsprint are among the most suitable; cardboard and specialist papers containing dressings such as kaolin and glues are much less suitable. The hollow fibres in the paper absorb water and will also draw up minute particles of clay. The latter effect results in a complex structure of fibre and clay slip, with amazing and unusual working properties that are of significant consequence to ceramic sculptors in particular.

Mixing the Pulp

Paper needs only to be torn up and soaked in hot water. Mechanical assistance may, however, be necessary to speed up the process: use an electric drill with a mixer attachment, or a domestic blender. Use paper that tears easily, as it will soak down more quickly than a tough paper. When the pulp is mashed down sufficiently, put it in a kitchen sieve to drain off excess water. This pulp is now ready to be mixed with clay. The most convenient method is to use casting slip; otherwise use slop, slurry and/or turnings. Allow the mixture to soak overnight if dry clay is added, and stir to blend it into a smooth, creamy consistency. Blend the two materials together in a ratio by volume of 10–50 per cent pulp.

DISADVANTAGES

- It is difficult or impossible to throw.
- It is equally disinclined to be kneaded.
- After a couple of weeks it can develop a nasty smell.
- Mould spores, if allowed to grow, are now suspected of causing respiratory problems in those with sensitivity to them. Instead of preparing large batches, do not normally mix up more than can be used immediately, or alternatively put any surplus into plastic bags and freeze, or allow to dry out.

ADVANTAGES

- The wet mix can be poured out onto plaster slabs to the appropriate thickness and allowed to dry.
- Can be used directly to lay up moulds.
- Can be used for coiling.
- Pieces can be joined at any stage: wet, leather-hard and dry pieces can be joined without problem.
- Incredible tensile strength develops as the material dries.
- Strength/weight ratio is increased by up to 50 per cent.
- Dry pieces can be cut using a craft knife or small saw blade, or scored and snapped off over the edge of a table.
- Thoroughly dry slabs or rolls of paper clay can be stored for later use, either used as formed, or …

- … can be returned to a malleable, leather-hard state by being immersed in water.
- It is easy to modify surface texture. In its original state it has a porridge-like surface that can be smoothed down using a fine sponge, sandpaper or file, depending on how dry it has become.

Firing

The material fires exactly as clay, and also looks and behaves like clay because that is what it is. If fired in an electric kiln, it is advisable to have both vents and door open, firing up slowly through 300°C up to 500°C. Increase the temperature at about 50° or 70° per hour to burn off the paper fibre and allow smoke to disperse before it becomes an unpleasant hazard. Doors and windows should remain open to allow maximum ventilation. Where fossil fuels are used and kilns are fitted with chimneys, there will be no such problem. After biscuit-firing, the pieces can be glazed and fired in the conventional way.

This unlikely material offers, in large measure, the sort of freedom this book seeks to encourage. The chance to build with preformed slabs and sludge, and the possibility of endless reassembly, offers creative adventure with none of the old craft skills and taboos. Paper clay has endless potential, and is open to development, new methods and ideas appearing almost regularly.

Slumping

This technique is borrowed from craftspeople working with glass. As the name implies, it relies on a body melting/collapsing into a mould during the process of firing. Firstly, the clay body used must be liable to bend without the need for excessive heat, that is, within normal kiln capabilities. This bending can be encouraged by the addition of 'accidental' fluxes. Secondly, the mould must be highly refractory: cradle formers can be manufactured from crank clay slabs, fired and coated with batt wash. These can be useful where repeated forms are required.

The critical collapsing temperature will vary,

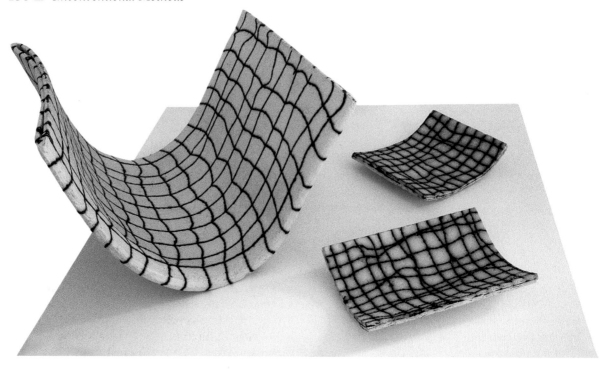

depending on the type of clay used. Porcelain is the obvious choice due to its translucent quality, and sheets of porcelain paper clay, for example, will slump readily at stoneware temperature.

Plaster/flint moulds suitable for slumping can be made in the normal way, except that 'the mix' is different. The recipe for refractory plaster is one part each of plaster, flint* and water by volume (i.e. one jug of each). Even with the addition of flint these moulds usually only survive one firing. They become very friable after being subjected to high temperatures, and require careful disposal, as the flint is still a potential hazard to health. Wearing a face mask is essential.

Try slumping into, or onto other, 'found' structures such as kiln shelves or lengths of kiln props.

* Health & Safety issue. Use *only* dampened flint purchased for the purpose from specialist suppliers. Do not use dry flint, as purchased for ceramics.

Slumped porcelain decorated with integral copper wire.

Moulds and slumped dishes, after firing. Notice how the moulds have disintegrated, requiring careful removal and disposal.

11 Glaze

Why bother with glaze? The answer is that clay, changed by heat into a new ceramic material, is hard, permanent and porous – and it is this latter characteristic that limits its utilitarian functions, as liquids will be absorbed into the body, eventually seeping out. Furthermore, liquid remaining within

the biscuit body will soon discolour the vessel and, more importantly, turn rancid. In short, the object is unhygienic and potentially dangerous. Porous bodies therefore need to be sealed, to prevent the absorption of liquids. Moreover, the porosity of a biscuit-fired cup would make it a most unpleasant drinking vessel – imagine the disgusting sucking sensation that would be caused by putting

Weighing out glaze ingredients.

moist lips to a porous mug! Thus from a purely practical point of view, glaze can be regarded as essential.

The warm colouring of unglazed terracotta plant pots is certainly quite agreeable, but grey clay bodies lack even this limited attribute. Thus in addition to their drawbacks in functional terms as mentioned above, pieces made from grey clays are also usually aesthetically unappealing. Glazes applied to such pots therefore have a cosmetic purpose: they enhance and beautify ware which otherwise would be drab and boring. Further, such wares would discolour very quickly in use and become even more unattractive, particularly if associated with food and drink.

As a general rule, wares intended for domestic use must resist absorption. Most people are at least unconsciously aware of glaze, and recognize the need for it when actually confronted with the question. It is quite surprising, however, that many students at the beginner level imagine that some sort of paint or varnish provides this protective, cosmetic coat. But just imagine what would happen if such a coating were applied to a mug containing hot tea, or if a casserole were subjected to the rigours of a domestic oven! Obviously such a solution would not do. Any covering to the clay should be similarly 'ceramic' in that it has a similar response to heat, and it should be at least as durable as the vessel to which it is applied.

What is Glaze?

To understand glaze, it is first necessary to know what it is. A student's second contact with glaze – the first being the thousands of glazed pots experienced in everyday life – is a bucket of runny white stuff in a pottery workshop. It is often white or off-white in colour, though sometimes it will be a pale red-brown, and sometimes it will be grey. It will have a label proclaiming it as 'Speckled Oatmeal', 'Tenmoku' or 'Lavender Blue'; but it will look nothing like this at all.

Like clays, glaze mixes change colour and character after being subjected to great heat, so do not be guided by the unfired appearance of the contents of the bucket. Apart from a label, the contents of a glaze bucket should be identified clearly by some sort of sample tile, firmly attached to the bucket rather than the lid. This sample will indicate the fired consequence of applying the contents of its parent container to subsequent pieces. Few, if any, clues as to what the glaze will look like after firing can be gleaned from the visual appearance of a glaze mix; neither does it indicate what a mix contains.

Perceptive students soon make the connection between glaze, glazing and glass. Based on the notion that glass is simply melted sand, it could be, and is frequently assumed, that the bucket will contain finely ground sand and that the heat in the firing process will transform this into a glass. Such a simple explanation is very appealing, but unfortunately it just will not do. If a hypothetical application of sand is given to a pot, and is then subjected to heat, it will be found not to have melted to produce glaze; further, most, if not all the sand will have dropped off too. So what is needed here? Rather than becoming involved with the chemical theory of glaze, it might be useful to refer back to paint, a material that although inappropriate in ceramic terms, will nevertheless allegorically offer clues as to what is required in developing glaze.

To work effectively, paint requires three basic ingredients: pigment for colour; vehicle to transport the pigment; and adhesive, to ensure that the pigment stays in place. Finely ground sand mixed with water is in no way a paint: as an intended coating, the mixture has only a pigment carried, in theory at least, by a vehicle. Even if the mixture could be held in suspension long enough for a coating to be applied to the porous body, there is nothing in the recipe to provide adhesion. The addition of some sort of glue would solve this latter problem and complete the triadic structure of paint, and so biscuit-ware could in this way be covered with a coating of sand, before its placement in a kiln.

The first drawback to this solution is that any glue which is animal- or vegetable-based will be burned away long before the sand has been converted to glass, even assuming that this is going to happen. Sand would simply drop off any non-horizontal surface, to leave the ware exactly as it was prior to coating.

The second drawback concerns the nature of sand. Although this familiar and very common material will contain large proportions of silica, the basis of glass, it will also contain other materials. Sand is a mixture of material broken down by weathering and ground down by mechanical erosion, so it is likely to contain other mineral content (such as ground-up shells) and vegetable matter, in addition to the desired silica content. Such additional material will not be quantifiable, it might or might not burn away during firing, and will inevitably have unpredictable effects upon outcomes.

Furthermore, in spite of the fact that silica, on its own, would make an excellent glaze in theory, in practice it is too refractory, requiring a temperature of $1713°C$ to melt, and such a temperature is beyond the bounds of practicality on both technical grounds and in simple economic terms. These technical difficulties arise from the fact that clay bodies will melt at relatively low temperatures that have no effect upon the highly refractory silica. Apart from the obvious consequences to over-fired wares, just about everything else used in the firing process would be at risk. Kiln furniture, and of course kilns themselves, make use of ceramic materials that are highly refractory. Inevitably, these would start to break down or collapse well before the required $1713°C$ can be attained.

The economic drawbacks, meanwhile, can be illustrated as follows. The thermal energy required to boil a kettle is relatively modest, but an immersion heater that is kept on twenty-four hours a day will very soon clock up a disturbing bill, even when heating water to less than $100°C$. As maximum temperature is increased, so too is the cost. Economically, it would be prohibitive for the craft potter, or industry for that matter, to attempt to melt unadulterated silica. Most of us consider the acceptable temperature in the range $1000–1300°C$.

The cost of purchasing pure silica is also a consideration. It is available to the potter in the form of quartz or flint, both of which will have been processed and packaged at the customer's expense. As flint is also very hazardous to health (see Appendix), its unnecessary use should be avoided whenever possible. A safer, more cost-effective source of silica is in a potter's most basic material: clay, having the theoretical formula:

$$AL_2O_3 \quad 2SIO_2 \quad 2H_2O$$
$$\text{alumina} \quad \text{silica} \quad \text{water}$$

Clay, therefore, clearly provides a natural source of silica. Alumina is also an important contributor to glaze, as will be seen below, and is more refractory even than silica, melting at $2050°C$.

But what about the chemical composition of real, natural clays? The formulae of secondary clays, such as ball clays, vary significantly, and these therefore have different basic properties. An average ball clay has the following composition:

$$Al_2O_3.4SiO_2.2H_2O.0·1K_2O$$

Where the silica content is less, the clay is said to be aluminous; if the silica content is higher, the clay is siliceous:

Content of Ball Clays				
Alumina	Silica	Water	Potash (potassium oxide)	
Al_2O_3	$4SiO_2$	$2H_2O$	$0·1K_2O$	average
Al_2O_3	$2SiO_2$	$2H_2O$	$0·1K_2O$	aluminous
Al_2O_3	$9SiO_2$	$2H_2O$	$0·2K_2O$	siliceous

Typical Ingredients in Different Ball Clays

	China clay	Ball clay (blue)	Ball clay (Devon)	Ball clay (Hymod red Devon)	Ball clay (Dorset)	Ball clay (or sedimentary)
Alumina	38.3%	33.5%	25%	25%	29%	33·3%
Silica	46.6%	46.5%	70%	60%	55%	47·3%
Potassium oxide (K_2O)	–	–	–	–	–	1·7%
Sodium oxide (Na_2O)	–	–	–	–	–	0·2%
Calcium oxide (CaO)	–	–	–	–	–	0·2%
Magnesium oxide (MgO)	–	–	–	–	–	0·3%
Iron Oxide (Fe_2O_3)	–	–	0·8%	2·5%	2·5%	1·0%

Note: The table suggests typical percentage ingredients, but check supplier's data for specific information

As can be seen, these ball clays have the additional ingredient of potash, not present in china clay (formulated above as theoretical clay). Natural red clays have collected other impurities in addition to the red iron oxide (Fe_2O_3) that imparts the characteristic terracotta colouring. Such oxides can cause the body to vitrify at lower temperatures than china clay, acting as fluxes on the parent body.

As we appear to be rushing headlong into chemistry and making use of terms so far undefined, perhaps a brief explanation of these is necessary here:

Vitrification: This is heating a clay body sufficiently to cause it to become malleable, or soft, and on the point of collapse. If subjected to pressure at this stage, a pot will sag unless supported by the strength of its form. This vitrification results from the fluxing of free silica and feldspathoids (see below) in the clay. On cooling, the mass is seen to have been welded together into a glassy matrix, which gives rise to a virtually non-porous body, and is usually considered as a characteristic of stoneware.

Flux: Ceramic fusion is promoted by one oxide interacting with other oxides. Alkaline oxides interact with the glass to form silica.

Feldspathoids: These are feldspathic minerals, the most common being Cornish stone and nepheline syenite. Others include granite, petalite and spodumene (these will be discussed in a later section).

To recap, therefore, clay contains silica, which cannot provide a glaze on its own, but probably can with additions of fluxes. These fluxes are also natural, mineral materials, almost as readily available as clay. Given this basis for experiment, perhaps it is possible to discover a mix of ingredients that will fire to become a glaze?

Above we have identified silica (to provide a glass) and flux (to melt the silica); the spare ingredient is alumina. This coincidentally acts as an adhesive, binding the glaze to the ware and adding viscosity to prevent the glass running off when molten. So:

Glaze = silica + flux + adhesive

The silica comes from mineral sources (see Appendix), including clay; the flux melts the silica; and the adhesive (alumina) sticks the glaze to its ware. A potter's individual requirements can be met by adjusting relative amounts in a glaze recipe.

Types of Glaze

Surface Texture

If a perfect balance is made between fluxes, alumina and silica, in theory we should have a smooth, shiny glass or glaze. The balance will alter depending on the intended firing temperature. Earthenware glazes, which melt at lower temperatures, require more flux and less alumina and silica than do stoneware and porcelain glazes.

A theoretical imbalance of materials will result in matt or semi-matt glazes. A matt glaze containing a surfeit of alumina is referred to as alumina matt; if silica is in excess, it is a barium matt. Where one oxide is predominant, or is even the only oxide present, matt glaze will often result. This is because certain fluxes act in reverse beyond a critical point, stopping the melt rather than precipitating it. As a general rule, the more fluxing oxides there are present, the better the glaze.

Surface Quality

Specific minerals will give a perfect or near-perfect glaze, certain characteristics of which are likely to be very subtle. Such loose terms as 'thin', 'lardy' or 'waxy' might be used to describe the appearance of such a glaze. Borax, used for earthenware glazes, gives a brighter, glassier look than lead-based glazes; high-fired glazes that are rich in feldspar have a 'fatty' quality, do not usually run, and tend to obliterate sgraffitoed or impressed decoration.

Beware of shiny glazes with a high calcium content (from whiting, for example) as they have a tendency to run. Although they seem ideal for sgraffitoed pots, such glazes are likely to channel down incised cuts, and then run off at the foot. Added, rubbed-in oxides and over-firing increase the possibility of this occurring – and of a ruined kiln shelf and damaged pot. On the other hand, these glazes often produce beautiful surfaces reflecting variations in thickness, fluidity and colour changes.

Magnesium, added to glaze in the form of magnesium carbonate or talc, usually gives rise to 'buttery', 'soft' or 'silky' surfaces, whereas dolomite glazes, however attractive, can have surfaces pitted with pin-holes. These, therefore, tend to be unacceptable for domestic wares.

Glazes with an opalescent quality can be obtained by the use of bone ash, comprised of phosphorus and calcium. Minute bubbles suspended below the glaze surface reflect light, thereby giving rise to this effect. The presence of small quantities of iron oxide can cause the reflected light to appear blue, as in Chun glazes. Other sources of phosphorous are wood and other vegetable ash, all of which will give glazes such an opalescence.

Any colouring oxides added to a glaze mix will react with different fluxes in different ways, thereby giving rise to endless subtle changes in colour, texture and quality. The effects and potential of such additions can be tested, using bought-in, refined ingredients. Locally found ingredients, lacking conformity and consistency, will offer exciting, if unpredictable possibilities and are well worth exploring. For example, a glaze using wood ash from a garden fire will almost certainly yield an unrepeatable combination of fluxes because next time it will contain a different mixture of woods and vegetable stuffs.

The table (*see* page 164) indicates a range of oxides that can be added to basic glaze recipes. It also suggests percentage amounts. If two or more oxides are added to a single recipe it will probably be necessary to reduce the amounts for each oxide, testing for colour and fluxing effect on the glaze. It also extends the possibilities of on-glaze decoration, as outlined in the preceding chapter.

Oxides Commonly Used in the Ceramic Decoration Process

Metal	% added	Comment	Colour*
Iron oxide (red)	1–10%	Fe_2O_3 haemetite fine, stable oxide	Burn sienna Yellow ochre
Vanadium stain ■	4–10%	V_2O_5 usually with tin oxide as a prepared stain	Yellow
Rutile	2–10%	Contains iron oxide and titanium oxide, used for texture	
Manganese ■	2–6%	MnO_2 black dioxide powder $MnCO_3$ manganese carbonate – very fine pink powder	Purple-brown to black if thick Purple response best in alkaline glazes
Chrome ■	2–5%	Cr_2O_3 green oxide of chrome depending on glaze	Red, yellow, pink, brown or green
Copper oxide or carbonate ■	2–5%	CuO – black powder $CuCO_3$ – light green powder 1250°C + – volatile, influences environs, not to be used with lead oxides	1% light tint 2–3% strong colour 5% dark metallic, often black
Ilmenite	1–5%	Ore similar to rutile (titanium + iron)	Speckled textures
Iron chromate	1–3%	$FeCrO_4$ – 2% gives significant darkening of colour	Grey-brown or black
Nickel ■	$\frac{1}{2}$–3%	NiO green nickel oxide Ni_2O_3 black oxide	Browns/greys
Cobalt Oxide or Cobalt Carbonate ■	$\frac{1}{2}$–1%	CoO black powder – very powerful $CoCO_3$ light purple powder – very fine	CoO – 0·25% will give strong blue

*Will depend on the precise amount added, the type of glaze and the nature of the atmosphere in the kiln chamber. The colours are indicated as a guide, in an oxidation atmosphere.

■ Use with care – ref. Appendix, Toxic Raw Materials

The Thickness of Glaze

Only experience can help in determining whether to apply a glaze thickly or thinly. In the same context, check temperatures in different positions in the kiln, in order to ascertain how variations in colour come about, or problems with running or under-firing arise.

UNDER-FIRING AND OVER-FIRING

A theoretically perfect, shiny, transparent glaze will only be perfect when fired to its designated fusing temperature. If it is fired below that point the glaze will not have melted or fluxed sufficiently to produce a shiny glaze, and will be matt and opaque. A glaze formulated to be matt at, say, 1250°C, may well flux to a shine at a higher temperature. So in theory at least, a matt glaze can simply be under-fired glaze. Similarly a glaze that turns to glass and runs can be considered as over-fired.

The firing cycle causes several changes to glaze, the precise order of which will vary from one glaze to another. Part one of the metamorphosis takes place when the kiln has heated to a red/orange colour, probably in excess of 1000°C. At about this temperature sintering takes place, where the glaze ingredients melt together loosely. As the heat increases there is interaction between the various ingredients, and the glaze begins to boil. If this vigorous activity is ended, by cooling, the glaze will eventually be seen to be pin-holed and probably matt; but if the kiln temperature is raised still further, then the maturing temperature of the glaze will be reached. At this point the surface settles down, filling in the pin-holes. Over-firing may cause the boiling to recommence, causing possible pitting or bloating of the surface, and very probably the glaze will run; its appearance and fit may well be adversely affected.

Firing Temperatures

As the foregoing will have suggested, glazes melt at specific temperatures. That is to say, they are designed to fit particular firing schedules and clay bodies, the critical variable in all this being temperature. Ingredients must therefore be selected to suit this variable, and should be seen as dependent upon it. Firing ranges usually fall into two basic categories:

1. Low/medium: 850–1100°C; earthenware/raku.
2. High: 1200–1300°C; stoneware/porcelain.

Earthenwares are porous bodies protected and enhanced by glazes; stoneware and porcelain have been subjected to temperatures that enable a further metamorphosis to take place, whereby the body of the ware vitrifies. This renders the piece impermeable, so that glaze is less functional and serves more of a cosmetic role. As the name suggests, earthenware tends to be softer and less durable than stoneware. The latter has virtually

undergone an igneous reversal process, returning it to a condition similar in some respects to its material of origin via a subjection to intense heat.

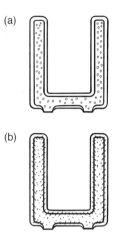

Glaze coating: (a) earthenware – a porous body with a distinct layer of glaze over; this is prone to chip, craze or flake off; (b) stoneware – a vitrified body, impervious to moisture, fluxed onto and 'welded' into the body; it is thermal shock resistant.

To summarize: a stoneware glaze intended for use at 1250°C and giving a shiny, transparent surface, will be matt, white and porous when fired to a typical earthenware-glaze melt temperature of 1100°C. Solution: re-fire to the correct temperature, possibly taking advantage of the sintered surface for additional decoration.

Earthenware glazes over-fired to stoneware temperatures cannot be rescued. The glaze will probably have melted and run off, with boiling, blistering and bloating, even to the body. The ware may well have collapsed, at least in part, and red clays may have been transformed into a bubbly consistency. The appearance of wares fired in this way is further disadvantaged as they become firmly stuck to kiln shelves.

If two transparent glazes are in use, one for stoneware and one for earthenware, clearly label both – on buckets and lids, ideally. The addition of vegetable stain to one or the other can provide an obvious visual warning to the person packing the kiln: knowing that the red-stained glaze is earthenware, for example, should ring warning bells when placing stoneware in the kiln.

Developing your own Glazes

Unlocking the apparent secret of glaze recipes is not as difficult as it might appear. As mentioned above, the basic ingredient can be clay, which provides both silica (the glass) and alumina (the glue). Some clay bodies also provide small amounts of fluxes, as indicated in the final column of the table on page 161. More flux is available from feldspars. These are precursors of clay, and have the same origins, but have not yet lost ingredients such as potash, soda and calcium salts, all of these being splendid fluxes. This phenomenon suggests that if feldspars and clays originated from igneous or metamorphic rock, we might even produce a glaze from ground-up rock. The problem with this idea is that rocks such as granite are not easily finely ground.

Would-be glaze experimenters could visit a local monumental mason's yard rather than Dartmoor to obtain suitable materials for eventual blending and firing. The slurry and dust that result from cutting, filing and grinding could provide a source of raw material that otherwise might be regarded as unwanted waste. Experimenting with samples of such materials can be very rewarding, both in terms of actual success and in appreciating the essence of the craft, steeped as it is, literally, in earthbound elements. Obviously such a source cannot always be regarded as consistent, and so, even with the extreme co-operation of the mason, samples might not always be pure or from a similar parent rock. Nevertheless, it is better to have had a beautiful glaze for your exclusive use than not, and the inability to repeat it exactly will lead on to the development of other, equally exciting glazes. The search for the ultimate glaze is, for some potters, almost more challenging than producing the ultimate form.

Assuming that the bought glaze route is not really for you, how then do you go about experimenting to develop your own glaze? We saw earlier in this chapter that a glaze consists of glass + flux + adhesive, and that these ingredients are all available, occurring naturally in clays and feldspars.

The other factor necessary to produce a glaze is heat.

As in any experiment, it is necessary to be methodical, varying only one factor at a time. To this end you might decide to experiment with a grey clay that is readily to hand, plus some feldspar which, like the clay, is on hand in reasonably reliable quantities, and which is also readily identifiable. As the table below illustrates, the composition of the feldspar varies. Manufacturers go to considerable lengths to provide products that are relatively consistent, so provided you know the supplier and catalogue details you should usually be able to repeat your recipes if they are found to be suitable.

As naturally occurring minerals, feldspars vary in composition so that each has different characteristics when used in the ceramic process. Referring to Table 3, orthoclast is used as a body flux, having a wide vitrification range. Albite is more suitable for low-temperature glazes, yields different colour, responds to potash feldspar, and is more vigorous. Nepheline syenites have a lower melting point than other feldspars, so these can replace others when lower maturing ranges are required. It is important to ensure that different feldspars are identified clearly with the supplier and catalogue reference number, or at least whether it is potash, soda or a mixture. All tests should similarly be clearly marked, coded and recorded to enable you to compare and duplicate recipes.

The First Experiment

This experiment consists of the independent variable, heat – 1250 °C – and the dependent variables clay (earthenware or garden), and feldspar, both of which vary in quantity. The ingredients (dependent variables) should be considered in terms of percentage/dry weight – in other words, 50 per cent clay, 50 per cent feldspar. In this example both must be in dry powder form. If the clay, for instance, is still plastic, you will actually be adding 50 per cent clay plus water to the other ingredient, and will not know exactly how much clay remains when the water dries off.

If the above example (50 per cent clay, 50 per

Typical Feldspars

	Potash (K_2O)	Soda (Na_2O)	Alumina (Al_2O_3)	Silica (SiO_2)
Feldspar potash (orthoclast; $K_2O.Al_2O_3.6SiO_2$	10.3%	2·5%	17·5%	68·2%
Feldspar potash	12%	2·92%	18·5%	65·8%
Feldspar soda (Albite; $Na_2O.Al_2O_3.6SiO_2$)	2·8%	8·5%	21·2%	66·4%
Nepheline syenites (typically $K_2O.2Na_2O.4Al_2O_3.8SiO_2$)	9·0%	7·0%	25%	56%

cent feldspar) is weighed out carefully, the quantities recorded and the ingredients blended with water into a single-cream consistency, this can be applied to test tiles or pots and fired up to the predetermined temperature (1250°C in this example) to check fusibility. If the resulting test appears matt after firing, presumably the silica was in need of more flux; if the result is too runny, there was perhaps too much flux for the available silica.

Rather than wait for individual test results to appear from separate firings, which take considerable time even when using small test kilns, most potters use variations on the line-blend method, and fire a range of possibilities in one firing. So, using the 50/50 mix in the table below as a starting point, it would be sensible to also weigh out a 60/40 mix of predominantly clay, and a 40/60 mix where feldspar outweighs the clay.

As suggested in the table below, it is possible to weigh out ingredients for a range of tests. Each sample needs to be made into single-cream consistency, and should be passed through a 120-mesh cup sieve before application to biscuit-ware tiles. When sieving, make sure that any lumps are broken down and pass through the mesh. All weighed ingredients must end up in the glaze if the test is to be useful.

Making Test Tiles

Step 1: Roll out a slab of clay.
Step 2: Cut out a rectangle approximately 4 × 10–12in (10 × 25–30cm).
Step 3: Cut the rectangle into 4 × 1in (10 × 2.5cm) strips.
Step 4: When leather hard, bend each strip into an 'L' shape.
Step 5: Use a hole-cutter to make a hole at one end of each tile so that the sample can be strung up for reference, or attached to a glaze bucket.
Step 6: An impressed pattern will indicate how the test will respond to textured surfaces. Press in a screw-head or interesting plastic fitting if you have not made a suitable stamp.

Biscuit-fire or once-fire. In the latter case, miss out the biscuit firing and apply the glaze direct to the raw tile, preferably no later than the leather-hard stage.

Line Blend Percentages

Clay	70	65	60	55	50	45	40	35	30
Feldspar	30	35	40	45	50	55	60	65	70

Step 7: Dip the tile in glaze to cover the vertical part.
Step 8: Use a wash of manganese dioxide to paint an identification code on the foot, where the glaze will not obliterate it.
Step 9: Glaze-fire; stand the tiles with the glazed part vertical to check for excessive running (flat tiles will not indicate how a glaze reacts to vertical use).

Weigh out small quantities of minerals on a simple digital kitchen scale that can record both ounces and grams. Laboratory scales are obviously ideal for quantities of 3.5oz (100g) or less, but they cannot handle large quantities, are rather slow to achieve their undoubted accuracy, and tend to get rather dusty. Note also that extremely small quantities, however accurate, do not always translate into large quantities without changing fired characteristics.

It is therefore sensible to test using reasonable sized batches. Even tests totalling 3.5oz (100g) sometimes fire differently than when used in working quantities. Having tested a 100g mix, it is advisable to mix a 100oz (6lb 40oz) (2.8kg) batch and re-test: if the result is acceptable, you will be able to commit it to your pots with confidence.

In the event of the larger batch not matching expectations, the recipe can be fine-tuned according to its shortcomings (for example, is it too 'fatty', or not fluxing enough?) using variations on the system outlined below. If you are testing ingredients that are easily and cheaply available, the best policy is always to test larger quantities. And to avoid much tedious weighing out, the following method might seem a reasonable alternative to the above:

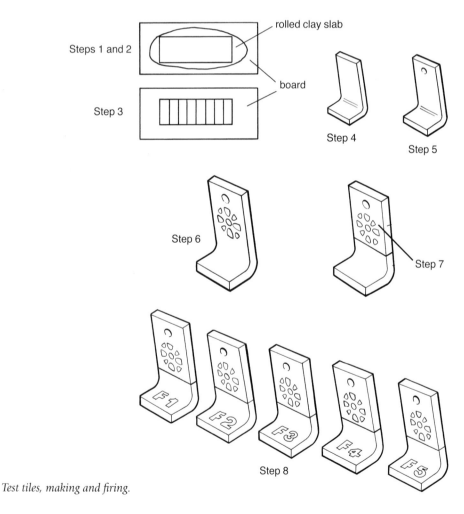

Test tiles, making and firing.

Subsequent Experiments

Step 1: Mix a double quantity of 50/50 mix (B).
Step 2: Weigh out standard quantities of 70/30 (A) and 30/70 (C) mixes.
Step 3: Apply mix B to test tiles, then divide it into two equal parts, and add one to mix A and one to mix C.

This will effectively give reasonably accurate 60/40 samples that require no weighing, assuming that the original test samples were all mixed to single-cream consistency.

If you succeeded in mixing exactly similar single-cream consistencies in the first experiment with 50/50 clay/feldspar, you will have noticed a difference in volume. The clay mix will have taken rather more water to achieve the correct consistency – in fact, 3.5oz (100g) of clay will make up into about

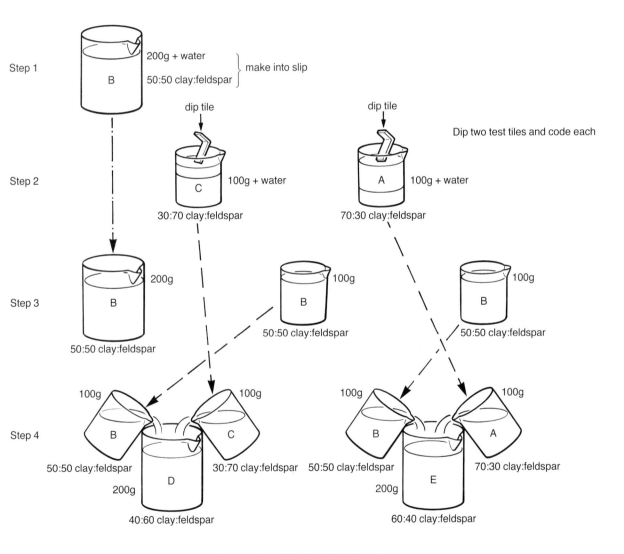

Line blends – by dry weight.

5fl oz (150ml) of slip, whereas the same amount of feldspar will only make 3fl oz (100ml).

When using slip mixes in line blending, you must therefore remember that the dry weight ratios need to be implicitly carried over into your tests, so volumes must be divided into quantity, not weight. If you use one or two graduated measuring jugs or beakers you should have no problem pouring off the required amounts. Remember, though, that some slips will settle out more quickly than others, so always stir well prior to blending, and when dipping test pieces.

The above experiment results in five tests: the first three are dry weighed, and the latter two blended in slip form from the originals. Where more tests are required across the range, the sides-to-middle line-blended method is very useful.

Sides-to-Middle Blending

Step 1: Two blends, A and B (be careful to mix slips to the correct consistency, then divide by volume), are divided to produce C, which is an equal mix of A and B. For convenience, these can be thought of as primaries.
Step 2: By combining two primaries such as A and C, again in equal amounts (taking care with amounts/volume), a secondary blend is made. Mixing the other combination of C and B will give a second secondary.

Step 3: The blending of a primary with a secondary produces a tertiary, four of which are possible.

The sides-to-middle system gives a test range of nine, which can be varied by the composition of the original A and B mixes. If you choose to test plain clay and feldspar samples as A and B mixes, five subsequent mixes will result. Using 80/20 or 70/30 clay/feldspar mixes as a starting point, you will restrict the range more within the bounds of possibility. As has already been made clear, clay is not likely to become glass/glaze on its own, but testing the feldspar on its own might give some interesting results.

Recipes to Try

If fired test results suggest that a 45/55 clay/feldspar ratio is suitable as a glaze, all that is necessary is to use the figures as percentages – in other words, 45 per cent clay, 55 per cent feldspar. A working batch can then be weighed out as shown in the table.

If fired tests suggest that a mix between, say, 45/55 and 40/60 might be better than either test result, add together the two batches (carefully saved in anticipation of such an eventuality) and fire the mixture. Alternatively, re-calculate and weigh out 42.5/47.5, this being the midway point (or average) between the two original test mixes.

The Ratios Arising from 80/20 and 70/30 Starting Points								
C/F	C/F	C/F	C/F	C/F	C/F	C/F	C/F	C/F
80:20	72·5:27·5	65:35	57·5:42·5	50:50	42·5:57·5	35:65	27·5:72·5	20:80
70:30	65:35	60:40	55:45	50:50	45:55	40:60	35:65	30:70
Note: Figures are based on a clay/feldspar order throughout – clay is given first in each ratio.								

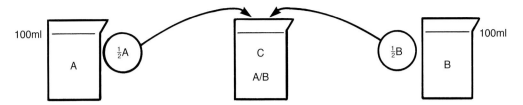

Primary blends

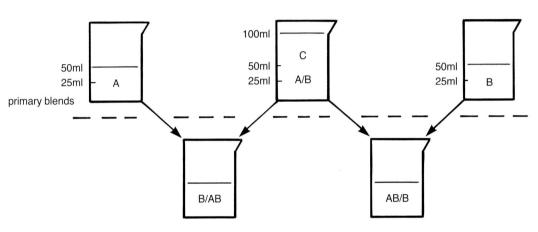

primary blends

Secondary blends

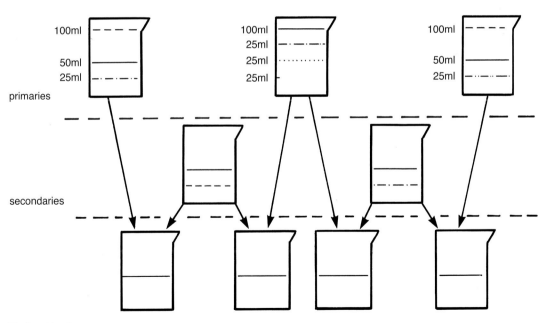

primaries

secondaries

Tertiary blends

Line blends – by volume.

Weights for a Working Batch

Ingredient	Percentage	Measure – dry weight	Volume – when mixed with water	Amount – average bucket
Clay Feldspar	45% 55%	45oz = 2lb13oz <u>55oz = 3lb 7oz</u> 100oz = 6lb4oz	At least 6.75pt, where 1lb dry powder will require approx 1pt water	Half a bucket or less
Clay Feldspar	45% 55%	450g <u>550g</u> 1000g = approx 1 litre	Approx 2pt (1.1litres)	Less than a quarter of a bucket
Clay Feldspar	45% 55%	4,500g <u>5,550g</u> 10,000 = approx 10 litres	At least 20pt (11 litres)	More than one bucket

Note: Amounts are approximate, and only intended as a rough indication of container size. It is hoped that the weight/volume figures will be helpful when using *any* recipe based on percentage amounts.

The Way Forward

So far only two ingredients have been examined, and these are only suitable for high-temperature glazes. This section looks at a range of other high-temperature glaze possibilities, and gives suggestions for lower temperature testing, together with observations concerning health and safety.

Amazing discoveries and inventions have often been the consequence of pure accident, or of doing something that seemed completely illogical but which proved, after the event, to have been a stroke of genius. The idea that simple glazes were discovered by accident is an attractive one. Imagine an early Chinese potter who, having placed clay vessels for hardening in a wood-fired kiln, stokes the fire with dry sticks. After many hours of careful, if tedious stoking, the temperature inside the kiln increases to an orange-red heat. The stoker, however, is mesmerized by magical vision within the fire; using a long stick to poke the ashes, he alters the scene and uses his imagination to transport himself elsewhere.

The poking action and the draught of the kiln, however, may transport ash up through the glowing

Making Up a Glaze

When preparing DIY or bought-in glazes, assume that 10lb (4.5kg) of dry glaze will make a useful bucketful by adding 10pt (5.7 litres) of water. Initially, however, add only 7–8pt (4–4.5 litres), allow to soak (overnight if possible), then stir well by hand prior to sieving two or three times. If the mix is too stiff, add more water. Once water has been added and stirred into the glaze it cannot be easily removed, so be careful to add a little at a time until the required single-cream consistency is reached. To remove excess water the mix must be allowed to settle out (this could take several days) so that surface water can eventually be drained off, either by pouring or siphoning.

pot so that some settles on their surfaces. The stoker returns from his reverie, decides that the fire has done its required work, and so ceases stoking. After clamping up the kiln to slow down the cooling, the stoker retires to rest before unpacking.

When eventually the kiln is opened, it is found that some pots (those that received a dousing with ash) have a glassy surface. Of course, it might then take a number of similarly spoiled firings to enable a connection to be made between the hot clay and the hot ashes, and maybe also the generally over-fired appearance of the contents of the kiln. The combination would, however, soon become apparent, eventually leading to someone to mix dry ash and dry clay into a slip.

This story is probably not far from the truth, for some of the most beautiful glazes used by early Chinese potters were simple blends of wood ash and clay, or limestone (whiting) and clay.

High-Temperature Glaze Suggestions

For stoneware and porcelain temperatures (1250°C–1300°C) it will be profitable to try the following pairs:

Blends for Stoneware and Porcelain Temperatures
Clay/feldspar (various – see the table on page 167)
Clay/wood-ash (will vary from wood to wood)
Clay/limestone (whiting)
Clay/granite
Clay/basalt
*Clay/talc
*Feldspar/ash (wood or vegetable)
Feldspar/basalt
Feldspar/dolomite
Feldspar/granite
*Feldspar/whiting
*Replace with basalt for further testing.

By adding several materials to the blend it is possible to increase the number of fluxes to a range of glaze tests. Such combinations of fluxes give rise to stronger melts than are likely with only one flux.

The permutations are almost endless, but if a few two-ingredient tests have already been tried, some more complex combinations as suggested above

Increasing the Number of Fluxes

50 Clay 50 Feldspar	+	50 Basalt 50 Ash
50 Clay 50 Wood Ash	+	50 Feldspar 50 Granite
50 Clay 50 Limestone	+	50 Clay 50 Feldspar
50 Clay 50 Basalt	+	50 Clay 50 Feldspar

will already seem more promising than others. For example, a simple test with a large quantity of flux and a small amount of clay might seem too runny. By increasing the number of fluxes and still retaining a predominance of the same, the first two couplings above seem likely to be more mobile than the following two at the same firing temperature. In any event, you are likely to get a good result on one or more tiles along the line-blend test.

Low-Temperature Glaze Suggestions

Usual earthenware glost (glaze) firings are at 1100°C, and very positive results can be obtained from the combinations in the table below:

Earthenware Glaze Firings		
Clay	+	Lead Bisilicate*
Clay	+	Lead Sesquisilicate*
1 part Clay + 3 parts Flint	+	Lead Bisilicate (4 parts)
4 parts Clay + 1 part Flint	+	Lead Sesquisilicate (5 parts)
Clay	+	Borax Frit*
*Test as in Line Blend Percentages table, page 167.		

The firing range of any particular glaze can be increased by adding 5 per cent whiting to any of these blends. Try combinations using ball clays for transparent glazes and red earthenware bodies for honey/amber glazes.

Health and Lead

Lead has been used extensively in glazes over hundreds of years. It was originally introduced as galena or lead sulphide, these later superseded by white lead (lead carbonate), which was found to stay in suspension longer than the granular oxides and sulphides of lead, due to its flaky structure. Deaths in the British pottery industry at the turn of the century ran at about 200 per year, due invariably to ingestion of small quantities of lead-bearing glaze over long periods of time. Both oxides and carbonates of lead are readily soluble in the stomach and can be taken into the bloodstream until their accumulation gives rise to symptoms of lead poisoning.

To overcome this problem, it is now customary to use lead only in fritted forms. By combining lead oxide with silica in specially constructed frit kilns, the pre-mixed ingredients are melted together to form lead silicate, lead bisilicate or lead sesquisilicate frits, as listed in the table: and these are not soluble in the gastric juices of the stomach. Together with good housekeeping practice, such as reducing dust, not eating and drinking in the workshop, and wearing dustproof protective clothing, frits have minimized risk to the potter. Raw lead glazes are now prohibited from use in factories and schools in the UK, having been replaced by low-solubility glazes.

If, in spite of the foregoing, you are attracted to the undoubted beauty of raw lead glazes, which make use of red and white lead and galena, remember that they are toxic. They can be used safely if handled with extreme care, and they produce exciting visual results. For all practical purposes, however, the fired raw-lead glaze must be considered potentially poisonous. Such wares should never be in contact with food or drink, either of which can act like gastric juices to dissolve lead from the glaze.

Suggestions for Raku

Raku is mentioned elsewhere, but involves soft, low-fired glazes (less than 1000°C) traditionally based on lead flux. The great British potter, Bernard Leach, suggested:

White lead	66
Quartz	30
China clay	4

Quartz is toxic as a dry ingredient and is therefore best avoided, as is white lead. So, start testing with:

Lead sesquisilicate	75
China clay	25

Or try soft-firing glaze or natural frit such as gerstley borate or calcium borate. Alkaline frits, borax frits and lead sesquisilicate frits will melt at temperatures below 1000°C, and can be used on their own or in combinations to provide a range of colour and surface possibilities. The glaze hardness can be increased by the addition of small quantities of flint. Clay will stiffen the glaze in firing and act as a vehicle and adhesive prior to it. Used as an auxiliary flux, zinc oxide promotes an even melt, and the addition of 1–2 per cent bentonite will help to keep the glaze in suspension.

For further testing it is suggested only that usually 75–80 per cent should be frit(s), the balance likely to be made up with clay, Cornish stone, flint, nepheline syenite (a soft feldspar-like flux), tin oxide to whiten and opacify, bentonite to aid suspension, and metal oxides to colour (*see* Chapter 6).

Glaze Ingredients

A number of very useful ceramic substances can be identified as hazardous, but cannot be avoided because there are no safe substitutes for them. It is therefore essential to maintain a common-sense approach to the matter. Risk from the occasional, careful contact with ceramics materials is probably less than is likely in other areas, such as photographic darkrooms or woodwork and metalwork shops. Adherence to good workshop and personal hygiene procedures will ensure that no ill effects are experienced, even by someone involved with ceramics throughout a working lifetime.

12 Mixing and Applying Glazes

Mixing Glazes

Commercially prepared glazes and most raw materials are usually sufficiently finely ground to pass through a 200s-mesh sieve. This makes it possible to use such glazes without further preparation if the necessary water is added, the mix allowed to soak at least overnight, and then thoroughly stirred. If the mix is passed through an 80s or a 120s sieve, this will ensure consistency and even dispersal of all the ingredients throughout the mix, and will not take too long to do. When preparing a glaze from raw ingredients, the mix should always be sieved at least two or three times through a 120s sieve.

The amounts of water required for dry mixes will vary according to the glaze. As a rough general guide, add sufficient water to allow the glaze to pass through an 80s or 100s sieve without too much difficulty. Make sure that *all* the ingredients go through the sieve (break down the lumps with a lawn brush).

After this first sieving, stir the mix by hand to check its consistency, which will probably be somewhere between single and double cream. Pass the mix through a 120s sieve, two or three times, and carefully add more water to bring the mix to an even, single-cream consistency.

To check its readiness for use, dip a hand into the mix and immediately withdraw it, giving it a quick flick to remove excess glaze; then inspect the coating left on the fingers: glaze should cover the fingernails, breaking to reveal the centres, the

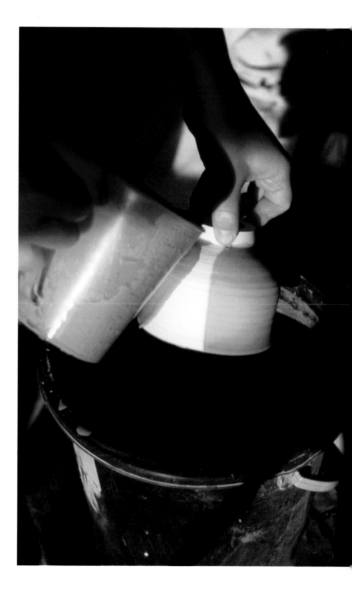

Pouring glaze.

higher parts, while filling the 'quicks'. Dip a piece of biscuit-ware quickly in and out, and allow it to dry (taking only a few seconds). It should have a coating of glaze as thick as a thumbnail, or about 1mm: check again by carefully digging in a thumbnail.

If prepared glazes are left to stand unused, they settle out. This is useful when the mix is too watery and needs to be decanted off, but it can be very inconvenient when the ingredients are heavy, when it requires considerable effort to get them back into suspension. It is advisable to stir frequently when using glaze, and an addition to the recipe of about 1–2 per cent Bentonite will help keep the mix in suspension when it is not in use.

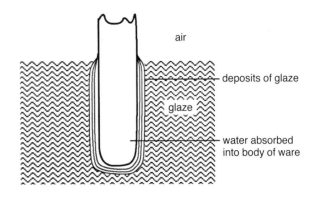

Dipping; showing a build-up of glaze. Long immersion = thick deposit.

Applying Glazes

Glaze can be applied by painting, pouring, dipping or spraying.

Painting Glaze

This is suitable for small pieces, where an even coat is not critical, or if it is intended to build up texture with different colours. Bear in mind that biscuit-ware is 'hot': that is to say, it absorbs moisture rapidly causing 'drag', when the brush seems to stick and pull, often removing more glaze than it deposits. Coatings will have to be built up, using single brush strokes, or blobs. The addition of 1–2 per cent of glaze binder (obtainable from pottery suppliers) will improve the viscosity, and subsequent hardness, of a glaze; or try a little glycerine, or gum arabic. Brush-on glazes can be purchased ready to use from most pottery suppliers.

Dipping Glaze

This is the quickest and most convenient means of applying glaze to pots that are small enough to be held in the hand or in a glazing claw. Coat the inside first, by pouring in enough glaze to fill the vessel, then immediately empty it out, avoiding drips to the outside, and allow the coating to dry.

To coat the outside, grip the pot at its base, then invert it and lower it into a bucket of glaze, trapping air to protect the inside, to form a high-tide mark of glaze about $\frac{1}{4}$in down from the foot – that is, leaving sufficient space to keep the finger-tips clear of glaze. Withdraw it quickly, place it on its unglazed foot, and allow to dry. This takes seconds.

Using a glazing claw, or by gripping the pot at lip and foot using a thumb and middle finger, both inside and outside can be coated simultaneously by a quick immersion sideways, and excess glaze shaken off to avoid thicker dribbles. In this instance glaze should be wiped off the foot, or the pot fired on a spur to prevent accidental adhesion to a kiln shelf. Unglazed finger marks can be 'spotted' in by dripping a small blob of glaze from a fingertip into the bare spots.

With practice, small pots such as mugs can be glazed inside and out in one overall action while keeping the feet clear of glaze. This is done by holding the pot firmly by the foot, using the thumb and finger-tips. Invert the pot, and lower it quickly into the glaze to the required depth. Tilt it a little, so that some glaze is admitted to the inside, and jerk the pot firmly upwards, downwards and a bit sideways, and up again, out of the glaze, moving it quickly so that a miniature tidal wave splashes glaze right up into the bottom of the pot. Practise this 'flick of the wrist' action using a glass tumbler when washing up, or using glaze, so that you can see the wave effect as it happens.

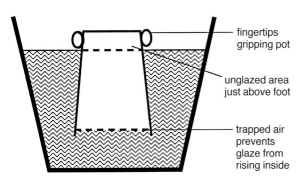

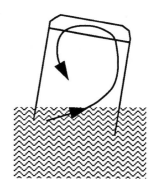

Dipping a beaker. Trapped air prevents glaze from rising inside for more than about $\frac{1}{4}-\frac{1}{2}$ in (6–13mm).

If the pot is tipped, glaze will enter and the inside can be fully glazed by jerking, causing a wave to splash glaze up inside.

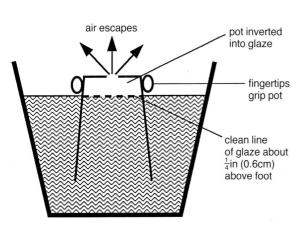

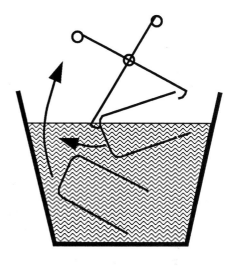

A planter or flowerpot will allow glaze to rise inside for simultaneous inside/outside cover.

A glazing claw allows the whole pot to be glazed in one movement: lower it in base first, tilted to allow glaze to flow inside; then lift out upside-down to drain off the excess.

Pouring Glaze

Wares that, as a consequence of size or shape, cannot easily be dipped, can usually be glazed by pouring. Glaze the inside, if necessary, by partially filling and then pouring off the glaze while turning the vessel to ensure complete inside coverage. While the pot is drying off, prepare the next stage. Place a banding wheel on the floor, and on that, a large bowl; for very big pieces use a dustbin lid or similar, inverted on a supporting bowl. Make a 'bridge' over the top of the container, using two strong wooden slats, ideally triangular in cross-section.

The pot can now be stood upside-down on the slats, over the bowl, so that glaze poured over it will be collected rather than running onto the floor.

When the pot is set up ready, check that you have plenty of glaze within reach, and that you can pour from a jug with one hand while turning the pot, by its foot, with the other.

Pour the glaze steadily but quickly, turning the pot to coat it evenly all round. Use plenty, quickly, for an even covering; or reduce the amount and the pace deliberately, to create variations in thickness and colour. Further, partial applications of other glaze could add to the arbitrary possibilities already opened up. Clean up, and save each glaze as you go, otherwise a bucketful of intermixed glaze will result. However, be careful not to build too many layers, as this can cause cracking before firing, and running or boiling of the glaze in the kiln.

Incidentally, odd ends of glazes, provided they all fire to the same temperature, can be put together in one container. This mixture, known as 'counter' glaze, and often of indeterminate colour, is useful for the inside of wares, where exact colour is not important. It makes economic sense, and avoids the need to store small quantities that, in all probability, will never be required anyway, even if the labels manage to stay legible.

When dealing with large or awkward shapes there is not always a need to dip or pour in one go; in fact it can be advantageous to dip one side or part, allowing it to dry before applying glaze to other parts. A double-dipped area can often spring a visually interesting surprise in contrast to other parts, glazed or otherwise, and it is worth using a little ingenuity and imagination to explore the creative possibilities on offer.

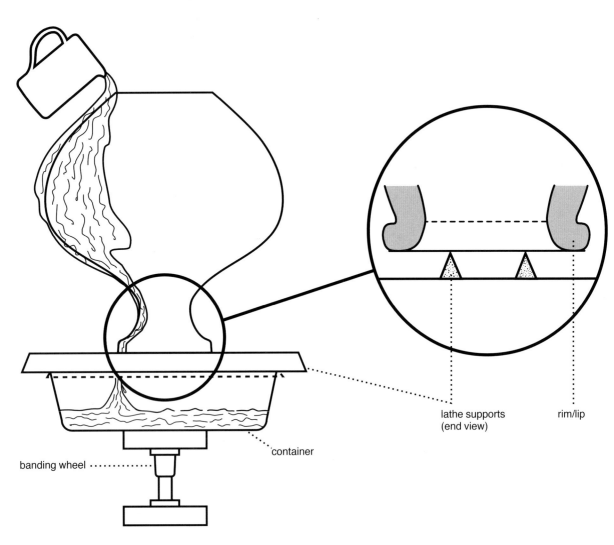

banding wheel ············

container

lathe supports (end view)

rim/lip

Pouring. Remember to shake off any excess glaze before it dries to ensure a smooth finish.

The foot, supported over a bowl on laths with a triangular cross-section, for minimal contact.

Spraying Glaze

This method has 'industrial' connotations, and does not always fit comfortably into a studio/craft context. The equipment is expensive, it has health and safety implications, requires careful maintenance, and takes up space. It is, however, an excellent means of applying glaze to larger pieces, it can effectively utilize quantities of glaze too small to allow dipping or pouring, and will deliver, with practice, an even coverage essential for some types of glaze, for example matt, pastel colours.

As with most items, ideally you should purchase professional quality equipment. In addition to a spray gun, a compressor is essential, and when spraying indoors, a spray-booth fitted with a filter/extractor system is essential. Alternatively, work outdoors on calm days, and use newspaper or an old sheet as a 'throw-away' backdrop, avoiding unnecessary dispersal and pollution by the glaze. *Always* wear a face-mask, and goggles.

Stand the item on a banding wheel, to make for easy turning while spraying. Keep the gun moving, and spray in bursts to build up an even coat. Deposits of glaze accumulate quickly, obliterating the colour of the surface below and making it difficult to gauge thickness, and the evenness of the coating. A useful device to aid this is to make pencil marks all over the biscuit surface, using a soft pencil: these marks will be slowly obliterated as the glaze coat thickens, giving a reasonable indication of the amounts of glaze deposited over the various parts of the pot; and will, of course, burn away during the subsequent firing.

Take care not to hold the gun too near, as over-thick deposits will rapidly turn into runs. On the other hand, if held too far away the fine spray will dry in mid-air, and most, in any case, will disperse into the atmosphere. A distance of about 12in (30cm) should be about right. Practise by spraying on old newspaper at first, using the print as a guide to thickness, as above. Remember to spray up or down under 'overhangs', and watch out for 'shadows' caused by protuberances such as knobs or handles. When glazing outdoors, keep upwind of the object to be sprayed. The same goes for any other people in the immediate vicinity.

Deflocculation

Glaze does not readily adhere to highly fired biscuit-ware or a previously glaze-fired – perhaps unsuccessfully – surface. In order to remedy this the second glaze can be rendered more 'stickable' so as to adhere to these seemingly impervious surfaces. The addition of a few drops of a deflocculant, such as sodium silicate solution, *to the dry mix*, will reduce the amount of water necessary to bring it to the desired consistency, described above. This will enable it to be applied to the vitreous surface by either dipping or spraying.

Summary

Glaze application is relatively easy. The simple methods are the cheapest, and usually the most convenient. Remember:

- Keep glazes in suspension by frequent stirring. Use your hand so that you can feel the consistency.
- Whichever means you use, be quick.
- Glazed feet require spurs or stilts when firing (earthenware). Or wipe the foot clean.
- Sponge glaze off about a $\frac{1}{4}$in (75mm) up from the foot to allow for glaze movement downwards when the glaze melts (stoneware).
- Avoid touching the glaze until it is completely dry – it will not take long.

13 Firing

'The kiln has the last word.' *Anon*

Transformations

The metaphysical image of a ceramic holy trinity – earth, fire and water – is significant in several ways. First, it reminds us that clay requires drying and firing in order to be truly ceramic. It also conjures up an interesting idea of decomposed feldspathic rock being changed back to something akin to its original state; the process is reminiscent of volcanic heat, the centre of the earth, intense trauma and transformation, and of considerable risk. Finally, it can act as a reminder that materials falling outside the trinity are unlikely to be suitable for inclusion in the ceramic process.

There are three basic reasons for subjecting clay (earth) to ordeal by fire:

- To bring about a metamorphosis, or a change from clay into a unique and new material.
- To render the object made in clay durable, and safer and easier to handle consequently.
- To similarly change other ceramic raw ingredients into glazes.

In some circumstances, the final two processes can be achieved as a consequence of the first, although it is usual to progress via two firings so that wares are rendered safer to handle before glazing is considered. Reference will be made to a single-firing process later.

For industrial and studio potters alike, the firing process will normally involve two separate firings.

The First Firing

This is known as the biscuit-firing: clay is changed through a one-way transformation (metamorphosis) into a new, hardened, porous and rather lacklustre state. As its name implies, this ware has a biscuit-like appearance; it is not suitable for storing liquids, and so for practical and cosmetic reasons requires further attention. In some respects temperature is not critical at this stage.

The Second Firing

This is usually referred to as the glaze-, or glost-firing, its prime objective being to melt or fuse a glaze mix onto the surface of the piece. In a glaze fire, the top temperature is determined by the fluxing, or maturing temperature of the intended glaze and the clay body beneath.

Opposite *Pulling out a sculptural form (raku) at peak temperature: Peter Hayes in his studio. Photo: Rud Dowrling*

Industrial and Studio Firings

The table below outlines the differences in firing temperatures used by studio potters and the industry. The advantages to the industrial potter are in some measure offset by the craft potter's ability to create a system to suit a particular circumstance – for example, it is relatively easy to alter a glaze or firing schedule. And because most studio pottery does not require complicated propping, or can be so designed, the problem of distortion to plates is minimal, particularly as most studio potters will not usually be involved in producing long runs of, for example, bone china.

The Properties of Fired Clay

Clay bodies react to heat in two ways, but to different extents and at different temperatures, depending on their body type. Stoneware clays, which have a high maturing range, will need firing to temperatures of 1250°–1300°C and are described as highly refractory. Earthenware clays, being less refractory, will mature in the range 1100°–1150°C.

When fired to about 1000°C, both types of clay will be porous. If firing temperatures are increased, this porosity is reduced so that at the maturing temperature the body begins to vitrify. Porosity and vitrification both refer to the degree of water retention of the clay body after firing. This suggests a second metamorphosis: the change from porous to non-porous or vitreous ware, the latter state being virtually non-absorbent for all practical purposes.

To summarize, earthenware is relatively porous after glaze-firing, and so glaze is essential for cosmetic and practical purposes. Glaze is a separate layer over the body. Stoneware is highly refractory, its body vitrifying at temperatures similar to glaze maturity. It is non-porous, and so the glaze is mainly cosmetic and becomes integrated with the body with no clear demarcation line.

Differences in Firing Temperatures Used by Studio Potters and Industry

Firing	Studio	Industrial
Biscuit	900 – 1050°C	1100°C or more
Glaze	1100°C	Approx 1050°C
	Biscuit readily absorbs moisture – accepts glaze by dipping and pouring	Hardier biscuit requires precise consistency of glaze (applied by spraying). Use of binders or flocculants
Advantages	• Easier • More convenient for the studio potter	• Tends to give better results • Warping and distortion are likely to be apparent after first firing, avoiding problems when glazed • Less chance of pin-holing during glaze-firing
Disadvantages	• Body more reactive over 1100°C in glaze-fire – escaping gases obliged to bubble some way through layer of melting glaze • Distortions to glazed wares possible – cannot be supported at extremities, as in plates on a pin rack	Hard biscuit/softer glaze allows horizontal forms – plates can be supported at extremities without risk of sagging

Correct Firing

A clay body can be considered to be correctly fired when its maximum degree of vitrification has been achieved without deformity, or when the body is capable of accepting glaze without problems of crazing due to imbalance in coefficients of contraction. The maturing ranges of clay bodies differ according to the nature of the body. Earthenware bodies, particularly terracotta, tend to vitrify early at about 1150 °C, eventually becoming rather bubbly in cross-section when overfired. Some stoneware bodies are safe even in excess of 1300 °C.

In theory, any clay that has vitrified to its maximum, whether glazed or not, could be described as stoneware. A highly refractory clay, fired below its vitrification point and glazed with an earthenware glaze matured to the correct temperature, could be described as earthenware.

In practice, however, deliberately vitrifying a red earthenware body will almost certainly over-fire its glaze, making the body colour much darker. Applying and firing earthenware glazes to an underfired stoneware body (which then does not reach its maturing range) will cause problems with the glaze, and result in a friable body. Nevertheless, the latter practice is widely used in the raku process, more of which later.

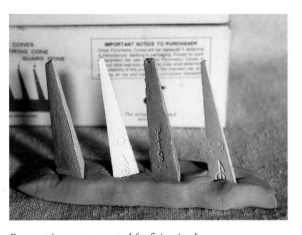

Pyrometric cones supported for firing in clay.

A rod supported by a pyrometric cone or bar, inside the kiln, drops as the cone bends, switching off power.

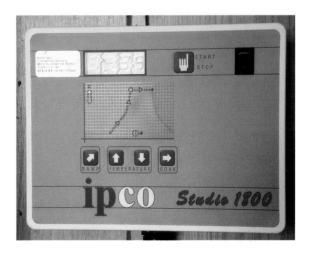

Right *A mechanical kiln-sitter. The knob (lower right) controls how long the electricity is 'on', per minute: 'full', it is on all the time, and pro rata, depending on designation. As a safety measure the knob (left) can be set to switch all off between $\frac{1}{4}$hr and $\frac{1}{2}$hr beyond the predicted firing time.*

Far right *A fairly typical simple microprocessor-type digital programme controller, allowing automatic firing.*

Correct Temperatures

The table on page 182 indicates the temperatures associated with different types of wares, but it begs the question of 'how'. In bonfires and other crude firing procedures, it is only possible to guess the temperatures reached, and it is almost impossible to predict with certainty where hot and (relatively) cold spots exist. Modern kilns are designed and constructed in such a way as to minimize internal temperature variations, and are equipped with some means of regulating and controlling temperature.

THE TRADITIONAL METHOD

Pyrometric cones, viewed through a spy-hole, reflect 'work done' by heat, equate to temperature reached, and inform the operator when to turn off power, or cease stoking (*see* page 195).

PYROMETERS

Provide an analogue or digital read-out of the actual temperature via a thermocouple (a probe inserted through the kiln wall), and are often used in conjunction with regulators.

REGULATORS

These control the supply of energy (usually electricity). They can be set to deliver percentages of power, usually approximately per minute, 100 per cent being on all the time, 50 per cent being 30 seconds 'on', 30 seconds 'off'.

CONTROLLERS

These are microprocessor based; they provide a digital read-out, and are programmed to provide a range of firing schedules and variable options to cater for the most demanding circumstances.

See Firing a Kiln, page 191.

The Simplified Chemistry of Firing

Several very complicated chemical changes are brought about by the firing process, and the firing must be scheduled so as not to hinder these reactions. From a practical point of view, however, these changes can be grouped into two stages. The first process is the formation of steam, while the second

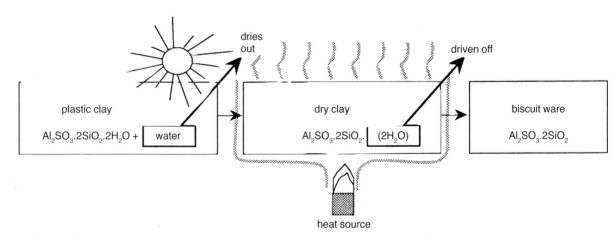

dries out

driven off

plastic clay

$Al_2SO_3.2SiO_2.2H_2O$ + water

dry clay

$Al_2SO_3.2SiO_2.$ $(2H_2O)$

biscuit ware

$Al_2SO_3.2SiO_2$

heat source

clay ($Al_2SO_3.2SiO_2.2H_2O$) = alumina + silica + water driven off by fire

The chemical changes that clay undergoes during drying out and firing.

involves the combustion of organic material (carbons) contained within the clay.

Most water is driven off in the form of steam during the initial temperature rise through 100°C to 300°C. Carbonaceous material begins to burn away at 300°C, combustion continuing right up to about 1100°C, and is released as carbon dioxide gas.

Silica – the Major Component

As indicated in an earlier section, silica (SiO_2) is a major ingredient of clay. The theoretical composition of pure clay is $Al_2O_3.2SiO_2.2H_2O$, or one molecule of alumina, plus two molecules of silica, plus two molecules of water, all combined chemically. Other sources of silica are crushed or finely ground quartz or sand, and calcined (burnt) flint; similarly, refined silica abounds in volcanic rocks, feldspars and clays as a result of decomposition of rocks such as granites, and in sandstones.

Because silica is such an important component of clay bodies and glazes, potters are mainly concerned with the way it behaves when heated. Silica occurs in several different forms. When heated, some of it changes from one form to another, and then reverts to the original form on the subsequent cooling. Other modifications of the material result in a permanent change to a new form, which remains that way after cooling.

Two important silica modifications are of major concern to the potter: quartz and cristobalite. Let us look at the quartz first. Before being heated, quartz exists as alpha (α) quartz, but on heating it changes to a new form called beta (β) quartz, and expansion takes place. As it cools, beta quartz reverts to alpha quartz and contracts.

The table looks in detail at what happens to the silica as it heats up. The higher the firing temperature, the more cristobalite is developed, which in turn increases the body's resistance to crazing. Underfiring a body, thereby restricting the development of cristobalite, is probably the most common cause of glaze crazing. A natural earthenware body has a small expansion/contraction rate (approximately 0.7 per cent), while the expansion rate of cristobalite (3 per cent) is sudden, and is exactly reversible on cooling. If sufficient cristobalite is present in the body, the body will contract a little more than the glaze, which is thereby compressed and unable to craze. This cristobalite squeeze, as it is known, happens at about 225°C. It is invaluable in controlling crazing, but if overdone it results in shivering, the opposite and equally undesirable result of an ill-fitting glaze.

Silica Inversions

Sudden expansions and contractions at about 225°C, and again at about 573°C, occur each time a body is fired – in other words, during both biscuit- and glaze-firings. If firing or cooling is too rapid, the stress set up by the inversions can cause dunting, or cracks right through the ware.

The Changes to Silica as it Heats Up

	Event	Cause
Gradual expansion until approximately 225°C	First sudden expansion	Cristobolite changes from alpha to beta form
Heating continues to approx 573°C	Second sudden expansion	Quartz changes from alpha to beta form
Heat increases	Other forms convert to beta cristobalite	
1200°C	Most other forms converted to beta cristobalite	

Firing Schedules

From the above it will be seen that two sets of criteria have to be taken into account when considering the firing schedule. Regardless of whether it is a biscuit- or a glaze-firing, the steam/carbon factor will be present to a greater or lesser extent. Silica inversions and accompanying sudden expansion/contraction trauma may occur in any firing, all of which seems rather technical and threatening. Everything hinges on temperature and time, both of which can be controlled, as indicated below. Before firing however, wares must be placed inside the kiln.

Packing a Kiln

Techniques for packing kilns vary only in as much as although raw, unglazed wares may be placed in contact with each other, glazed wares must not. The aim in either case should be a good solid pack, making maximum use of setting space. Not only does this make good economic sense, but it also assists even firing and a good atmosphere in the chamber.

Packing Biscuit-Ware

Raw pots must always be handled with care, and this is particularly true when packing them. The main preoccupation is often to try to find something to fit a particular space, rather than to take note of exactly where a handle might be relative to a kiln wall. Take care to avoid even very slight accidental damage. When lifting an unfired pot, ensure that it is supported from underneath, putting a hand under the foot and steadying the pot with the other. Do not pick up raw pots by handles or spouts.

With care, small pots can be placed inside larger pots, and smaller-sized pots can be stacked one on top of the other. One bowl can be inverted on another and the pattern repeated several times, possibly to the top of the chamber. Obviously, vessels with vertical walls provide better support than very shallow, open forms. Care should be taken not to impose too much stress on such walls, which would almost certainly be split under the strain. This can be a problem if packing school-children's work, for example, when there is little or no uniformity of form or size. If in any doubt, put in a shelf rather than put work at risk.

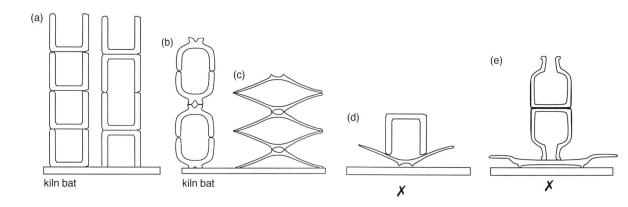

Packing biscuit wares. (a) This arrangement allows maximum support, vertical walls carrying the weight straight down onto the kiln shelf. (b) Shapes with a concave interior provide good support, utilizing the circular structure to carry the load. (c) Greater stress will be imposed upon 'coathanger' curves, particularly when the pieces are extremely shallow. Do not over-stack such shapes. (d) and (e) These are two stress-inducing arrangements.

When stacking odd shapes, try to find solid and heavy forms for the bottom, keeping shallow, open forms for the top. Remember that pots under stress during firing are more at risk than when simply stacked in a cool kiln. So although everything might look all right, survival at this point does not guarantee eventual success. Provided wares can be placed in the setting chamber with due regard for weight and are stable enough not to shift in firing, there should be no problems.

Packing Glazed Wares

Packing a glaze kiln requires that pots should not be in contact. As a general rule, if you can get a finger between items they will fire without problem. If the gap is less, glaze can pull across, joining up between two objects. Moreover, if there is glaze on the foot of a pot it will melt and fuse the pot to the kiln shelf. Again, as a general guide, all glaze material should be removed, or prevented from

The Stages in Kiln Firing

Stages	Temperature	Characteristics
Initial heating – water smoking stage (0–150°C)	0- 150°C	• Free or mechanically held water is driven off in the form of steam. Replacement of free water will return the clay to a plastic state; the chemical structure of the clay is unaltered by its removal. As water boils at 100°C, it is reasonable to assume that by 150°C this first stage will have been accomplished • Surface water is easily driven off and first to go • Moisture at the clay's centre will warm up more slowly and require an easy passage to the outside • Similarly, clay is heated first on the outside – see below • Application of glaze causes the absorbent biscuit body to soak up water from the glaze mix
Dehydration – first inversion (225°C)	150–600°C	This is the removal of chemically bound water. Once gone, such water cannot be returned to the body; it is now a new material. This process takes place from 150°C to 600°C, with most chemically combined water being released between 200°C and 460–600°C, although some traces still remain up to about 900°C
Oxidization – combustion of carbons and second inversion (573°C)	400–1000°C	Carbon will be burned out in this period. Basically, carbons combine with oxygen, escaping in the form of carbon dioxide. When oxidization is complete, a black core will result, as can often be seen at the centre of old broken house bricks. Occasionally, blistering or crawling glazes result from small black holes formed on the surface of biscuit-ware, arising again from insufficient oxidization
Maturation/vitrification – (900°C upwards)	900°C+	The period when fluxes in the clay body start to react with the clays, softening as the temperature increases until they virtually melt. Fired beyond this point, the body would almost certainly boil, giving off gases which give rise to bloating or blistering, and leaving the pot on the point of collapse. There are two causes for the subsequent bloating: carbons oxidizing at this late stage; and temperature rising too quickly or too far

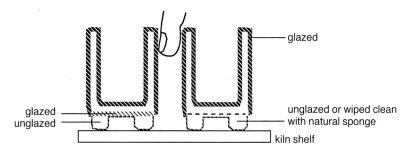

The 'finger test' ensures there is sufficient gap between glazed wares, preventing 'pulling' across from one pot to another.

getting there in the first place, from the foot and for about $\frac{1}{4}$in (0.6cm) up the pot's wall (*see* pages 176-7). This will allow for a slight downward movement of fusing glaze if it becomes too viscous. This technique is suitable for all temperature ranges, is probably the most reliable and, because the use of stilts and spurs is avoided, is certainly the cheapest. Furthermore, if kiln shelves are given a coating of bat-wash, there should be little risk of adhesion.

When glazing earthenware bodies it is sometimes felt necessary to glaze the whole item to make it absorption-proof. Wares are supported on stilts or spurs, refractory pieces providing support with minimum contact to glazed undersides of wares. By elevating the glazed surface above the surface of the kiln shelf, and having minimum contact with the

pot via only three sharp points that are chipped off after firing, virtually no part of the pot's surface remains unglazed. When pots are removed from the kiln, stilts can be released from bases by easing or tapping with a sorting tool or screwdriver; they may be used at least a few times if they are not too damaged by the glaze and the removal process.

Small particles of very sharp refractory material may remain stuck to the glaze. These should be carefully removed using a sorting tool, and then rubbed down with a piece of carborundum stone or similar to clean up the foot. Take care not to run a hand over the foot of a pot before ensuring that every slither of refractory has been removed, because whenever there is broken ceramic there will be razor-sharp edges. When clipping off it is advisable to wear goggles, too.

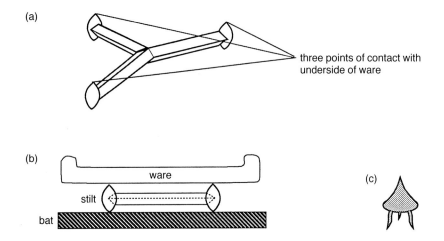

When glazing earthenware all over, use stilts or spurs to ensure minimum contact with shelves. (a) A three-pronged stilt; various sizes available. (b) Cross-section showing the stilt in use. (c) Spurs are an alternative to stilts; used in threes, they come in various sizes, and can be arranged to suit any size.

Stilts or spurs should not be used to support stoneware because the body tends to warp. At peak temperature the body is approaching the point of collapse, and will sag around a stilt with the very real possibility of falling sideways, not only collapsing itself, but damaging other pieces in the process, too. Wares with glazes in a state of flux coming in contact with each other and kiln walls can create a dreadful amount of damage when, as the firing cools, glazes weld everything together.

When firing very small pieces such as ceramic jewellery, nichrome wire can be used as a support. Beads or earrings that are glazed all over and strung up between two supporting props can be safely fired in this way. Small items can often be packed into spaces too small or the wrong shape to fit larger items, and an even more economical setting can be achieved.

Kiln Furniture

Kiln furniture is necessary to support wares in the kiln. Shelves, props and other accessories are usually made from high-grade alumina refractories so that they will withstand working temperatures up to 1300°C. Furniture as supplied with a kiln may not be to excess in terms of quality, but will be adequate for normal loads packed into that kiln. The trick is to have refractory kiln shelves of sufficient thickness to carry the weight likely to be applied over their span. Shelves of excess thickness will absorb heat (and money), which could be better used for firing wares.

Kiln shelves are rather expensive items, so are worth looking after carefully. Before use, ensure that they are dry, and not cracked. Check by supporting the suspect shelf at its centre by hand, or suspending it between thumb and finger. Tap it with a metal tool: if a clear, ringing sound is heard, it is probably not cracked. If a crack is present, the sound will be muted, and if the shelf is wet, the ring will be dull. They should always be stored on edge in a dry place.

To prevent shelves absorbing glaze, or contamination by direct contact with it, they should be coated with a proprietary bat wash; a mix of one part china clay and two parts alumina hydroxide makes a good DIY alternative. Do not coat props or kiln bricks.

Props and large pots create 'hot spots' on a cooling kiln shelf. Do not 'crack' or open the kiln prematurely or uneven cooling will result, possibly damaging wares and causing glazes to craze, or will cause bunching to the elements, shortening their life.

Do not place shelves right up against kiln walls, and do ensure that air can circulate throughout, possibly by leaving gaps between them, particularly in large kilns where they are used in pairs or quadruplet.

If overall dimensions are kept to a minimum, their thickness and consequent bulk or volume can also be reduced. Where two half-sized shelves are used instead of one full size they can be correspondingly thinner. Where four 'quarter' shelves are used it is not possible to use a three-prop system so rather more setting area is encroached upon.

In the diagrams of shelf arrangements (*see* page 190) it can be seen that, assuming that in each case the overall size is the same, plan (b) is the least impinged upon by props, although (a) might actually be better if one large plate were set on each level. Plan (c) might be more useful for this purpose than (d). In the case of (e) there might be considerable loss of setting space depending on the size of pots. In any event, kiln setting can be something of a puzzle, and it is often necessary when packing assorted shapes and sizes to unpack and start all over again.

When building up layers of shelves, prop systems should be vertically in line wherever possible, especially at the bottom of the pack. Where a large shelf is supported at the outer edges, and loaded to excess centrally, there is liable to be considerable stress on it.

Kiln shelves and props carrying the weight of upper layers should, therefore, be well supported above and beneath so that weight is transferred vertically down to the kiln floor. Only in the top layer or two may props be moved over to accommodate odd-shaped pieces, and only then when it is clear that props and shelves will not be transferring weight to a critically weak part of the structure.

A thermocouple can be accidentally damaged sometimes, when placing pots. The porcelain

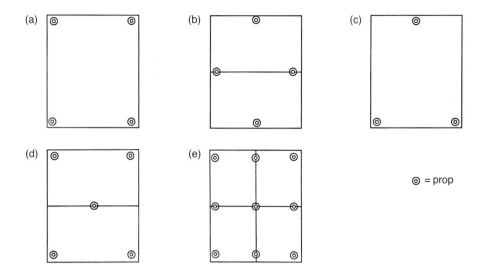

An arrangement of shelves and props within a kiln: (a), (b) and (c) could all be subject to stress if loaded excessively at the unsupported centre. (d) Slightly restricted placing, centrally, but well supported. (e) Maximum support for high firing and smaller shelves allows ease of handling.

sheathing is obviously fragile so take care not to knock it. The instrument can gently be partly withdrawn so that it does not protrude into the setting space while pots are being placed. Do not forget to replace the thermocouple before firing, and before doing so check that nothing is in its way before easing into place.

There is a special satisfaction in achieving a good pack. Whether biscuit or glaze, it is good to know that you have made maximum use of available space and have ensured a safe firing by your careful placing of wares. The stage that follows is at least as satisfying, but is also an exciting challenge. A very first firing can also be a somewhat daunting experi-

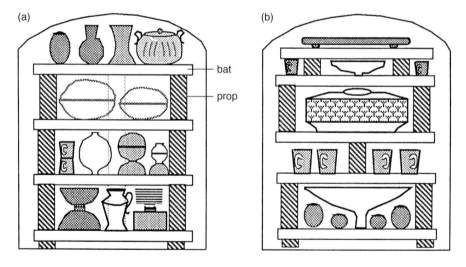

Propping shelves. (a) The weight is carried down by vertically placed props; a very stable pack. (b) The second shelf up is liable to central stress, and the third could be warped by insufficient support at the outer edges. It is also rather unstable.

Mike Powers packing a gas kiln.

The pack almost complete.

ence, and nerve-racking to say the least. But if the principles are reasonably well understood before the first switch is thrown, the whole process is likely to be trouble free.

Firing a Kiln

If you have recently set up a workshop, at home or at a school, your first firing will be for biscuit. All wares must be thoroughly dry. If there are excessively thick or heavy pieces among the work, these might be best left until the next biscuit-firing, stored above or near the kiln to ensure that free water trapped inside the clay walls and bodies has completely dried out. If in doubt, leave for weeks rather than days; trapped moisture has an explosive effect when subjected to sudden heat.

The purpose of a biscuit-firing, as has been said, is to expel water chemically combined in the clay, and to convert it into a new material strong enough to support itself when handled. Biscuit-ware is therefore much easier to glaze than raw ware.

The dry, raw clay requires very slow, gentle heating in the early stages. Heat has to penetrate through the body gradually enough to prevent expansion of the surface, while the material inside remains cool. If heating takes place too rapidly, the surface clay would expand and break off in much the same way as rock does if exposed to constant changes of extreme temperature. At the same time, chemically combined water has to be allowed to escape without damaging the wares due to excessive build-up of pressure within the body.

Firing a Hypothetical Electric Kiln

This could be an old model used in a home workshop. It might have an electro-mechanical interlock to isolate the mains supply before the kiln can be opened, nowadays frequently fitted as 'standard' to conform to health and safety regulations. Ensure that the main switch – the one on the wall that cuts off all power to the kiln – is 'off'. Only then proceed to pack the kiln.

Before closing the door or lid, check the pyrometer reading. The instrument will be calibrated in degrees Centigrade, so should be currently reading the room temperature, probably between 12°–22°C, depending on conditions. If it has a digital read-out, it will be accurate, and easy to read. If it is of the analogue type, it may be less so, but a rough idea can be obtained as to whether or not it is wildly inaccurate and in need of recalibration. Compare the reading to what seems like a probable room temperature, add or subtract the difference to 'guesstimate' the required target temperatures, and use cones (*see* Firing a Gas Kiln, page 195) to ascertain the precise heat/work done.

If the kiln is fitted with a removable bung in the top of the chamber or lid, remove it to allow water vapour to escape. Then close it up. Where there is no bung, it may be possible to leave the door or lid slightly ajar. If there is any possibility of someone inadvertently opening the kiln while the power is 'on', secure the door in position by some means. A padlock and chain will suffice.

The kiln is now ready. First the wall switch, supplying energy to the whole outfit; check that any mechanical isolator switch has been locked on. Activate the heating elements by switching the energy regulator to about 10 to 20 setting on the dial to warm the kiln slowly. Traditionally an overnight, low temperature 'soak' is used, to build gradually to 100°C or a little more, allowing moisture to be exhausted slowly. By morning it will be possible to increase the power slowly to bring the temperature up to about 500–600°C.

With a little experience it may be possible to increase the rate so that the overnight soak builds to 200–300°C.

After the soak, close the door or lid completely, and continue firing. Keep any spy-holes/bungs open until 600°C is reached, then close them up. Once this 600°C point is exceeded, it is safe to increase power to maximum, allowing temperature to rise as fast as the kiln will allow, until the required temperature is reached. (Check the pyrometer and cones.) All bungs and spy-holes will remain closed.

Switch off the power and allow the kiln to cool down in its own time. Do not be tempted to 'crack' the door or lid until the temperature is down to below 100°C, although bungs can be opened a little earlier if required, provided there is no inrush of cold air to cause trauma to pots or kiln.

There is always a temptation to open up as quickly as possible, to unpack while wares are still too hot to handle, using leather gloves to protect the hands. Ideally, leave everything to cool sufficiently for bare hands to be used. This, particularly in the case of glaze firings, can increase excitement or nervous tension for you, but will safeguard the wares from thermal shock.

The Firing Log

Adjustment of the regulator setting, time and temperature increase should all be recorded in a firing log, and is essential for building up a picture of the capabilities of a particular kiln and its associated equipment. It can be used to record information about glaze results from each firing, in addition to changes in schedules and weather conditions – often critical in firings other than electric – and it will boost confidence in your ability to manage firings effectively, and without undue apprehension. After all, people have been firing with much less sophisticated facilities for thousands of years, so with a few simple cones, and basic control equipment, you can too.

Summary of Biscuit-Firing Schedule

A safe and simple procedure is usually best: you should identify the major objectives:

- Avoid excessive, premature heating as this would result in the traumatic production of steam and hence damage the piece.
- Oxidize as much carbonaceous material as possible in the first firing.
- Make the temperature (probably 1100°C) safely, without mishap.

Observe the following procedure:

Step 1: A long, low soak (overnight perhaps) to gradually increase the temperature from cold to 150 °C or so. The vent plug should be out during this period to allow free water to escape.

Step 2: If necessary, increase the heat input to build temperatures gently (over a maximum of two to three hours) to over 300 °C. This will take it gently past the first inversion point.

Step 3: Increase the firing rate a little more to pass 700 °C. This will allow any lingering H_2O to be released safely, and will allow the second inversion point to be passed with a minimum risk of trauma. (Depending on the kiln, insert bungs, or close vents – probably at about 600 °C.)

Note: Beyond 700 °C, full power can be applied to bring the temperature to the desired maximum; vents at this stage should be closed.

Kiln Variations

The time taken to complete the schedule depends to a considerable extent on the type of kiln in use. Older kilns were built using refractory bricks that are usually dense, rather heavy and inclined to absorb heat. Because the bricks heat right through, heat loss is reduced by the use of thick kiln walls, which then act rather like storage heaters. Much energy in the early stages goes into heating the bricks, so wares inside the kiln are consequently allowed to heat up slowly and gently, with an even temperature rise throughout the kiln. Due to heat loss at the upper end of the firing range, advances in temperature are similarly protracted. However, the disadvantages of the time required to reach temperature, and the cost of firing at the top end, are offset by a natural schedule appropriate to the wares – in other words, the slow build-up at the early stages allows plenty of time for water to be driven off, inversion points to be passed safely, and carbon oxidization to take place. Cooling down also takes time, again avoiding stress and shock to the wares.

Modern, hi-tech kilns make use of refractory insulation bricks, which, because of their open porous nature, are much more efficient insulators. When the inside face of the brick is heated, the air pockets within the brick ensure that heat loss is kept to a minimum, air being a very poor conductor of heat. The outer face of the brick therefore remains relatively cool.

Other very efficient insulators used in kiln construction are ceramic blanket and ceramic paper, both basically made from ceramic fibre. This amazing product has become an important component in low thermal mass kilns due to its refractoriness, extremely light weight, and incredible insulation properties. As a consequence, modern kilns are lighter, use less energy to achieve their temperatures, allow greater internal volume compared to external dimensions, and are quicker and more economical to fire.

Modern kilns do, however, have a down side. Their very efficiency can be a problem, as temperature increases can be extremely rapid: this can put contents at risk during the early stages of water smoking and dehydration, it ignores critical inversion points, and it can reduce the period of carbon oxidization so severely as to leave excessive amounts that will affect glazes later. The major disadvantage, however, seems to be the rapid cooling down of such kilns. A kiln packed with short wares, requiring a number of shelves and props, and having a very dense pack anyway, will probably be less prone to problems that an open kiln with virtually no storage heater potential and plenty of air space. The latter will cool very quickly, possibly causing problems to the wares (of which more later).

The good news is that accurate and very convenient systems of electronic control have been devised that complement the hi-tech nature of the low thermal mass kilns. These are usually programmed to provide schedules for biscuit, earthenware and stoneware glaze-firing while enabling individual programmes to be added, or the programme schedules to be changed temporarily as circumstances might dictate. They usually maximize on fuel input, resulting in extremely economical firing cycles. Some of these controllers even take note implicitly of the rapid cooling potential of the parent kiln by providing a firing down facility. At risk of offending some suppliers, it is worth noting that such a facility might actually be essential in certain circumstances – something not usually mentioned in product descriptions. If you are thinking of buying a new kiln it is well worth visiting showrooms so that you can actually see items, rather than relying on descriptions in catalogues. You will be able to check out the thickness of the insulation, enquire about appropriate control units, and check the usual weight and external measurements, rating and power supply required.

Glaze-Firing Schedule

This is the easy bit, or so we are frequently led to believe. All you need do is turn on the kiln at about one-quarter to one-half power, depending on the kiln, to drive off any water absorbed in the glazing process and to allow the kiln to heat to somewhere just over 100°C; as water boils at that temperature, all is well once it is exceeded. You can then turn on full power and let it rip until maximum temperature is reached.

With some of the older refractory brick kilns, this method may well be sufficient. The nature of the kiln, with its tendency to absorb lots of precious energy, is probably slow enough to allow steam to escape safely. The slowly but steadily increasing temperature will proceed through the inversion points without threat, only to slow up via a progressively flattening heat curve until it has reached its absolute maximum. Carbon will have plenty of time to burn away, while the increase progresses slowly toward stoneware-maturing temperatures.

The reverse process can almost mirror the upward cycle, except for an initial relatively fast drop in temperature. There is likely to be another chance for carbon oxidization to take place as the kiln cools, and there is little risk to the wares at this time. The final drop from 300°C or so can seem an endless wait, however, and here there is a threat, because in order to advance cooling enough to get pots out, one might be tempted to crack the kiln door at about 300°C. This will often cause dunting, as sudden cooling and contraction coincide with the inversion contraction encountered at 225°C. This is the most likely time for dunting to take place; and it would be a rash person indeed who would open a kiln while it was still at 500–600°C,

when in the region of the second silica inversion point. So, avoid temptation and allow the kiln to cool in its own good time.

Modern, low thermal mass electric kilns utilize a combination of HTI (high thermal insulation) bricks and an outer layer of ceramic fibre protected by a reflective steel sheet as outer casing. They are capable of achieving high stoneware temperatures very quickly. By trial and error, it will be found that an energy setting of about 25 per cent power will increase temperature slowly enough at first, and an increase to about 45 per cent power will then speed up the process sufficiently so that the temperature exceeds 700°C over the next six hours or so. By setting the controller (if there is no microprocessor-type programmed unit) to 80 per cent power, the kiln will still reach 1000°C in another couple of hours or so. For earthenware glaze-firing, a soak for twenty minutes at the maturing temperature of 1100°C will give a toasted (slightly vitrified) look to red bodies. Where a slightly lighter, more traditional terracotta body is required, the temperature can be confined to a maximum of 1080°C, with a similar soak period.

The soak period allows final oxidization to take place when the quicker increase rate would cause problems (small bubbles, craters or pin-holing) with the glaze. To simplify, gases have time to escape and the glaze time to melt over before cooling and stiffening occurs. This extra time enables more heat-work to be done, so the body and glaze will be more mature.

COOLING DOWN

When firing traditional kilns, whatever the type of fuel or design, the major concern will almost certainly have been to actually reach temperature. The preoccupation with temperature increase would have arisen partly from the need to stoke, and therefore the necessity of having sufficient fuel to hand, and partly from awareness of the vagaries of the kiln and weather. Once the magical temperature had been reached and the kiln clamped up by closing the stoke hole, the potters were obliged to wait. If the heating process took a lot of time, so too would cooling. Some older electric kilns of my acquaintance have taken longer to cool down than to heat up – although this cannot be said of the high-tech kilns we use today.

Contemporary technology, at least in some respects, leaves little margin for error. There is a fine line between what is efficient when used exactly to design, and what is not if used even marginally outside its specifications. In this respect, some modern kilns tend to work only just within the range of tolerance of clays. The consequence is that, if a kiln is not tightly packed with wares, has little in the way of kiln shelves and props to store up heat, or if the weather is extremely cold at cooling time, it may cool down too quickly.

There is very little that can be done to avoid such rapid cooling. If the kiln room is a potential icebox, it could perhaps be better insulated, or firings could be scheduled for mild weather only. Vent openings and spyholes can be closed securely to prevent heat loss or draughts, and doors or lids should be checked for tightness of fit. A ceramic blanket laid over the top of a kiln during the firing and cooling will also help to reduce heat loss. In the case of top-loader kilns, it is helpful to add an extra shelf above the wares to help contain heat; the loss of firing space is likely to be more than compensated for by having fewer dunts.

If a kiln continually cools down too quickly, the only recourse is either to fire it down or to rebuild it. Usually the practical solution to this is to fit an electronic temperature control system. Savings made on fuel and elements will soon offset the modest cost, to say nothing of the undoubted convenience.

Firing a Gas Kiln

The major difference between electric and gas kilns is, of course, fire. Controlling heat requires a hands-on approach, sometimes adjusting the burner/s, sometimes altering the distance from the chamber. Consequently, biscuit firing tends to be more difficult, bearing in mind the need for a very slow build-up of heat.

'Reading' temperature inside the kiln can also be a problem if there is no pyrometer; which, in any case, may give only an approximate idea of the heat/work done. For precise information, pyrometric cones must be used and placed where they are visible during firing. These cones are made of refractory mixtures graded to bend over as they are affected by particular amounts of heatwork. Each cone is coded, indicating an amount of heatwork it will withstand, and, because this reflects both temperature and time, is generally regarded a more precise means of indicating a completed firing cycle. (*See* Appendix 1, Bending Temperatures.)

When packing the kiln, remember to site cones where they will be visible later. Use a candle or torch inside the kiln to check visibility. Arrange them as illustrated (*see* diagrams below), at the correct angle, and if space and viewing allow, add an extra guide cone. If plastic clay has been used to support them, make sure this is completely dry before firing. Alternatively, use commercially produced supports. This is an excellent means of verifying pyrometer readings in any type of kiln, and individual guide cones can also be used to check

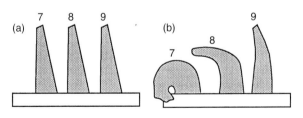

An arrangement of cones. (a) Incline at about 80°, (b) showing cone 7 down, cone 8 at the quarter hour, and 9 beginning to bend. For a stoneware firing to 1250°C this would be the time to shut down the fire.

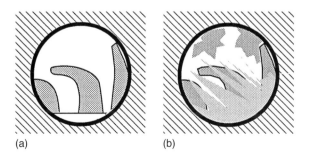

View through the spy-hole. (a) At best it is often difficult to arrange cones for easy viewing. (b) The background is confusing, and the atmosphere smoky, making it difficult to read the cones.

Jim Malone stoking his wood-fired kiln. Photo by Alex McErlain

heatwork – hot and cool spots – in different parts of a kiln.

Cones are best viewed against a plain background, such as a large pot. When other vague outlines can also be seen it can be difficult to see exactly what is, and what is not, a cone. This is particularly true as bending temperatures are achieved, and/or when a reduction atmosphere exists. A dark blue glass filter will sometimes enhance visibility, and it is helpful to leave the spy-hole open a moment or two to allow the atmosphere immediately inside to clear. Constant vigilance is the best recourse, although a pyrometer is always useful as a general guide to progress. It will warn of the approaching critical period before it happens, so that you will be able to identify all three cones before the first goes down.

Gas kilns and their burners and controls differ from one model to another, so it would not be appropriate to give a detailed description of how to fire a particular kiln. Even so, a few suggestions might be in order.

Igniting a gas kiln can be a rather tricky opera-

tion if you have to rely on matches: a gas poker or blow-torch will make it much easier. Familiarize yourself fully with the operating instructions accompanying burners, and particularly with flame-fail devices. The idea of these is that they automatically close down the gas supply if the flame goes out, and are a significant safety feature. It can be very frustrating when, apparently, the equipment is conspiring to prevent ignition. Read the blurb, act in the order stated, and there should be no problems. Once ignited, and with burners turned to full power, the sequence becomes similar to that of an electric kiln.

While temperature builds, all you can do is wait, ever watchful and vigilant. Listen to the burner/s: if for any reason the firing is automatically shut down (a sudden gust of wind could blow out a low flame), you will notice and set it off again. You will also be at hand to notice that either the pressure gauge is showing the need for a new cylinder of gas, or a less intense sound will suggest the same thing. In this respect it is useful, but not essential, to fit a two-way valve system, enabling switching from one bottle to another without disconnection and subsequent loss of flame.

Reduction Firing

A gas kiln is an excellent vehicle for reduction. This process, described below in the Summary (*see* page 200), involves starving the internal atmosphere of oxygen, thereby changing not only the chemical composition of metal oxides on pots and in bodies, but also their visual appearance. By this means, the ubiquitous green from copper oxide can be transformed into amazing reds, and iron oxide from terracotta to green/greys.

Reduction is developed during the final stages of heating, by deliberately creating a smoky atmosphere inside the chamber by closing the dampers and thus reducing air flowing through, and, consequently, oxygen supply; or by increasing fuel. At about 1,000°C, for stoneware, these changes to the firing tend to slow or halt heat-rise, so maximum attention to burner/s and damper/s is imperative.

Reduction is usually completed as the maturing temperature is attained, and fuel can be shut off and the kiln allowed to cool down. However, there is a likelihood of re-oxidization, so it is important to prevent the incursion of air. Closing all air ports and flue may be sufficient, but it may be necessary to fire the kiln down if heavy reduction is desired, depending on the circumstances. Again, there is no substitute for experience, or trial and error. If this all seems rather daunting, *see* Raku, page 200.

Types of Kiln

Front-Loading Kilns

The front loader reflects its historic antecedents, conforms to a traditional concept, and can be constructed to fire with virtually any type of fuel. This type of kiln tends to be very robust, logical in design (based on the fact that heat rises) and is convenient to use. Packing and unpacking involve a minimum of stooping, enabling wares to be placed safely. Shelves can also be placed with similar ease, as the inside of the kiln is easily accessed and visible.

Top-Loading Kilns

The top-loading kiln does not share all the advantages inherent in the front loader. Some models are less robust, and packing and unpacking can be a chore, putting stress on the potter's back. Placing shelves is not always easy either, and lids sometimes threaten to fall on the packer, although in fairness it has to be said that such a thing has never happened to me. Many years ago a student did end up head down inside one such kiln, after her feet had slipped away as she stooped to place a pot inside. Only a modicum of dignity was lost in the event, although it did highlight a problem!

A major advantage that top-loading kilns have over their front-loading counterparts is that they tend to be cheaper. They can, however, be less than tough to look at, and they sometimes do seem somewhat meanly insulated, putting them in the marginal bracket when it comes to critical extremes. Controversially, it could be said that they are cheaper not because of their basic format, but because materials have sometimes been pared back to the minimum. Some versions on the market appear to be more substantial than others, but the thinner-sectioned models appear to be no less reliable except in the coldest weather.

Choosing a Kiln

When looking to buy a kiln it is therefore sensible to check the manufacturers' specifications, examine a range of alternatives and, best of all, talk to owners of the models wherever possible. It can also be helpful to have a clear idea of how the kiln will be used, or rather what it will be used for. A kiln which is fine for biscuit and high-fired stoneware, but which cools rather quickly, may not cope with the more 'precious' tendencies of slip-decorated earthenware. A combination here of, possibly, vitreous slips, inadequate oxidization, excessively rapid cooling and insufficient glaze compression can lead to disappointing firings not encountered with other kilns.

Where cost is not of prime concern, there are probably three practical ways forward, purchasing a new top-loader being only the first of these.

Second-hand kilns are usually offered in local newspapers, craft and ceramics publications, such as *Ceramic Review* in the UK. These can be extremely good value, having been purchased perhaps by someone whose enthusiasm has waned or who has used it irregularly over the years, hence leaving it in virtually new condition. Such 'low mileage' kilns will have originally been purchased at pre-inflation prices well below current costs. Taking depreciation into account as well, they are likely to be half-price deals at worst. The cost of transport is another factor to consider, and if you have access to a sturdy trailer and a few strong bodies you have the edge on the competition. This may be a cynical point, but kilns are difficult to move, and vendors do like to clear the space and put the cash in the bank.

Building a Kiln

Another cost-cutting alternative is to build your own kiln. This has several advantages. First, it will be built on site, so actually getting it there is not a problem. Second, the various materials and pieces of equipment can be purchased as work progresses – in fact, it may be possible to purchase second-hand or surplus HTI bricks, burners and the like around which to design the kiln. Finally, alternative sources of energy can be considered.

Building a kiln puts one in touch with the fundamentals of ceramics in a very real way. Firing it up for the first time is awesome, exciting and rewarding – an experience not to be missed if at all possible. However, further reading is suggested before you start, there being insufficient space here to deal with the details of such a specialist project.

It is possible, nevertheless, to experience at least some of the anticipations and excitement of firing your own work, without the need for expensive materials and equipment. The latter part of this chapter indicates methods that are possible in the smallest back garden and which cost very little; they tend to be at the primitive edge of the ceramic experience, but they are utilized by some of the leading ceramicists to produce extremely sophisticated work. As someone once said: 'Jazz ain't *what* you play; it's the *way* you play it.'

Pit- or Sawdust-Firing

This process can, literally, be as simple as its name suggests, and is a slightly improved version of the bonfiring illustrated in Introducing the Ceramic Process (pages 34-5):

Step 1: Dig a pit sufficiently large to hold the intended pot with about 6in (15cm) excess depth.
Step 2: Cover the bottom of the pit with sawdust to a depth of about 4in (10cm).
Step 3: Place the piece onto the sawdust.
Step 4: Pack in more sawdust until the pot is covered to about 3in (7.5cm) over its top.
Step 5: Ball up some old newspaper, add some bits of kindling wood and ignite.
Step 6: Cover the pit with a metal sheet or old dustbin lid when the sawdust has caught fire properly.
Step 7: Allow the fire to burn down as slowly as possible.
Step 8: When cool, remove the pot.

So what exactly happens here? The heat generated by such a fire is just capable of biscuit-firing clay. It also smokes the pot, causing arbitrary patches of unburnt carbon to discolour the body. If the fire is allowed to burn down too quickly, this reduction process, or smoking, will be ineffectual and thermal shock may cause dunting. Raw pots are more susceptible to reduction than is biscuit-ware, although they are rather more at risk. This process, together with its improved version, sawdust reduction firing (below), attempts to control the distribution of heat and accommodate bigger, or more, pots in one safer firing.

Because burnishing takes rather a long time, it is probably sensible to keep the size of the pot reasonable – say, not much more than 12in (30cm) high. The larger the pot or the greater the area to be burnished, the more the vessel will dry out during the process; burnishing thereby becomes progressively more difficult, until some parts have to remain rough. Thrown pots can be burnished more quickly if worked on immediately after turning. As the pot revolves when still attached to the wheelhead, pressure can be applied via a suitably smooth tool.

After biscuit-firing, the burnished pots can be

polished to enhance the surface and to accentuate the warm appearance of smooth wood. Applying fine slips prior to burnishing can also enhance the surface colour. This will provide a superfine layer over an otherwise open body. Colour traditionally comes from the use of haematite or iron ore, which is almost pure ferric oxide (Fe_2O_3). This can be mixed into a creamy slip and applied to the pot, or can be deposited on the surface by actual burnishing with a smooth lump of the ore, as was once the practice in Iran and India.

The smooth, red gloss finish of *terra sigillata* is achieved by using an incredibly fine slip refined by numerous levigations. In other words, after lawning, a thin slurry of slip is left so that coarser, heavy particles settle out. The slurry is then decanted, leaving the sediment behind. This process is repeated until only the finest particles remain.

After biscuit-firing, such pots can be polished to enhance the surface quality and accentuate the wonderfully warm appearance of smooth wood. To add an extra dimension to the process, the unpolished pot can be reduced in a sawdust fire as mentioned above: the resulting black and grey gunmetal effect can be quite stunning. Where results are not to your liking, the pot can simply be re-oxidized in another biscuit-firing.

Sawdust Reduction Firing

Rather than dig a pit, any raised container can be used instead. As the basic idea is to create a smoky reduction atmosphere in the kiln, only a minimum of oxygen (air) is allowed. An old metal bin or brick box will suffice. Some sort of lid will be necessary, to act like a damper restricting the supply of oxygen, as will a pair of protective leather gauntlets, worn when removing the lid by hand.

Old house bricks can be used to build the walls of the kiln; as this will be only a temporary structure, it will not require mortar. Just fit the bricks together closely enough to exclude excess air, bonding in as shown in the diagram: using twelve bricks to each course and building five courses high, a total of sixty bricks will be required. If a square of chicken wire is readily to hand, lay it in the kiln to form a ventilated floor one course above ground level. This is not absolutely necessary, but it ensures an adequate layer of fuel below the wares.

Pack the wares in the kiln, allowing room for plenty of sawdust. Fine sawdust will burn more slowly than wood chippings or shavings, but both will require regular topping up to prevent premature completion – and more so if shavings are used. Once lit, the lid can remain in place, totally closed

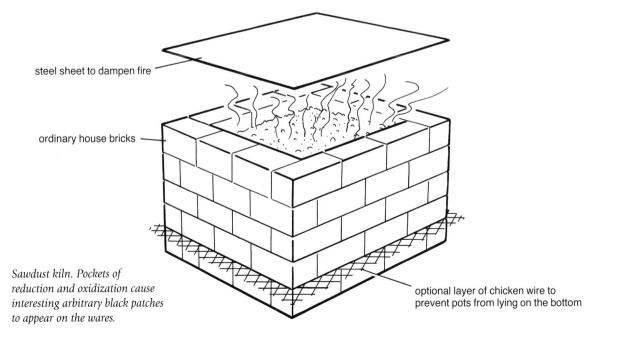

steel sheet to dampen fire

ordinary house bricks

optional layer of chicken wire to prevent pots from lying on the bottom

Sawdust kiln. Pockets of reduction and oxidization cause interesting arbitrary black patches to appear on the wares.

or slightly open as firing requires, except when adding more fuel. As a general rule, the slower the fire burns, the better will be the results.

Some potters achieve a similar reduction firing within a conventional kiln using lidded saggers. The pot intended for smoking is packed in sawdust contained inside the sagger.

Reduction in Electric Kilns

Current advice is that reduction should not be attempted in an electric kiln, but the occasional introduction of one or two saggers into a firing will not cause significant premature deterioration to the elements. In fact another view suggests the occasional reduction firing in an electric kiln does not necessarily threaten instant death to the elements. Provided that the greyish layer of protective oxide built up on elements fired over a temperature of 1150°C is not significantly reduced, no serious deterioration should take place. Two or three successive reduction firings will probably be necessary to remove the protective layer, whereas an oxidizing firing will restore the coating to its usual thickness. It would seem sensible practice, therefore, to allow two or three normal oxidizing firings between reduction firings.

Whether a reduction atmosphere is detrimental to kiln elements or not, it is not actually easy to achieve and maintain these conditions in an electric kiln. Many years ago, along with other enthusiastic exponents of reduction firing, the author attempted to introduce carbon into electric kilns in the form of mothballs. Suffice to say that a huge quantity was required, plus more patience than most of us possessed, and anyway it gave rise to the production of horribly noxious and toxic fumes. Naturally, we gave up.

More successful methods include drip-feeding oil, or inserting a gas burner into the kiln. The best time to attempt such reduction is when top temperature is reached, continuing to add carbon, possibly in the form of charcoal, until the kiln has cooled to about 750°C. This excess fuel can be fed in via a spy-hole or vent, but it is essential that the bungs or plugs are replaced as soon as possible to prevent incursion of air re-oxidizing the atmosphere. It is necessary to stoke in this way every fifteen or twenty minutes to maintain reduction.

Summary

Reduction occurs when insufficient oxygen is available for the kiln to burn clearly – in other words, there is too much fuel and too little air. The result is often a slowing down of the heating process, and a chemical reaction whereby the fire burns oxygen that is bonded within metal oxides – it is part of the molecular structure – particularly at high temperatures; for example, Fe_2O_3 (ferric oxide) is reduced to FeO (ferrous oxide).

Raku – An Introduction

Raku originated in Japan during the sixteenth century. Its recent popularity in the West is due to its process of rapid firing, plus being able to remove the ware from the kiln while red hot, also the spontaneity and drama of the technique, and the direct contact with the ceramic process. Recently, the added drama of almost instant reduction has been developed in the West, thereby contributing exciting colour, texture and metallic lustres to the process. Raku has the additional merit of being relatively instant, in that wares can be glazed, decorated, reduction fired and completed all within a single day.

My introduction to raku was through building and firing a wood-fired raku kiln with students. Our principal aims were to experience at first hand the challenge of achieving glaze temperatures using natural fuel, and to obtain a better understanding of kiln construction. It turned into a revelation to us all, as we witnessed the melting and boiling of glaze – something not usually visible as it takes place inside a closed kiln and is beyond our control in a very real sense. Another valuable outcome was that the group developed a system of dealing with the various stages involved, almost without thinking. Co-ordination of stoking, placing and drawing out pots, and submerging the pots first in combustible material to obtain the reduction, then removing them and plunging them into cold water prior to cleaning, generated a group dynamic and experience that was unique and essential to the success of the project.

The results of this introduction to raku were visually exciting: the contrast of the blackened body to the lustred and reduced glazes was in marked contrast to the subdued results of a typical stoneware firing. On the other hand, there were inevitable casualties due to the several traumatic processes involved, and although the decorative qualities could be instantly appreciated, they soon became somewhat laboured. The completed items were also, in conventional ceramic terms, non-functional, so the very considerable effort involved in the raku process seemed somewhat inconsistent with the usefulness of the vessels that resulted from it.

Over the years, raku has been developed by numerous practitioners into a rather more refined art. Decorative techniques have become more sophisticated, with individual potters evolving novel and ingenious methods of controlling reduction, lustring and firing.

The Basic Process

Pieces for raku can be made by any process or combination of processes. They need biscuit-firing before being submitted to the extraordinary processes typical of raku. The usual procedure is as follows:

Step 1: Glaze and decorate the biscuit-ware, and allow it to dry thoroughly.
Step 2: Preheat the raku kiln.
Step 3: Preheat the pieces to beyond hand-hot, to drive off moisture and reduce (a little) the thermal shock.
Step 4: When red heat is reached inside the raku kiln, carefully place the ware inside, and close up the kiln to prevent heat loss.
Step 5: When the pot glows red and the glaze turns viscous and begins to boil, remove the piece using tongs. (This usually takes between ten and twenty minutes.)
Step 6: Immediately lower the ware into a metal bin containing combustible material such as dry leaves, sawdust or chippings, and cover. This is the reduction stage and takes about twenty minutes.

Raku is a team event, enjoyed here by interested spectators as well as participants.

Andy Mason placing audience-decorated pots in a cool raku kiln. The pyrometer's thermocouple can be seen protruding through the kiln wall.

Kiln, with top in place, and heating under way. Note the orange interior just visible through the vent in the top.

Removing a red-hot pot with metal tongs.

Placing the same pot into a 'reducing' container filled with combustible material.

Step 7: Remove the piece with tongs or fireproof gloves, and plunge it into water. This prevents oxidization by instantly cooling the piece. However, closed bottle forms should not be dealt with in this way, as the hot air trapped inside, when coupled with the sudden cooling of the exterior surface, may cause violent fracture.

Step 8: When cool enough, the piece can be removed and carbon deposits carefully scrubbed off under a tap.

Making a Start

THE CLAY BODY

Special raku bodies can be purchased already blended to suit the raku process. They are usually very plastic but open, and make use of grogs to assist resistance to the thermal shock that arises from imposed rapid heating and cooling. In fact, any clay that can withstand the shock will suffice. Much depends on how you use the clay (what will be your method of production?), whether there are extreme differences in thickness, and whether you work on a large or small scale.

Your first attempts could be experiments with various bodies – including fine, coarse, coloured and white clays – to see what might best suit your requirements. Bearing in mind what has already been said about clay bodies, it is worth repeating that some clays mature at lower temperatures than others. Predominantly stoneware bodies can be given a higher biscuit-firing to about 1050°C; others should be fired at only 850°C or so, given their much lower maturing or vitrifying temperature. The more mature a body is, the less it will be affected by carbon, thereby reducing possible black areas to greys. Burnished surfaces are diminished by high firing. You are thus free to select the qualities you consider most appropriate to your own work.

More hay (in this instance) added on top, before shutting down with a lid to ensure a good 'reduction'.

After smoking in the enclosed bin, pots are removed and immediately immersed in water.

Scrubbed off to reveal 'accidental' lustres, glazes and a blackened body.

DECORATION

To start with, keep things simple. Biscuit-fired ware can be painted with thick, bought-in glazes, making use of unglazed areas and their ultimate blackening as contrast. Oxides can be applied on glaze; try silver nitrate on a white crackle glaze. Coppers will reduce later, in a dramatic way, especially if dead leaves are used to provide combustion in the reduction bin. Try to build up a repertoire of promising techniques based upon your own experience. And be adventurous, take risks, there is nothing to loose. Some basic suggestions for glaze recipes are included in the chapter on glaze (*see* page 174).

THE FORM OF THE PIECE

Your piece need have no constrictions, provided only that you take note of thickness and practical considerations. Not only are there inherent dangers to the piece from thermal shock, but there are also the physical ones – fragile appendages that survive firing can still fall victim to imprudent handling. A student scrubbing a wonderful teapot recently, and holding it by its handle, saw it shatter on impact with the sink: such handling had caused it to part from its not immensely functional handle, even though ironically it had survived all preceding traumas. In the spirit of raku, however, the piece was reassembled later using an epoxy resin glue, and remains as aesthetically pleasing as it was before the accident.

Raku Kilns

These have become popular of late. A widely available design is the propane gas top-loader, although numerous alternative DIY designs exist, again usually making use of convenient propane gas as a fuel.

But is a special kiln necessary? In theory, it is not. Glazes can be brought up to fluxing point in any kiln, provided only that subsequent steps can be carried out conveniently. The crucial word here is 'conveniently'. An American Raku fanatic known to the author used to use an electric top-loading kiln, a largish model that stood almost chest high when open, with the inner floor at just above ankle level – so removing pieces from the bottom of this kiln was not just inconvenient, it was downright dangerous.

Other inconveniences can bear listing: some top-loaders are not fitted with lid-operated isolation switches; groping inside a kiln with live elements using steel tongs is certainly not good health and safety practice, and neither is attempting to look down inside such a kiln when tremendous heat is surging up into one's face. Sudden incursions of cold air do not prolong the life of the kiln elements and linings, either.

Returning to the American raku fanatic briefly, his kiln, in common with most kilns installed in institutions, was located indoors. The reduction bins (sawdust, conflagration, smoke) were therefore indoors too – not to be recommended. So by this route, the answer to the question 'Are special kilns necessary?' is, in practice, yes. Any raku or similar process requires adequate ventilation, preferably located outdoors, and also totally unconnected to electrical power supplies. Propane is a safe and convenient fuel, and raku kiln designs can be simple, and their use convenient.

BUILDING A RAKU KILN

The major disadvantage with any top-loading kiln used for raku is heat loss. In order to place or withdraw wares it is obviously necessary to remove the lid, but by doing so, most of the heat will be released, prolonging the firing time and increasing fuel costs. Even with a smoothly operating team working closely together, there will inevitably be a significant loss of heat each time the lid is lifted and pieces inserted or extracted. One answer is to use a bottom-loader, more commonly referred to as a 'top-hat' kiln. As its name implies, this kiln is raised from its floor or base, thereby affording direct access while retaining valuable heat up inside the 'hat'. Pots can be placed on the bottom, or floor, of the kiln, and the entire structure lowered into place. This enables firing to continue with minimum loss of time and heat.

The oil-drum kiln (illustrated in the diagrams)

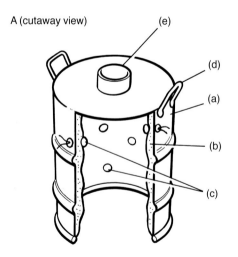

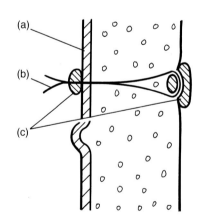

Top-hat/drum kiln. A: A general view showing (a) drum; (b) insulating ceramic fibre wired into place; (c) ceramic buttons; (d) handles; (e) metal pipe 'chimney'.
B: Detail showing fastening of ceramic fibre: (a) metal drum; (b) element wire, used as 'thread'; (c) ceramic buttons, home-made.

can be constructed from half an oil drum, lined with ceramic fibre, sitting on a kiln shelf or brick base. A hole about 3–4in (7.5–10cm) in diameter cut in the centre of the top will provide an exit vent or flue. Drill the body at intervals to allow the ceramic-fibre blanket to be wired into place – 'sewn' to the walls, the wire 'thread' protected from heat by ceramic 'buttons', which also prevent the wire cutting through the blanket. Attach lifting handles so that the lid can be lifted using gloves, or, preferably, by inserting a long shaft through them to make the lifting even easier, and safer.

SIMPLE FRONT-LOADER

For your first sortie into the exciting world of self-built kilns, you may feel that the above is rather too daunting, or it may simply be that cutting up an old oil drum is beyond the scope of the tools available to you. A simple and effective alternative is to assemble a small brick kiln. This will have a capacity of only 1cu ft (0.03cu m) or a little less, and will fire up with a normal gas-gun burner fuelled from a propane-gas cylinder. You will need about forty hot-face insulating bricks, off-cuts of ceramic-fibre

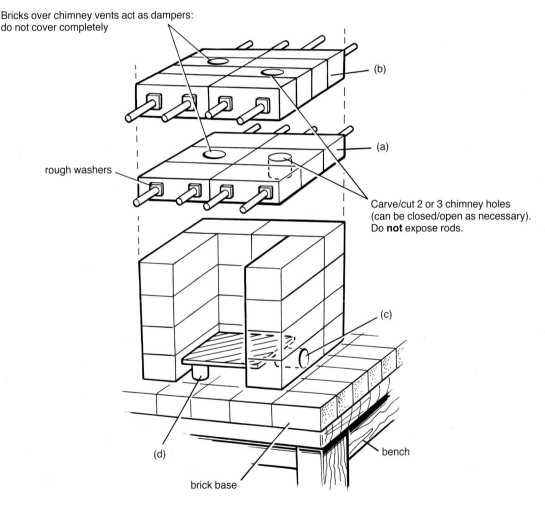

Bricks over chimney vents act as dampers: do not cover completely

rough washers

Carve/cut 2 or 3 chimney holes (can be closed/open as necessary). Do **not** expose rods.

(b)

(a)

(c)

(d)

brick base

bench

The construction of a front-loader: build up with this from a common brick base. The burner port (c) is either carved through, or a gap (a half brick) can be left. Experiment with the angle and/or size of burner, and the height of the kiln shelf (d). The roof can be 3in (7.6cm) (a) or $4\frac{1}{2}$in (11cm) (b) thick. Use mild steel rods to connect the HTI bricks.

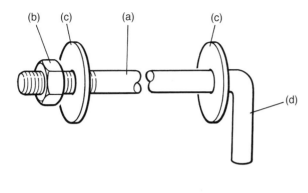

(1) Rods with added 'compression': (a) threaded both ends, or one end bent as (d); (b) retaining nut; (c) washers or plates to protect the bricks.

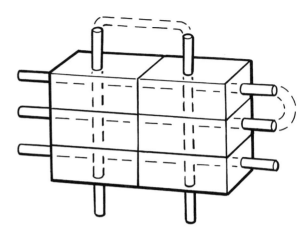

(2) Kiln door, either 3in (7.6cm) or $4\frac{1}{2}$in (11cm) thick.

blanket, a few lengths of $\frac{1}{4}$in (6mm) or $\frac{1}{2}$in (13mm) tubing, and half-a-dozen or so old house bricks. The gas gun and cylinder more or less complete the list, but an old bench or table, suitable for use outdoors, will make life easier. The final capacity will depend on the size of the bricks. The diagrams indicate the basic construction of the kiln. Assembling it on a bench and base of bricks will bring it up to a more convenient working height.

Builders' merchants can often obtain HTI bricks for you; alternatively, you can contact specialist firms direct. Although HTIs are expensive and fragile, with careful handling they can be used over and over again. The bricks are unlikely to be adversely affected by raku firing, and even if broken, they will usually fit together and work as effectively as ever. HTI bricks, which are approximately $9 \times 4 \times 3$in ($22.5 \times 10 \times 7.5$cm), can be stacked up into place one against the other without the need for mortar. The bricks are very easily cut or drilled as they are extremely soft, so a hacksaw blade and screwdriver (to drill through the bricks) are the only tools that might be necessary. The roof and door sections can be supported by internal rods or tubes. If sufficiently tight fitting there is really no need for nuts and washers at each end, although the compression thus provided would give extra rigidity.

The internal chamber will be 9in (22.5cm) deep, 9in (22.5cm) wide and 12in (30cm) high, with

$4\frac{1}{2}$in (11cm) insulation; ten bricks can be used to form the roof, giving $4\frac{1}{2}$in (11cm) insulation there also. A lid utilizing only six bricks laid horizontally and giving 3in (7.5cm) insulation will be sufficient, but a layer of fibre blanket laid over the top will ensure good heat retention where the bricks are not packed together tightly.

To close the kiln, the bricks forming the front, or the door of the kiln, can simply be stacked up. If vertical stacks can be fastened to form two individually movable doors, access will be easier, but for maximum ease both stacks can be joined using horizontal supports.

Bricks required to build the basic box		
Back and sides	16	HTI bricks
Front/door	8	HTI bricks
Roof	10	HTI bricks
	34	
Base (ideally)	10	HTI bricks
TOTAL	44	

ECONOMY VERSION

A cheap version of the simple front-loader kiln can be made using any available refractory bricks, or humble house bricks. The latter are not always so successful: they are liable to split apart as a result of uneven and excessive quick heating, they will take a long time to heat up in any case, and will form a much less efficient insulation. An inner facing of ceramic-fibre blanket could be added to overcome these problems; however, as the bricks are likely to be cheaper than the fibre itself, their damage or loss will hardly be a problem.

The Actual Firing

With biscuit-ware ready, and a kiln and fuel to hand, it is only necessary to check that you have all you need to carry out the firing. This includes:

- A reduction chamber. A large metal bucket, drum or old dustbin will be fine, depending on the size and quantity of the wares to be fired, together with a metal cover (dustbin lid); this should be filled to a third or a half full with sawdust, dead leaves or virtually any combustible (waste) material. Ensure that you can understand and deduce the controlling factors giving rise to the effects you will have produced by keeping everything simple – in other words, introduce only one factor at a time. So, see what effect is obtainable from sawdust alone before adding another combustible to the equation.
- Another bin/container with additional fuel.
- A container with water – metal for preference, as plastic buckets have been known to melt.
- Leather gauntlets such as old gardening gloves.
- Metal raku or blacksmith's tongs, to handle red-hot pots. Long handles are essential.

Insulating the Kiln from its Foundation

In spite of the fact that heat rises, the base or floor of any kiln gets almost as hot as its upper parts. It is therefore essential to insulate the kiln well from its foundation, whether it be constructed on the ground or on a bench. Concrete paving slabs will crack if not protected, and any wooden base will be an even more serious risk. A base of old house bricks will usually be all that is necessary, but to be on the safe side either ceramic-fibre blanket or board can be used in addition.

Raku is essentially a group activity, so have two or three friends to assist in placing and drawing the pots, lifting lids, adding combustibles and so on. It also tends to get rather frenetic, so brief everyone about safety before you start. Ensure that gloves are used when lifting lids, always ensure that propane gas-supply pipes are well away from sources of heat, and warn anyone putting red-hot pots into the reduction chamber to keep clear of the conflagration, as this can be quite dramatic.

Raku's universal appeal is due in part to the excitement of the process and the often unpredictable nature of results, but also to the fact that raku potters tend to evolve their own systems, equipment and preferences, becoming, as it were, their own experts. And so can you.

Some suggested glaze recipes are included in the glaze chapter (*see* page 174), and may serve as a starting point for developing your own. Ready-mixed glazes can be obtained from a supplier, are more easily stored than a range of raw ingredients, are reliable, but deny you the sense of achievement in making your own.

Fuming – a Variation on the Raku Process

The series of photographs that follows illustrates a technique refined and demonstrated by John Wheeldon; together with the captions, it is self-explanatory.

1. John Wheeldon's DIY gas kiln with the lid in place.

2. Spreading sawdust onto a kiln shelf, ready to receive hot pots.

3. Lifting out a fired pot with long-handled tongs.

4. View from another side.

5. Conflagration commences as soon as the pots are in contact with the sawdust.

6. More fine sawdust is sprinkled on, through a sieve.

7. *As each pot is added, a metal bin/reduction chamber, of suitable size, is lowered down and clamped up with more sawdust to seal the pots (and smoke) inside.*

8. *When reduced pots are not quite 'right' they are removed, again while still hot.*

9. *Supported and revolved on a banding wheel, and further heat applied.*

10. *Using a fan-tail flame.*

11. *The colour is 'washed' on with heat ...*

12. *... until the desired 'best' result is obtained.*

14 Personal Approaches

This chapter offers a glimpse into the working methods and thought processes of just a few contemporary ceramic artist-potters. In addition to the colour illustrations in this book, they have contributed insights into personal approaches that are often avant-garde and idiosyncratic. Traditional values and techniques are embraced, distended or extended to suit their own visions, these often broadening the boundaries of ceramic experience in some unique way. Their comments highlight and/or expand on ideas or themes suggested elsewhere in the text, and reflect the richness and breadth of the contemporary ceramic scene. Their accounts also reflect the fraternalistic generosity of a vast majority of potters, for they have been willing to share the products of their very significant hard work, successes and frustrations, a great deal of which goes unseen.

Bryony Burn

Fallowfield, Manchester

The initial designs for my vessels come from the studies of tropical fish. These include the tails, the fins and the way in which they move in the water. The colours and patterns of the vessels also originate from the markings of tropical fish. Much of my resource work has been done at Kew Gardens and the aquariums at London Zoo.

Recently, I have been drawing inspiration from the textile collection at Bankfield Museum, Halifax, where I have been working as an artist in residence.

I have had access to their archives, and have become particularly inspired by their collection of domestic textiles from the 1940s and 1950s.

All my work is slab-built. It is a technique that suits me as the building work is immediate. I make initial maquettes in card to help me achieve simple, controlled shapes for my vessels, and these are then used as templates. I roll the slabs by hand, as it is the easiest way to get a thin sheet of clay; the slabs are then left for a few hours to go leather hard. I clean up the slabs of clay with a metal or rubber kidney and then emboss the surface with stamps and texture. The shapes are then cut out with a template. I curve the clay around a cardboard tube and stand it up. Both sides are then scored, slipped and joined together. This is left again for another hour for the slip to dry off, after which the edges are neatened with a kidney and a surform. The bottom of the pot is then smoothed down using wet and dry paper to create a flat area for the base. I stick the pot down onto an oversized piece of clay, and do any trimming away after it has had a chance to bond together.

After being bisque-fired, each piece is hand-painted to ensure individuality. A coloured slip is poured inside and left to dry. A clear glaze is then poured in and the outsides are cleaned down. The surface is built up with layers of slips and glazes. These layers are often scratched away to reveal the clay, or written on to create depth and intrigue in the work. The text, if you can piece the words together, comes from different sources including poetry, songs and snippets of conversation.

Opposite *Square and spot pots, by Byrony Burn.*
Photo: Steve Teague

Richard Godfrey

Holbeton, near Plymouth, Devon

My decision to become a potter was initially motivated by the desire to spend my life doing something creative, making something that I could sell in order to earn a living. Now, after twenty-nine years as a professional potter, I still love the job. For me it is important to hang on to that original reason that sent me down this road: it was fun and seemed like a great way to earn a living. I had thought that architecture might be a rewarding career, indeed I had a place at York University, but a brief visit to an evening class where I had my first go on the wheel made me change my mind. I touched the clay and like so many others, I was instantly hooked. So now, all these years later, I am still a full-time potter, and getting the same buzz from going to work.

Teapot, by Richard Godfrey. Photo: Richard Godfrey

I now have a studio that looks out over the unspoilt coastline of South Hams. This coastline, the beaches and cliffs, the beautiful countryside with its winding lanes and lush hedgerows full of flowers and insects, are my inspiration and source of ideas. I love to search the beaches and coves after a storm looking for interesting objects. My studio is full of bits of plastic, metal and wood, seashells, bones and pieces of rock. I use these as starting points for drawings and doodles. I have a large table covered in polythene where I store clay slabs and extrusions that are ready for use, so I can try out an idea in clay without having to spend time on preparation.

The teapot in the illustration started life as a drawing of a shell, and as it was a bivalve, it had to have two spouts. The idea for the handle came from an Art-Deco sideboard, and the exhaust pipes just add the necessary visual balance. It is built out of two press-moulded halves, with extruded additions. The slabs are very thin, only about $\frac{1}{8}$in (4mm), so careful handling and support is necessary. I use a lot of old cushions to rest teapots on while the slabs firm up. The decoration was applied

using a range of brightly coloured engobes that I have developed over the last twelve years. These are sprayed, brushed, trailed and/or sponged onto the dry pot. The inspiration for the design comes from many different sources. The black and white arrow is from a drawing of a Jersey Tiger Moth, a spectacular visitor to the south Devon coast. Other elements include telegraph poles and wires, wild flowers and pieces of driftwood with chipped layers of paint.

Peter Hayes

Bath

For me, one of the most significant introductions to ceramics was digging Neolithic, Iron Age and Roman samien shards on archaeological digs somewhere in Wales while trying to survive as an art student in Birmingham.

I have always been interested in the history of ceramics – why and how 'things' are made in clay. This interest deepened after spending several years travelling through Africa working with various tribes and village potters, and being intrigued how, with limited technology and basic tools, they were able to achieve such exquisitely beautiful surfaces.

I found the same inherent skills in India, Nepal, Japan and New Mexico, and tried to adopt the ideas picked up from my travels in my own work. By building up layers of textured clay combined with burnishing and polishing of surfaces, I try to achieve opposites of rough and smooth. For the last two years I have been working on large-scale ceramic forms that I have placed in the landscape. My main aim is that the work should not compete with nature, but evolve within the environment. With this in mind, I have introduced other minerals into the 'Raku' ceramic surface, such as iron and copper. With the elements of time and erosion, the individual piece takes on its own developing surface.

In practice, I go by the seat of my pants. I have always worked in this way, and not by following any particular rules or methods. For instance, I like

Raku bows, by Alan Tabor. Photo: Alan Tabor

doing raku firing with completely the 'wrong' clay, which I know will crack or explode in the kiln (especially when wet). But when all the pieces are stuck together, and the surfaces ground down, it gives me a piece, a found object, with a pleasingly bruised and battered surface that has been carefully and lovingly honed down.

I also place pieces in the sea or the river bed next to the studio, to be forgotten about, then to be found and treasured again, or to be discarded.

I find it joyful to work with many different clay bodies, from bone china to crank. Each has its own character, its own limits, its own tolerance – some fight back, some play the game.

Finally, I think it is the clay that is in charge, and it will only let you make what it wants. It is my job to push it to its limits, and somehow an equilibrium is reached between maker and material.

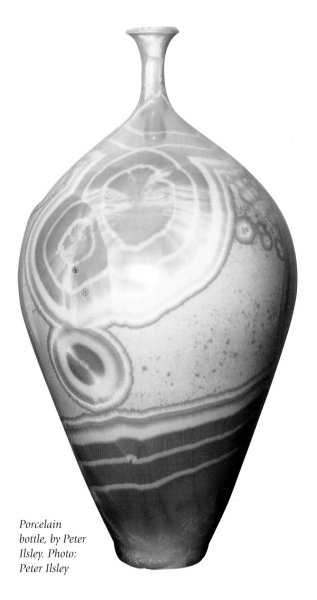

*Porcelain
bottle, by Peter
Ilsley. Photo:
Peter Ilsley*

Peter Ilsley

*Whilton Locks Pottery, Daventry,
Northamptonshire*

I have been a potter for almost forty years. I have concentrated on high-fired stoneware, which was ideal for the domestic/decorative ware and one-off sculptural pieces that I have always produced, though it was interspersed with various types of raku. In 1989 I made a total commitment to macro

crystalline glazes, using a white stoneware body and a porcelain body, used individually or in a 50/50 mix. Then in 1996 I discovered a porcelain that worked very well for me, and am still using the same body. My work schedule is currently divided into approximately 75 per cent crystalline work and 25 per cent stoneware, with a little raku. This is because I thoroughly enjoy the challenge of producing good crystalline pieces, not to mention their rarity and total unpredictability.

Crystalline glazes were discovered and developed by the large ceramic factories of Europe in the 1850s. They needed a pure white and smooth body, because impurities in the body and coarseness in the surface would encourage the crystals to seed and so spoil the finished piece. This is why porcelain has always been the preferred body, although a number of potters do use a smooth white stoneware, which can work almost as well.

Any method of manufacture can be used to create pots of crystalline glazes providing the surface is smoothed off, either when bone dry, or with carborundum paper after biscuit-firing. My work is mainly thrown bottles and bowls, although I do produce a small amount of slabbed ware and some tiles.

The bottles and bowls require a catcher: this is a little like an old-fashioned posy ring, in that the centre is the same diameter as the foot-ring of the pot, and the outer trough acts as a reservoir to catch the molten glaze as it runs off the bottom of the pot. Crystalline glazes must be as fluid as this, to allow the crystals to grow.

It is very important that the bulk of the glaze is applied to the top third of the piece – this can be up to 2mm thick. When the pots are taken from the kiln the catcher must be removed from the foot-ring; this is done by applying the flame from a needle-flame blow-lamp just below the joint, and expansion does the rest. The sharp edge of the glaze on the foot-ring is then ground down.

Firing crystalline glazes requires an oxidizing atmosphere, as reduction inhibits the crystal growth; this is why I choose to fire in a programmed electric kiln. The schedule is quite complex in that the temperature is taken up to peak between 1260° and 1300°C, the last 200°C being completed as fast as possible; this is to render the glaze fluid as quickly as possible. Having peaked, the temperature is reduced as quickly as possible by 200°C. This takes us down to the crystal growth band, which is approximately between 1100° and 975°C; and the pots are soaked in this band for anything between three and eight hours, to allow the crystals to grow and develop in the glassy matrix.

The body I use is called Audrey Blackman porcelain and is produced by 'Valentine Clay Products'.

A Typical Crystalline Glaze Recipe to be Fired at 1270°C

A base glaze	
Ferro frit 3110	44
Calcined zinc oxide	27
Flint	21
Titanium dioxide	8
Calcined alumina	0.5
Molochite	0.5
Finnfix	0.2

This glaze will give white crystals on a white background. However, the real joy starts when you play with colorants in the form of oxides. Try starting with 3 per cent copper carbonate, then do another test with 0.5 per cent cobalt carbonate. In the main the best results are when two or even three oxides or carbonates are used in the same glaze. Finnfix is a glaze adhesive/hardener that can be substituted with gums, arabic or tragacanth.

Hazel Johnston

Marton, Rugby

Like most potters, I played with raku for the fun of it. Then a few years ago I tried a sawdust firing and found that, for me, it balances the serious business

of my porcelain work with the fun and excitement of working without the pressures of exhibition deadlines.

My work for over twenty years now has been entirely in porcelain. It is a challenging clay to work with, but its luminous body and the enjoyment of its plastic qualities quite won me over.

I have always used electric kilns, and it is generally thought that glazes resulting from such a firing are entirely predictable. However, it doesn't have to be so. The glaze I use for my work provides constant surprises and sometimes disappointments, but I have stayed with it because of its ability to show visual texture whilst feeling beautifully smooth.

I enjoy the contrast between the cold, hard feel of high-fired porcelain and the soft, warm feel of a low-fired pot. Work can be made, and fired, for very little cost. A kiln such as the one I use, can be built from old house bricks.

The clay used needs to be suitable for burnishing, as this gives a smooth surface that is particularly receptive to smoke and vapour marks. I use my porcelain clay, then burnish before biscuit-firing in an electric kiln, giving me control at this stage. The sawdust kiln is made from sixty bricks sitting on a couple of 'side-by-side' paving slabs. Twelve bricks

Smoke-patterned pot, by Hazel Johnston. Photo: Simon Johnston

make about a 30in (75cm) square, and five such courses make the kiln walls. A metal sheet is an adequate cover, though metal dustbins and/or oil drums, perforated to let in the air, and dustbin lids would do just as well.

When packing the kiln, start with about 2in (5cm) of sawdust or shavings, then a layer of pots. I sprinkle salt and copper oxide as I am packing the kiln, and often spray copper oxide on the pots. Steel wool can give brown speckles, and copper wire linear marks. Banana skins, orange peel and so on, can be placed touching the work. Try anything! What I enjoy most of all is using seaweed to wrap around the pots: it can leave delicate rose-pink spots, or interesting negative shapes by masking the pot from smoke. Resisting the smoke is an area full of decorative possibilities. Dry clay shapes can be placed on flat forms. Biscuited clay or broken kiln shelves can be placed over, or alongside pots: this leaves a light area where they touch. Some potters use masking tape as a resist, thus introducing a more formal type of mark.

Cover the top layer of pots with sawdust. Light from the top, cover the fire, and leave it alone. Air moving between the bricks keeps it burning. Pots that you don't like can be biscuit-fired again before sawdust-refiring. Wash and apply beeswax.

Anticipation and excitement over unexpected results keeps one hooked on this type of firing.

Tony Laverick

Leek, Staffordshire

After studying ceramics at Preston Polytechnic (1981–84), I worked for a period of four years in the ceramic industry in Stoke-on-Trent. This included two years as a designer/product developer for Coalport China, part of the Wedgwood Group. This experience gave me a broader appreciation of ceramic forms and processes that previously I had dismissed as a student. When I set up in my own studio in 1988 my work was influenced by Pilkington's Royal Lancastrian, Bernard Moore, Royal Doulton's Chang and Flambe wares, the French potters Ernest Chaplet, August Delaherche and

Tall bottle (approximately 14in/36cm), by Tony Laverick. Photo: Tony Laverick

particularly Clement Massier, along with the work of the Zsolnay factory in Pecs, Hungary. I was also influenced by the work of contemporary British potters, including Alan Caiger-Smith, Derek Clarkson and Sutton Taylor.

The type of work I produce has changed a little over the last twelve years, the most obvious developments being in new techniques, which have allowed for greater expression. Form is of primary importance, and I feel there should be harmony and balance between the rim, neck, shoulder, belly and foot of the pot, giving it that 'right' feeling. The decoration as well as the form has historical references, and there is a constant play between three-dimensional volume and a two-dimensional illusion of space.

I have always been attracted to the hardness, permanence and feel of high-temperature porcelain: it is unlike anything else. Most of my work is thrown in one piece and turned, and all of my work is now fired in electric kilns: bisque to 1000°C, glaze to 1270°C, and re-fired five to six times at 750°C. I use a Valentine porcelain body with the following glaze:

Nepheline Syenite	70
Zinc Oxide	9
Whiting	9
Flint	10
Lithium Carbonate	2
China Clay	10
Titanium	2

I use many techniques to apply the different colours, most of these derived from liquid gold. I also use tin chloride, an ingredient frequently used by glass-makers, which is basically transparent but, depending on the colour underneath, iridizes the surface. The techniques I use mainly involve masking areas (usually with electrician's tape), spongeing, stamping and using brushes to decorate inside areas. I also use latex resist for masking out. Marbling is another technique that I have used.

Liquid Gold Preparation

The most important requirement of a metal used for ceramic decoration is the ability to resist oxidization. For this reason, only gold and platinum are used. Silver was used in the past, but on exposure to a sulphurous atmosphere it was found to tarnish quickly. The use of copper, similarly susceptible to oxidization, was also discontinued.

Liquid gold consists of a viscous solution of organo-metallic resonates in a mixture of solvents that may include turpentine, nitrobenzene (toxic and highly dangerous) and chloroform. The metals contained in the preparation are gold (10–12 per cent), rhodium (0.02–0.03 per cent), chromium (0.035–0.08 per cent) and bismuth (0.4–0.5 per cent). The procedure is to compound the various metallic resinates and then blend these with organic solvents to produce liquid preparations of various consistencies which, when applied and fired, will produce different decorative effects.

Basically, gold is being dissolved in acid with the addition of resins to produce a liquid gold that it is possible to burn. The resinates burn away, leaving a thin film of gold. This is achieved by heating a dilute neutral solution of gold chloride and a complex sulphur balsam compound, on a water or sand bath. During the heating, the metallic part of the gold salt is 'absorbed' by the sulphur balsam. The metallic resinate that this forms is then separated from the non-reacting part of the sulphur balsam, washed free of any acids left in solution, and then dissolved using either lavender oil, turps or synthetic resin solutions. Thinning agents such as turps can be used to vary the viscosity that will alter the fired colour. After firing, the gold deposited is brilliant and lustrous, with a thickness of 0.00005 to 0.000001in. The bismuth is used as a fluxing material, and is added to the liquid gold in order to 'fasten' to the body during firing and not rub off. It is firmly bonded at 600°C, but a rise in temperature means it is easily burnt away. The addition of rhodium and chromium resinates give more heat resistance and also make it more durable.

Whilst techniques, colours and so on are important as they can help to sell a piece (after all, I have to earn a living solely from the pots I sell), they are only 'dressing up' the form, which is the really important bit. No matter how nice the glaze/colour/effect is, if it is a badly made pot the result will still be a badly made pot (with a nice glaze!).

Roger Lewis

Bradford

Development of Ideas

Clay is a particularly good material for people, like me, who find it rewarding to develop ideas with a medium that they can get physically involved with. It is relatively cheap, it can be re-used (so long as it has not been fired), and some of the processes are relatively immediate. It is not surprising that there is considerable historical evidence of it having been used to imitate other materials. Its versatility of use – thick or thin, soft or stiff, worked by hand or tool – can signal many potential directions worthy of investigation. Exploring this natural versatility is a good way to develop ideas for ceramics. My main motivation for using clay is the excitement of making discoveries based on experimental investigation into the way it responds to manipulation. When these discoveries are unexpected, I have a strong feeling that the resulting work is more likely to be original.

Frog pot, by Roger Lewis. Photo: Roger Lewis

A large part of my work is the result of exploring ideas developed out of experimenting with thin sheets of clay. My working method is similar to a journey: it is always exciting to see what is round the next corner, but at the same time there are always favourite places to go back to that can sometimes be seen afresh. About fifteen years ago my journey took me to a point where I was folding over thin sheets of clay to produce double-skinned forms that had decorative windows cut out of the front surface. Even at that time, I had to be careful to put pinholes in any area that was likely to capture an air pocket.

Later, when I was improving a zigzag-shaped window, I folded back the clay in a way that resulted in the formation of triangular cushions – these definitely needed pin holes to stop them exploding in the kiln. I soon realized that I could make bigger forms by making these cushions of air-filled clay individually, and then fastening them together like patchwork. The cushions were blown up with a straw and sealed at the edges by the pressure of a thin stick. I decided to try a stick that had a decorative edge. This produced an interesting effect, so I tried cutting out images in thin sheet wood to press into the clay cushion to give a kind of instant modelling.

The basic form for these pots with pictorial elements was a box. However, I felt that the appearance of these needed softening, so I started to add rims made with elongated cushions of clay. I became attracted to these simple rims, and realized that they offered a new direction to explore. I started by using some of the wooden templates that I had made for the pictorial pots, to produce shaped, panelled cushions of clay. Several of these were joined together to produce one form. The resulting work was of a different character, and took me back into a more three-dimensional area of work. As the work progressed, new, simplified templates were cut. Even slight changes to these, either in the profile or the way they are used, results in pots of subtly different character.

There are several other facets to my work. One of these is the geometric work that led to the discovery of cushions in the first place; another has some relation to textile cushions and upholstery in general.

Working Method

Initially my working method involves experimenting freely with clay until an interesting direction reveals itself. Work then proceeds in a simple but logical way – each subsequent manipulation with the clay is a development from the last. At such stages it is important not to try to make a finished piece of work – to do so would cut the inventive process short and probably result in work that is preconceived. However, a point emerges naturally, where development into final forms is appropriate.

The process of solving technical problems can prompt new work. Because of this, I alternate between developmental work, producing thematic variations in areas of interest that have emerged from initial exploration, and refining older forms.

Technical Information

The clays that I currently use are Potclays White Stoneware (1145) (for medium and larger work) and Potclays Fraser Porcelain (1149) (for smaller work); I use an electric kiln. The work is biscuit-fired to 1000°C, and glaze varies between cone 8 and cone 9, depending on the glaze used. I use too many glazes to mention (and they keep changing).

Karen Lyons

Nottingham

I have recently established my own workshop in Nottingham after graduating with a degree in Decorative Arts, from the School of Art & Design, Nottingham Trent University, where I explored and experimented with the process of slip casting. As an undergraduate, I utilized this process to produce a series of sculptural ceramics, some of which have an ambivalent functional/non-functional nature. I regard myself to be at the beginning of what I hope will be a long and rewarding career as a ceramicist, and in particular as an explorer of that medium.

Ideas are largely inspired by nature. I draw on

Two tall bottle forms, by Karen Lyons. Photo: Karen Lyons

matter as diverse as shells and other sea life, as well as cacti and stones. It is through the painting and drawing of these that ideas are triggered. Drawing is, for me, an integral and exciting part of the development of designs, and it is an activity about which I am passionate. Designs are primarily concerned with scale, and the ability of forms to stand alone as interesting artefacts, whilst often working in a group at the same time. I find that the forms develop throughout the making process; this is most evident when plaster models are constructed. They are turned on a lathe, and are often further manipulated and carved by hand. Alterations and adaptations can also occur when casts are removed from the moulds.

I use a white earthenware body to cast with, and the cast is then left in the mould for approximately twenty-four hours. It is then removed from the mould, and dried slowly over a number of days to reduce the possibility of cracking. After sanding to remove visible joining lines, the cast is bisque-fired in an electric kiln to 1100°C.

Recently I have been experimenting with stained engobes as a means of colouring the forms. In particular I am drawn to the dry, matt and even covering that they produce, which has the interesting texture of sprayed and unfired glaze. This surface adds to the sculptural forms, as they remain porous even after firing. Colour plays an important part in my work, and I have recently been using a range of subtle and neutral tones teamed up with others that are denser and more intense. Contrasting colours are placed on the inside and outside, highlighting differences in inner and outer form. The forms are masked off, and engobe is sprayed onto the bisque-fired ware, which is fired to 1100°C; the process is then repeated.

Jim Malone

Ainstable, Cumbria

Most of the things that have influenced me have been oriental – glazes, techniques, forms, even kiln design; however, it has always been particularly important that mediaeval jugs have influenced me a lot because I am English, and they are a home-grown product. Early on, the intriguing and frustrating thing about them was the fact that to make a tall jug you obviously need a certain amount of throwing skill, and when you start out you don't have it – obviously it develops as time goes by. So, for example, you can make quite nice bowls, let's say, without a great deal of skill; in fact with these, skill often gets in the way, because it can become slick and that's something to be guarded against – but you can't get away from it. In order to make a tall pitcher or a tall bottle, you need a certain amount of throwing skill just to lift the clay. I used to see photographs of Bernard Leach's jugs or mediaeval jugs and think, I want to make something like that, and couldn't do it, or else they were terribly heavy; and so it became a challenge really very early on to make good jugs.

The clay body that I use most is high in both fire-clay and iron with added sand, and for bigger pots, grog. The clay is blunged and dewatered, pugged and stored for use. In addition, I use a fine white ball-clay body for more delicate items.

Jim Malone seated with his pots. Photo: Alex McErlain

My wheel is really a Korean/continental hybrid. It demands sensitivity in use, and for larger pots, patience. It means you have to coax the clay to do what is required – you cannot force it. These pots have a certain character that is just not obtainable on any other sort of wheel. I have never used an electric wheel in my life, except when obliged to do so, for instance in a demonstration situation.

I have two white slips in use at present, one for normal slipping use, and the other, thicker and whiter, for hakeme. In addition I use two ochre slips, one a Cornish ochre, the other a Cumbrian one. I have also been known to use – though it is very seldom these days – a red clay slip. Currently I use three black or high iron glazes, an ash glaze that employs a local granite, and two other (lighter) ash glazes, each with its own special character. Other than this, there is a transparent ash glaze for use over hakeme, and a ying ch'ing celadon. These are my standard glazes, but sometimes I mix up a 'special' glaze as a result of my continuing tests with local clays and suchlike.

Glazes principally make use of various wood ashes blended with local granite or feldspar and clays. The majority of glazes are based on three basic ideas:

- blends of granite, ash and clay in the ratio of 2:2:1;
- blends of feldspar, ash and clay in equal parts;
- blends of ash and one other material in equal parts.

By applying the glaze over different clays, over different slips, and in varying thickness, a very wide range of effects can be achieved.

I use an oriental climbing kiln. It is the third one I have built, and its design has been modified according to my experiences with the previous two (it retains the virtues whilst I have eliminated some of the faults). The last two were fired with wood alone, whilst this one has two oil burners on the front of the first chamber only. Each chamber has about 50cu ft capacity, and the whole kiln takes twenty hours or more to reach cone 11 all round. Chamber one is taken up to 1000°C on the oil burners, after preheating with wood the previous day.

At that point I may go on to wood, or I may not, depending on what is in the kiln (some glazes do not react well with fly ash). In any case, the chamber is finished with wood in order to spread the heat. When chamber one reaches cone 11, chamber two will be about 1000°C from the exhaust heat, and is finished with wood alone. There is a temperature variance within each chamber, and also an atmospheric range from heavy reduction through neutral and on to oxidized. I try to make creative use of these factors, but it involves careful planning at the start of each making.

Making sessions are usually quite long, and it is my practice to biscuit-fire both chambers, glaze all the work, and then glaze-fire both chambers. Glazed work left over will accumulate over a year, and then give an additional kiln-load free, as it were. Making can go on for anything up to three months, and this is done deliberately so that considerations of technique can be forgotten and I can concentrate all of my energies creatively. The best pots tend to make themselves. The quiet space within, from which pots come, can very easily be destroyed by constant interruption – deliveries, low-flying aircraft – and when this happens I will spend a day or two in the garden, or make some clay, or carry out some other menial task until quietness returns and making can resume.

Honey jar, earthenware, approximately 7 × 4.5in (18 × 11cm), by Sarah Monk. Photo: John Meredith

Sarah Monk

Eastnor Pottery, Ledbury, Hertfordshire

I am a potter who specializes in breakfast ware, designed to start the day on a cheery note! For this reason I choose to work in white earthenware clay. Once fired, the whiteness of the bisque provides the perfect canvas for my bright 'sunshine' yellow glaze.

Pretty much everything I make is functional. It gives me great pleasure when customers express their delight in regularly using my work. My product range at present is made up of thirty-five items, and these are usually made in small batches. The objects in it include toast racks, egg cups, lemon squeezers, cutlery drainers and ceramic spoons.

Inspiration is drawn in part from nature, and also from an interest in Victorian art pottery. My father collects antique china, so I grew up surrounded by weird and wonderful objects from history. An ornate ceramic wig stand from the Victorian era comes to mind!

The decorative images drawn from nature are slightly stylized, often humorous, cartoon-like representations. Again, my intention is to put a smile on the face of the user.

I employ a variety of techniques to produce my work. Jugs, mugs and bowls start their life on the potter's wheel. After turning, the leather-hard ware is decorated with bees, bugs and other grubs. These are press-moulded in tiny plaster sprig-moulds, and attached using the scratch and slip method.

I enjoy working with plaster, often devoting one or two days a month to sprig-mould development. Firstly I make a series of low-relief clay models. I then surround each model with wet clay walls, and seal all the joints. The plaster is mixed, then poured into all the models at the same time, and left to set. When the plaster is 'cheesy' I remove the clay and carefully fettle each individual mould to remove all undercuts. The fettling process takes quite a long time, and a number of 'dry runs', with scrap clay being pressed into the mould to check release. When I am satisfied, the plaster mould is dried thoroughly and put into production.

The rest of my work is slab-built. Initially the clay is rolled into large sheets, then card templates are used to cut the wet slab to produce enough sides for a butter dish, or whatever it is I am making. The elements are left to go leather hard, and then assembled. Sprigs, bolls and modelled finials are attached, and the completed piece left to dry.

I bisque-fire to 1120°C, dip-glaze in yellow, and finally brush on blues, greens and reds in selected areas. The pots are then glaze-fired to 1080°C.

John Pollex

Plymouth, Devon

My work is made with a white earthenware clay, biscuit-fired to 1050°C, and glaze-fired to 1120°C. Most of the work is thrown, and then the shapes are altered whilst the pots are still soft: this is done either by lifting the pot and then gently dropping it, or by striking it with pieces of wood. After the alterations have been made, the pot is further assembled by adding handles, spouts and the like. Once this has been accomplished, it is then covered with a black slip.

My ideas for decoration are mainly derived from the study of abstract paintings, my major influences

Square dish, 11.5 × 11.5in (29 × 29cm) 'La Promesa', by John Pollex. Photo: John Pollex

being the works of Howard Hodgkin, Robert Natkin, Patrick Heron, Ben Nicholson and Hans Hofmann. First I apply coloured slips with a variety of sponges, then I use brushes to bring a more painterly quality to the surface. I consider each pot as a painting regardless of scale, the object being to make each one different. The use of a transparent glaze completes the process.

Mike Powers

Powers Pottery, Ruddington, Nottinghamshire

I like the idea of pots being deceptively useful. Because the work is so highly decorative, I am often asked if they can be used. First and foremost the pot must serve a purpose and do it well, i.e. lids must fit, spouts must pour, handles must feel comfortable, and the pot must feel balanced.

Once utility has been resolved, then I can go mad with the brushes and slip trailers. The decoration can be described as abstract/floral. I've borrowed from different sources, remembering the

Stoneware pots, by Mike Powers, on display at Powers Pottery. Photo: Doug Wensley

adage 'to borrow from one source is plagiarism, to borrow from many is research'. Thus there is Dutch delft, Japanese and a touch of Spanish/Moorish, filtered through a peasant Irish sensibility, which tends towards over-decoration, a trait I haven't cured in seventeen years.

I work with a thrower, Chris Marsden, who fulfils all the above criteria, leaving me to concentrate on the decoration and firing procedure.

I use two main glazes; both are feldspathic bases but with different opacifiers – zircon for white and titanium for oatmeal-style. Both have been formulated to cope with the high temperature and heavy reduction, and, vitally, not to craze; a cardinal sin, in my opinion.

I glaze the pot by dipping, even the large pieces. The outside of the pot is glazed first to ensure an even layer for the decoration.

With stoneware the bases must be clear, and I use a glaze mat to wipe the bases of the pots. It is basically two layers of sponge, one dense sheet pinned to the table, and another thinner layer that is kept wet; when it becomes saturated with glaze from the pots, it is simply rinsed and re-used.

After the glaze has dried, the pots are banded; this is carried out on an old kick wheel for speed. This is an important start, as I am effectively creating set spaces and filling them in. I have a basic design, which I hold in my head and modify to suit the pot. After banding I do the brushwork, using different brushes: Japanese, flat liners, sign writers and even glaze mops for filling in.

I then add the colours, which are slip-trailed on. They are base glazes with colouring oxides, to give yellow, green, orange and red. I've modified the slip trailers to give me a much thinner line. The copper-red berries are 'dobbed' on using a specially widened nozzle, as it has to be applied so thickly. All the decoration is applied onto the dried glaze to keep the colours bright.

The use of copper red dictates the firing cycle. I have a 30cu ft gas-fired kiln, and I have to start the reduction early to 'catch' the copper, about 980°C. I have the flue heavily dampened, and the air to the burners cut right back for the fist hour, then a light reduction until reaching cone 9. I then turn off and push the damper in. It takes about twenty-four hours to cool down. A good firing is one in which all the copper glaze has come out a rich ruby red. Every time I open up the kiln I am reminded of Mick Casson's advice, that 'decorated pots sell': thanks again, Mick!
www.powerspottery.co.uk

Fran Tristram

West Bridgford, Nottinghamshire

I set up Lady Bay Pottery in 1993 after completing the old ceramics HND at Derby College of Higher Education. At the time I was producing single-fired, wheel-thrown domestic stoneware with zircon white glaze and sponged, brushed and trailed over-glaze decoration. I started decorating in response to

Tall jug, by Fran Tristram. Photo: Rod Bailey

a challenge when still at college, and continued for seven years!

My formative years were dominated by the seventies wholemeal aesthetic, so the work that drew me to clay in the first place was much earthier and more natural. I love the timelessness of weathered surfaces in nature – the way the directional blast of the elements polishes one face of a rock, while seaweed or moss grow on the sheltered side – a natural counter-balance that I see mirrored in Japanese Oribe ware. I was drawn to the Leach tradition through early exposure to Michael Cardew's work; a distant family connection to Cardew made him a romantic figure in my imagination long before I had any interest in working with clay myself. I love the warm flashing of wood-fired work, and the natural embrace of salt glaze on surface; although living in the suburbs of Nottingham I can't reasonably indulge in such dirty habits! These are the aesthetics that I wanted to celebrate, but not to imitate, in developing my new style of work.

Glaze development can be a long and arduous task, especially when it has to fit in with your production routine; I was lucky to hit upon a glaze that suited me quite quickly.

Working with a new surface treatment liberated my approach to form. From dedication to pure function (shapes stripped down to the bare essentials, the better to wear their decoration) I have broken some of my own taboos, developing a range of wheel-thrown sculptural ideas, and – prompted by the potter's plague, back pain – adding some slab-work and also pinched work to my domestic range.

All my work continues to be single fired, the glazes applied to the unfired pot when completely dry. I glaze the insides by pouring as I always have, but rather than dipping or pouring the outside glaze, as with the zirconium, my current work is sprayed. Before I took up spraying I believed it to be an easy option; now I see that it is far more time-consuming than a single dip, and it takes experience to judge the correct thickness of glaze – and I'm still learning.

Pots are wheel-thrown in white St Thomas stoneware body, and fired in gas reduction to 1300°C. The basic glaze recipe is:

Potash Feldspar	12
Whiting	27
China Clay	23
Red Clay	13
Borax Frit	1

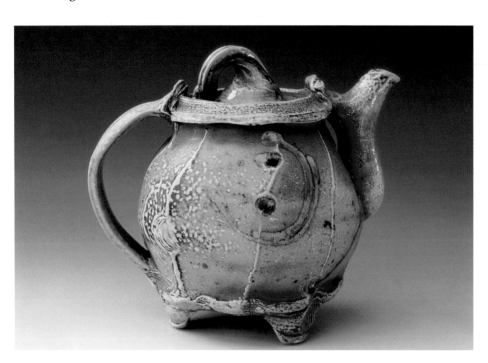

Teapot on three feet, by Ruthanne Tudball. Photo Ruthanne Tudball

Ruthanne Tudball

Earley, Reading, Berkshire

For me, manipulating soft clay on a revolving wheel and feeling the material respond to the merest touch is like setting out on an exciting journey. The dialogue that goes on between the maker and the clay is carried on through the use of the pottery, in as much as you pour, you eat, you store, you serve and you drink from them.

All of my work is thrown and manipulated while wet on the wheel. In an attempt to capture the soft, organic quality of the clay and to preserve it in the finished piece, I do very little turning (trimming), and when trimming is done, it happens at the soft side of leather hard. After firing and transforming the clay to stone, that softness can still be seen. Sodium vapour glazing emphasizes the marks and rhythms of making, picks out every line. Spouts and lips for pouring, handles to invite lifting and balance, feet for stability and elegance – these are all aspects of looking at function and sharing with others, which hold my attention when making pots. My inspiration comes from the natural world around me, and the energy in the evolving landscape, celebrating the rhythms and creative forces of the earth and the human body. Drawing, particularly life drawing, is an essential activity for me in the training of my eye and the development of my inner sense of form.

My work is raw-fired in a 27cu ft gas kiln to cone 10 (about 1300°C). Most of it is stoneware, although I do occasionally use porcelain. I use 1.3kg of sodium bicarbonate sprayed into the kiln, starting at 1260°C (cone 8) and spraying a small amount every 15 minutes until all of the soda is gone. The kiln is soaked for about one hour at the firing at top temperature while re-oxidizing. Rapid cooling ceases at about 950°C, when the kiln is sealed up, and left for two days before unpacking.

Carlos van Reigersberg-Versluys

Vine Farm Pottery, Stamford, Lincolnshire

For inspiration, I am indebted to the times I have spent in the arid, bleached landscapes of Africa, Asia and the Mediterranean, and some of the simplicity of that parched beauty has, I hope, trickled into what I make. I approach my work intuitively, and sometimes accidents reveal new creative directions.

I carve directly into the wet clay at the wheel using simple hand-made tools. These forms are further manipulated or stretched until their edges

Vase with handles, stoneware, Carlos Versluys. Photo: Carlos Versluys

begin to tear. I am interested in texture that is integral to the vessel, and I use layers of dry ash glaze to accentuate this. I produce individual, related forms. My work is reduction fired to 1300°C.

I have exhibited both in the UK and abroad. I currently have my studio at home on the Lincolnshire/Cambridgeshire border.

Doug Wensley

Papplewick, Nottinghamshire

After a predominantly Fine Art-based training as a sculptor, it was a revelation to realize the potential of ceramics. The immediacy of clay, fired to permanence (relatively speaking) without the need of complicated intermediate processes, and its directness and spontaneity were, and continue to be, greatly attractive. I am interested in the arbitrary nature of casual hand-building, the feeling of drawing with clay, and allowing surface and form to grow 'according to the laws of chance'. My work reflects a preoccupation with eroded forms as found in the landscape, and variations on the human form. It attempts to examine the assumed permanence of form in medium and manner, these incorporating metamorphosis and change.

For refined, modestly sized sculptural pieces I usually use T-material; more robust structures are built with heavily grogged raku bodies. I have also used fireclay and locally dug brick clays. The latter are cheap and totally unreliable, but they do occasionally produce spectacular eruptions of colour from the unpredictable impurities contained therein. I sometimes use integral plinths, resins and cold-cast metals as appropriate to the piece.

Work is usually fired to stoneware, cone 8 or 9, after biscuiting the pieces, partly to ensure that any weaknesses are identified in the first firing, partly to enable oxides to be applied to the piece without disrupting the surface of the clay. Most are fired in an oxidizing atmosphere in a 5cu ft (0.14cu m) top-loading electric kiln ideally suited to my work. For

Turquoise torso form, 'T' material, stoneware fired, by Doug Wensley. Photo: Doug Wensley

reduction firing I have a twin-burner propane-gas kiln.

Surface texture/pattern is often emphasized by washes of usually manganese or cobalt oxide, allowed to settle in the crevices and joins. An iron-bearing matt glaze is applied over, and often this is covered with light coats of body stains applied with a sponge, deposited mainly on raised surfaces.

John Wheeldon

Wirksworth, Derbyshire

My first contact with ceramics was unplanned. I became interested in graphics at school, and subsequently enrolled on a foundation course at Chesterfield College of Art. It soon became apparent that, compared to graphics, the pottery facilities were rather more exciting, and the pottery tutors

Two fumed pots, by John Wheeldon. Photo: Doug Wensley

much nicer. I was enthralled by the atmosphere, fascinated by activities that included building and firing kilns, and drawn to the altogether more attractive social life. So, after completing the foundation course, I stayed on for another year, concentrating on ceramics and drawing before taking a place on a mixed media degree course at Wolverhampton.

The Wolverhampton course here included a considerable element of industrial processes, which I found fascinating, including the industry's tendency to shroud some materials and processes in secrecy, closely guarded, presumably from competitors, but sadly also from studio potters. We can learn much from industry and its huge resource of technical and scientific expertise.

My early work was influenced by the traditional Leach, studio pottery approach, by contemporary movement away from it, and by the more industrial thinking encountered at Wolverhampton. I made stoneware, reduced but not brush-decorated, and developed forms that moved away from the traditional. I developed a method of spongeing coloured glazes onto a pale oatmeal/white base glaze together with a range of shapes on which to decorate.

Then in the early eighties the work changed, when I began using a similar (rubber) stamping method to apply lustres onto a black body. These pots were richer, decorative rather than utilitarian, and more expensive; but more appealing in the currently subdued economic climate.

The move away from lustres towards raku technology seemed to arise in part because I needed to change direction, something which, in my case, seems to occur in approximately ten-year cycles. The spontaneous nature of this process, particularly as far as decoration is concerned, was also a factor. In other words, the attraction was that raku seemed to be freer, although it has now become just as controlled; I had to develop that in order to determine – at least to an extent – colour, for example. So the process appears to be a lot less critical now, even though there is still more to learn, especially with the larger, flat forms.

The ten years seem now to be coming round, and I am hankering for the next thing. This will probably involve an up-grading of the raku principle (for practical convenience) and a shift towards earthenware. But watch my space.

Technical Notes

Pots are thrown, and allowed to become leather hard. They are then decorated with slip, and dried out thoroughly before biscuit-firing to 950°C.

A 'glaze' consisting of 90 per cent copper oxide (black), 10 per cent frit, with added glaze suspender, is applied by pouring and dipping.

Firing is in a gas-fired, top-loading raku kiln, and is to about 1070°C; various factors contribute here, such as type of clay, pyrometer and thermocouple, and even the weather. The critical thing is to fire as high as possible before the glaze melts. It is therefore important to become familiar with all the idiosyncrasies of the kiln, flame and so on.

The ideal body is white stoneware; it needs to be able to withstand all the trauma. The colour response is better than a terracotta or grey clay, and reduction is critical.

Glossary

agate ware Made from a stratified mixture of different coloured clays.

alumina Aluminium oxide (Al_2O_3), highly refractory, reduces drying shrinkage in raw clay.

bat Highly refractory shelf for kilns: plaster or wooden circular base on which to throw open forms.

bat wash Protective coating to the kiln shelves consisting of two parts alumina hydrate to one part china clay.

bentonite Primary clay from decomposed volcanic ash, which is fine and very plastic. Used to introduce plasticity into clay bodies and aid suspension in glaze mixes; add 2 per cent to bodies and 1 per cent to glazes. As an aid to raw glazing, add up to 10 per cent, thereby replacing china clay.

bloating Trapped gases in the body cause blistering in stoneware or between slip and body in earthenware.

blunger Container with mechanized paddle wheels used for preparing mixtures of clay and water as casting slip.

borax Hydrated borate or sodium, a chief source of boric acid for glazes. It is soluble in water, so is used in fritted form.

borax frit A frit made with borax and silica. Used with feldspars and clays to produce leadless glazes.

bung A stack of saggars packed vertically and containing wares requiring protection from direct flame, or to generate local atmospheric conditions within the saggars. Sometimes confused with a vent plug.

burnishing Rubbing the surface of clay or slip to polish it. Usually makes use of a smooth pebble, spoon or similar tool, causing compression and consolidation of the surface.

calcine Carbon dioxide and chemical water driven off by subjecting ceramic substances to moderate heat ($350-700°C$).

carbon soak Kiln temperature held at about $900°C$ for thirty minutes or more to facilitate oxidization.

deflocculant A sodium silicate or sodium carbonate solution. A few drops added to the glaze assists application to vitrified wares, retards the settling of glaze and slip, and results in harder setting when dry.

deflocculation The addition of soluble alkalis called deflocculants to slips and glazes to enable the creation of mixes containing smaller proportions of water. Advantageous in formulating casting slips and glazes capable of adhering to non-porous surfaces.

dunting Cracks in a pot resulting from stress during firing or cooling and caused mainly by silica inversions at $226°C$ and $573°C$. Crack occurring during firing up will have soft edges where glaze has melted later; cracks will have very sharp glazed edges when occurring during cooling.

elephant's ear A natural sponge of fine texture, flattish in shape and about 5in (12.5cm) across. Excellent for press-moulding.

enamel A soft melting glass coloured with oxides and used to decorate ceramics, metal and glass. Onglaze enamels are usually used by potters.

engobe Also vitreous slip. A covering for clay, which, like a slip, can be used as a vehicle for oxides. It usually contains glaze materials, will be more vitreous than the body it covers, but does not fire to a glassy state. Being neither simply clay (slip) nor glaze, it applies to any covering mix which falls somewhere between the two.

faience Colourful decoration or glaze used on earthenware.

feldspar Also felspar or fieldspar. They contain alumina, silica and alkalis, and are natural frits or glazes.

fettle To fettle is to trim off excess clay on leather-hard or dry clay, as in removing seam marks from slip-cast pots.

fireclay Often refractory clay that is associated with coal measures. Used for firebricks. Usually contains volatile impurities.

firing The process by which clay is changed into ceramic material, i.e. pottery.

flashing Coloration and fusion caused by volatiles settling on pots during firing. Considered by some to add interest, but by others as an unwelcome detraction.

flint SiO_2. Main source of silica, is a variety of quartz. Insoluble and chemically inert. Serious health hazard in powder form. Avoid use if at all possible.

friable Crumbling; easily broken up.

galena Also lead ore and lead sulphide (PbS). Dangerous source of lead oxide; should not be used.

grog Refractory material, usually consisting of fired and ground fireclay. Used as a filler to open the clay and reduce shrinkage.

high thermal insulation (HTI) brick Modern replacement for the less energy-efficient refractory brick in kiln linings.

impressed decoration Decoration pressed or stamped into the clay using wood, metal or biscuit implements.

inversions – silica Changes to the form of silica giving rise to sudden expansion or contraction of the body. The processes take place at 225 °C and 573 °C and are exactly reversible.

kaolin Also china clay ($Al_2O_3.2SiO_2.2H_2O$). Contains no impurities, and is valued for its whiteness, its high alumina content making it highly refractory. Lacks plasticity but is used to introduce silica and alumina to glazes.

kiss Occurs when two pots become connected in the kiln by fused glaze. After separation, the scars are known as kiss marks.

kneading Rolling and stretching plastic clay to homogenize it. Usually done on a plastic or concrete wedging bench or slab.

lead frit Also fritted lead or lead silicate. The most popular is lead bisilicate, widely used in earthenware glazes as a flux with smaller quantities of china clay, feldspar.

levigation A process that allows heavy particles to settle out while lighter ones remain in suspension in a slip.

line-blending A practical way of testing requirements for glaze recipes.

low sol Also low solubility. Glazes and frits containing lead oxide with a solubility rating of less than 5 per cent (UK standard).

lug Projection on a pot that acts as a handle.

lustre The metallic surface on glazes, involving reduction from compounds to pure metal, either applied deliberately or arising accidentally as in raku reduction processes.

lute Joining two pieces of leather-hard clay and slip for fine bodies.

marbling The partial blending of two different coloured clays to produce a variegated stain.

marl Natural red earthenware clays containing high proportions of calcium compounds.

matting agent A ceramic compound added to glazes to give matt surfaces after firing.

mochaware Decoration applied at the wet-slip stage by a rapid dispersal of alkaline liquid and pigment into the slip.

muffle Chamber made of refractory material inside a fuel-burning kiln that protects ware from direct contact with gases and flames.

once-firing Applying glaze and firing raw pots without an initial biscuit-firing.

opacifier Used to make glazes opaque. The most widely used is tin oxide, although other oxides can also be used.

oxidization Kiln atmosphere with an adequate oxygen supply.

plastic Malleable; can be modelled and reworked.

plasticity Has the capability to be manipulated, retaining its shape as it is modelled.

porosity The ability of biscuit ware to absorb moisture.

primary clay Clays that remain in their place of origin – for example, China clay.

pyrometer Used to record temperatures within a kiln.

quartz *See* **flint**, above.

reactive glaze The softer of the two glazes combined by fluxing after application over or under the harder glaze.

reactive slip As with most engobes, this is fusible, thereby creating a patterned, textured or mottled appearance with its covering glaze.

reduction Reduced oxygen supply in a kiln atmosphere, which causes changes to the colour of bodies and glazes. The combustion process is effectively reduced to 'stealing' oxygen from compounds contained within the wares; so Fe_2O_3, for example, is reduced to $2FeO$, the O_2 being used up by the fire.

refractory Resistant to high temperatures; will not melt at normal ceramic firing temperatures.

saggar A fireclay container used to protect ware from flashing when there are no muffles in a kiln.

salt glaze Characteristic 'orange peel' surfaced glaze formed by introducing salt into a hot kiln. Not environmentally friendly; see also sodium glaze.

sgraffito To carve or scratch through a slip to reveal the colour of the clay body beneath.

shales Compacted clays, characterized by a flaking tendency.

silica Chemical formula SiO_2; a fundamental oxide of glasses and glazes. Sixty per cent of the Earth's crust consists of silica, so it is usually easy to find and pure. Melts at $1,713\,°C$.

silk screen A printing process using stencils supported on a nylon or silk screen.

slip Clay with water added to make a creamy consistency. Used to coat clay bodies for decorative purposes. Colour can be added in the form of oxides.

sodium glaze Using bicarbonate of soda (sodium bicarbonate) instead of salt (sodium chloride) avoids the production of chlorine gas which converts to hydrochloric acid when in contact with a damp atmosphere, causing acid rain.

terra sigillata A very fine-grained precipitated slip used as a surface coating prior to burnishing or as a decorative medium.

underglaze Oxides modified by the addition of small quantities of glaze (flux) and assisting adhesion to the biscuit-fired body to which they are applied prior to being covered by transparent glaze.

vent A small opening in a kiln wall to ventilate the firing chamber, usually circular or square in section. Used to assist adjustment of the kilns atmosphere.

vent plug Often referred to as the bung, and used to close or open the vent.

vitreous slip Slip containing some flux to enhance the vitrification process.

vitrification The point at which a clay body begins to lose its porosity when fired.

vitrify Fired successfully to the point where fluxing takes place between the feldspathoids and the free silica in the clay body without deformation. Vitrified wares are virtually non-porous.

Appendix I

Toxic Raw Materials

Care should be exercised when using and handling the following materials. (Bold headings refer to basic materials that are toxic; compounds that contain the basic materials as a constituent are listed after the headings.)

aluminium oxide Feldspar, clay
antimony Antimony oxide
barium Barium carbonate, barium oxide
boron Borax (sodium borate), boric acid, calcium borate frit, colemanite
cadmium Cadmium compounds
calcium oxide Whiting, dolomite
chromium Chromium oxide
cobalt Cobalt oxide, cobalt carbonate
fluorine Fluorspar (calcium fluoride) traces in minerals. To remove fluorine from the kiln atmosphere, good kiln room ventilation is essential
leads, raw Lead carbonate, lead oxide (red lead), lead sulphide (galena), litharge (yellow lead)
lithium oxide Spodumene, lepidolite.
magnesium oxide Magnesite, dolomite talc
manganese Manganese compounds (such as manganese dioxide) are also regarded as injurious to health
nickel Nickel oxide
selenium Selenium compounds
silicon Quartz (sand), flint, cristobalite (also present in free silica in most clays)
sodium oxide Soda feldspar, pearl ash, nitre (soda nitre)
strontium Strontium oxide, strontium carbonate
titanium oxide Rutile
vanadium Vanadium pentoxide
zinc Zinc oxide

Hazardous Combinations

While many potters use what are now called 'low-solubility lead frits', which by themselves do not present a health hazard, they can become toxic with the addition of certain oxides, such as copper and chromium. This can greatly increase the lead solubility and hence the health risk, especially if acid foods are stored in receptacles glazed in this way. The reason for their continued use in glazes is that they give a wide firing range, a low melting range, smoothness and a high gloss. They also give enriching qualities to colours and, if used correctly, are highly acid-resistant.

The compounds of barium, antimony and zinc are also toxic by nature, and most of the basic colouring oxides, such as copper, manganese, cadmium and cobalt, tend to be toxic. Regular mopping up and vacuuming is the best protection against these health hazards. Rubber gloves should be worn when handling soda compounds that are not fritted, and some form of respiratory mask should be worn whenever you are handling powdered glaze materials.

If in doubt, contact the supplier, who is responsible for labelling all raw materials appropriately, and will be pleased to provide additional information or clarification.

Appendix II
Bending Temperatures

Bending temperature of Harrison and Orton cones at a temperature rise of 150° centigrade per hour

Temperature (° centigrade)	Harrison Cone	Orton Cone	Comments		Kiln interior
100	–	–	boiling point – free water driven off	crack kiln door	
200	–	–		bungs out	
300	–	–	in excess of domestic cookers	biscuit slowly up to here	
	–	–	chemically compounded water driven off		red glow appears and steadily increases
400	–	–			
500	–	–		bungs in	
600	–	–			
700	–	–	bodies harden	rate of firing increased	
	–	–			
720	018				
747		017	⎫	lead glazes (Galena) (700–800°)	
770	017				
792		016			
795	016				
804		015	⎬ lustres fire on		
805	015				
830	014				
838		014	⎫		
852		013	⎭	between 850° and 900° slow firing for approximately $\frac{1}{2}$–1 hour	
860	013				
884		012			
885	012				
894		011	⎬ enamels fire on		
910	010				
923		09		carbon soak as necessary	
930	09				
950	08				
955		08			
984		07			red heat – bright cherry
999	07				

To calculate 100° centigrade per hour, subtract 5° centigrade.

Bending temperature of H & O cones at a temperature rise of 150° centigrade per hour (continued)

Temperature (° centigrade)	Harrison Cone	Orton Cone	Comments	Kiln interior
1015	06		soft, biscuit	red heat –
1040	05		(porous)	bright cherry
1046		05		
1060	04	04	earthenware and	
1070	04A		bone china glazes	
1080	04B			
1090	04C			
1100	04D		hard earthenware glazes	bright orange
1101		03	usually 1100°C maturation,	red
1115	03		some with short soak	
1120		02	(30 min)	
1125	02		red bodies begin to lose porosity	
1137		01		
1145	01		red clay vitrifies dark brown	
1154		1	overfired begins to blister	
1160	1			brilliant orange
1162		2		
1165	2			
1168		3		
1170	3			
1185		4		
1190	4			
1196		5		
1205	5			orange
1222		6		turning yellow
1230	6			to white
1240		7		
1250	7		grey clays begin to vitrify	
1260	8			
1263		8	stoneware glazes mature,	
1280		9	also soft porcelain	
1285	9			white
1305	10	10	hard porcelain vitrifies	
1315		11		intense white
1325	11			
1326		12		

To calculate 100° centigrade per hour, subtract 5° centigrade.

Bending temperature of British cones at a temperature rise of 150° centigrade per hour

Temperature (° centigrade)	British Cone	Comments
940	08	
960	07	
980	06	
1000	05	earthenware, biscuit and soft glazes
1020	04	
1040	03	
1060	02	
1080	01	
1100	1	earthenware glazes
1120	2	
1230	7	
1250	8	stoneware and porcelain glaze
1280	9	
1300	10	

British cones have generally been superseded by Orton and Harrison cones.
Use British cones as above.

Index